W9-AVY-526

# PREPARE FOR THE WORST, PLAN FOR THE BEST

# PREPARE FOR THE WORST, PLAN FOR THE BEST

## Disaster Preparedness and Recovery for Small Businesses

**Second Edition**

## Donna R. Childs

**WILEY**

John Wiley & Sons, Inc.

Copyright © 2008 by John Wiley & Sons, Inc. All rights reserved.

Published by John Wiley & Sons, Inc., Hoboken, New Jersey.

Published simultaneously in Canada.

For general information on our other products and services, or technical support, please contact our Customer Care Department within the United States at 800-762-2974, outside the United States at 317-572-3993, or fax 317-572-4002.

Wiley also publishes its books in a variety of electronic formats. Some content that appears in print may not be available in electronic books.

For more information about Wiley products, visit our Web site at http://www.wiley.com.

The first edition of this book was entitled: *Contingency Planning and Disaster Recovery: A Small Business Guide*

**Library of Congress Cataloging-in-Publication Data:**

Childs, Donna R.
    Prepare for the worst, plan for the best : disaster preparedness and recovery for small businesses / Donna R. Childs. – 2nd ed.
       p. cm.
       Rev. ed. of: Contingency planning and disaster recovery / Donna R. Childs, Stefan Dietrich. c2002.
       Includes index.
       ISBN 978-0-470-17091-5 (cloth)
        1. Emergency management.   2. Small business–Planning.   I. Childs, Donna R. Contingency planning and disaster recovery.  II. Title.
    HV551.2.C45 2008
    658.4'77–dc22

                                    2007051421

Printed in the United States of America

10  9  8  7  6  5  4  3  2  1

# About the Author

**Donna R. Childs** is the founder and chief executive officer of Childs Capital LLC, a Wall Street firm dedicated to alleviating poverty in the developing world by broadening access to financial services. Childs Capital LLC was located in the so-called "Zone 1" of the World Trade Center on 9/11 when lower Manhattan was declared a federal disaster area. Owing to its unusual level of disaster readiness, Childs Capital LLC is included in the "Ready for Business" public awareness campaign of the Department of Homeland Security. Donna began her career as a research associate of the Harvard Business School, worked as an investment banker in the financial institutions group of Goldman, Sachs & Company and, more recently, was based in Zürich, Switzerland as a director and member of senior management of the Swiss Reinsurance Company. A recognized authority on risk finance, Donna was a contributing editor of *Risk Financier* and a frequent speaker at reinsurance industry conferences. She holds a B.S. from Yale University, an M.A. in International Economics and Finance from Brandeis University and an M.B.A. from Columbia Business School. In 2007, Donna was graduated from the Owner President Management Program of the Harvard Business School. In that same year, she was given the *Woman Business Owner of the Year* Award by the National Association of Women Business Owners and Wachovia Bank.

# Contents

# Foreword

The afternoon of September 15, 2006 marked a bittersweet occasion for America's Small Business Development Center Network. It was the 26th Annual Conference of the Association of Small Business Development Centers (ASBDC) held in Houston, Texas. We had assembled a reunion of the dozens of Small Business Development Centers' (SBDC) counselors from across the United States who had volunteered to go to the Gulf Coast to help their SBDC colleagues assist local small businesses recover from the devastation inflicted by Hurricanes Katrina and Rita. Helping small businesses is what America's SBDC is all about.

The SBDC national program is a partnership of private enterprise, government, higher education, and local nonprofit economic development organizations. Since 1980, the SBDC national network has been dedicated to helping our nation's small business owners and aspiring entrepreneurs by providing free business management consulting and low-cost management training. Approximately 1,000 SBDC service centers nationwide assist over a million small businesses at the local level each year. Our work helps strengthen the U.S. economy, as small business is the engine of our nation's economic growth. There are currently over 25 million small businesses in America. Approximately 700,000 small businesses were started last year. Small business accounts for 99% of all U.S. businesses, employs 52% of the private work force, and contributes over half of the nation's private gross domestic product.

At the ASBDC 2006 Annual Conference in Houston, we recognized the contributions of SBDC counselors who had assisted small businesses in the Gulf Coast during a time of unprecedented need. The counselors had helped the affected small businesses who sought help to apply for Small Business Administration (SBA) disaster loans, to process their insurance claims, reconstruct financial records, get in touch with their customers and employees from whom they had been separated, and other urgent tasks associated with a major disaster recovery effort.

But most of all, they listened. As our Katrina volunteers reunited to share lessons learned, one common theme that emerged was that their first task was to listen to the stories of the disaster victims, even before they could commence the tasks of gathering information needed for disaster assistance. Many of our counselors reported that they had not appreciated just how emotionally demanding this aspect of their work would prove to be, to relive, over and over again, the most frightening and traumatic experiences of those who had suffered terrible personal and financial losses.

The authors of the first edition of this book learned this lesson as well. In *Contingency Planning and Disaster Recovery: A Small Business Guide* (John Wiley & Sons, 2002), Donna Childs and Stefan Dietrich advised their readers that they should:

> listen to others who want to share. One of the common reactions that surprised us was the need people had to tell their stories. The experience was like the reverse of the poem by Samuel Taylor Coleridge, *The Rime of the Ancient Mariner*. Instead of being obliged by the gods to *tell* our stories to everyone whom we meet (the fate suffered by the ancient mariner), we were obliged to *listen* to the stories of everyone whom we met! People really need to talk about it—where they were when it happened, what could have happened and thank God it didn't, what were the consequences to them of what happened, what happened to other people. You can be dashing out the door for a meeting and the mailman will stop you and tell you his story and you have to listen. People really do need to talk and feel better after having done so—even those with whom you are only casually acquainted. We have learned to allow people to get the relief they need; if our listening helps them, we are glad.

The ASBDC understands the need to help small businesses become disaster-ready; it is part of our tradition. Former ASBDC Board Chairman and State Director of the North Carolina Small Business and Technology Development Center Network, Scott Daugherty, led efforts to get eastern North Carolina small businesses up and running after Hurricane Floyd struck in 1999. New York SBDC State Director Jim King led efforts to help small businesses in New York City after 9/11. ASBDC Board Member and Florida SBDC Director, Jerry Cartwright, led efforts in Florida to assist in the recovery of small businesses adversely impacted by the multiple hurricanes that hit the Sunshine State in 2004.

We are proud of our support of small businesses, but we also know that the emotional pain and economic losses brought on by major disasters can be mitigated through preparedness efforts. Unfortunately, our SBDCs across the country often report that their local small businesses, all too frequently, seek our assistance only *after* experiencing a disaster, when their options are more limited.

If you are a small business owner or manager, what you do *before* a disaster will determine, in large part, whether or not you will be able to remain in business *after* the disaster. It is emotionally draining for an SBDC counselor to meet a client, sometimes for the first time, after his or her business has experienced a major disaster, and to learn that the firm's tax records and financial data were lost because they were not properly backed up and stored off-site, or to learn that the firm does not have proper insurance, such as business interruption insurance. Please don't jeopardize the future and security of your business and your family by being unprepared for a disaster. Preparing for disasters is not complicated and does not have to be expensive. A few simple steps can enhance the security and safety of your business, your employees, and your family. Let's resolve to make our small businesses disaster-resilient. Visit your local SBDC to benefit from the resources it can offer you. To locate your nearest center, visit www.asbdc-us.org. Small business is our passion and we are eager to help.

DONALD T. WILSON
President and CEO
Association of Small Business Development Centers

# Acknowledgments

Launching my business is the fulfillment of a lifelong dream. It represents the opportunity to chart my own course, do meaningful work, develop new creative talents, encourage the potential in others, work with a talented team of friends whom I both love and respect, leave a legacy, and have great fun in the process. I often have to stop to consider how blessed I am to be able to pursue my passion. I would like to thank my parents for their hard work and sacrifices for my education, which has opened up a world of opportunities for me. I would also like to thank my brother for his encouragement and cheerful words when they are most needed. Jeffrey Silow has been invaluable for counsel and support; I am very indebted to him. I can always rely on Eileen Moccaldi to be a practical sounding board; I appreciate her help. Sheck Cho has been a most patient editor; I suppose that each author is a challenge, but my work takes me from Kenya one week to India the next and he keeps up with me!

I must thank Stefan Dietrich. Stefan was my coauthor for the first edition of this book. He received his diploma and doctorate, *summa cum laude*, from the University of Stuttgart in Germany. He did his postdoctoral training at Cornell University, where he also served as the lead developer for one of the U.S. National Science Foundation's "Grand Challenge" supercomputer projects. As a senior executive at Deutsche Bank, he contributed to the disaster recovery and contingency planning for one of the largest trading floors in Europe following the bomb attack on Bishopsgate, London. Stefan was responsible for all of the data backup and information technology work that kept our business up-and-running after 9/11. The content he contributed to our first edition continues to be timely and relevant. His engineering talent has helped me to appreciate the power and beauty of simplicity.

Lynn Russell, the professor responsible for communications courses to the Executive MBA (EMBA) students of Columbia Business School, has taught me critical lessons. I had enrolled in the EMBA program while starting my business to develop other skills that I knew my business would need. Lynn was very sensitive that students not perceive the communications course as fluff and in fact, I probably put more work into that course than any other. But it was worth it, because I consult Lynn's course materials almost every day.

I have to thank the Harvard Business School. I began my career as a research associate at the School, where I wrote case studies for the financial institutions course. I recently returned to the School, this time as a student in Owner President Management (OPM), the executive education program for founders of fast-growth, entrepreneurial companies. I cannot thank Jackie Baugher enough for making this possible and my thanks to Kathleen Mara, Lonya Smith, Chad Gordon, and Ann-Marie Wilson for their enthusiastic support. I am also grateful to the OPM faculty for their dedication to the program: Lynda Applegate, Robert Austin, Dwight Crane, John Davis, John Deighton, Linda Doyle, Regina Herzlinger, Bob Kaplan, Deepak Malhotra, Cynthia Montgomery, V.G. Narayanan, Laura Nash, Krishna Palepu, Forest Reinhardt, and Howard Stevenson.

I am very grateful for the support of small businesses shown by the team at Hewlett-Packard: Robyn West, Eric Brennan, Lisa Wolfe, Carolyn Bosco, SuChen Gee, Philip Lee, Dina Cretaro, Paul Brousseau, Marilyn Johns, and Tiffany Smith and HP's channel partners, particularly Michael Goldstein of LAN Associates. I owe particular thanks to Brian Wiser of Ingram Micro, Carin Falconer of CompUSA, Charles Royce of Dell, and Kevin Turner, Cynthia Bates, Frederick de Wolf, and Bill Rielly of Microsoft. And to Peter Alexander, Joe Diodati, Julian Lighton, Mimi Jackson, Madhu Anand, and Devin Hood: I am profoundly grateful for the passion and commitment of Cisco.

Finally, I have to thank the dedicated staff of the Association of Small Business Development Centers (ASBDC) and Don Wilson and Betsy Kaufman. I had the great privilege of leading workshops on small business disaster preparedness for the annual conferences of the ASBDC in Houston and in Denver, as well as for the local SBDCs. When I see images of disasters on television, it evokes a strong response from me, because I know the challenges ahead for the small businesses in the affected areas. I find it very gratifying to meet SBDC counselors from across the United States who struggle with the same issue: how to motivate their local small businesses to prepare for what they believe will never happen. I am particularly grateful to Peg Callahan, Jill Dickman, Deidre Pattillo, Carmen Sundra, and Mark Galyean. Their enthusiasm and commitment is like a shot of adrenaline for me.

Truly, the most rewarding aspect of writing this book was to have benefited from the enthusiasm and commitment of all the people I have named here. I cannot do enough to thank each of them.

# Preface

On August 31, 2005, I was beginning a workshop for executives in the healthcare industry in Huntington, California. My presentation focused on using technology to build disaster resilience, thereby reducing insurance and other costs even if disaster never strikes. But fate intervened to prove my points in a way I had not anticipated and could not control. I had relaxed in the hotel lobby café with a coffee before I was to begin my workshop. The hotel lobby had a big screen television and my timing for this workshop could not have been better: Images of the aftermath of Hurricane Katrina were ubiquitous, with cable television news broadcasting scenes from the Gulf Coast 24 hours a day. I was embarrassed to become tearful before the group, which had never happened to me. While the vivid images of the devastation in the Gulf Coast undoubtedly evoked powerful emotions in all who viewed them, they had particular resonance with me.

On the morning of 9/11, I was in the World Trade Center when the two planes struck the towers. I lived in Battery Park City then, the residential neighborhood in the shadow of the World Trade Center. Indeed, Battery Park City was built using the landfill excavated during the construction of the World Trade Center. Like many of my neighbors, I chose to live in Battery Park City both for the beauty of this community (my apartment afforded a view of the Statue of Liberty, Ellis Island, and the Hudson River) and its proximity to the financial district. I am a small business owner and my company, located on Wall Street, is just a 15-minute walk from home. Like most residents of this community, the World Trade Center formed the "anchor" of my neighborhood.

On September 11, 2001, I had a 9:30 A.M. appointment in my office with a former classmate, Alex Krutov. On my way to work, I stopped by the pharmacy in the shopping concourse of the World Trade Center. After the first plane struck the World Trade Center, firefighters and police officers rushed into the towers and began the evacuation. I left the building and, as it was unsafe to walk about, I went home and immediately called the office to advise people of what had happened and to urge everyone to leave the area. I was among the thousands of residents of Battery Park City who were evacuated. Along with my neighbor and his dog, I boarded a New Jersey police boat and crossed the Hudson River to safety. The Mayor's Office of Emergency Management closed our community for months, although I was permitted to re-enter my home once during that time under the escort of a National Guardsman, to retrieve some clothing and personal items. During this period of homelessness, I stayed with a friend in an apartment on New Jersey's side of the Hudson River, facing Lower Manhattan and my neighborhood.

The next two weeks were extraordinary. I remained glued to the television set, watching events unfold in New York City and across the world; I could also see firsthand what most people could see only on their television sets. It was as if I had two screens displaying different images: the television screen displaying images broadcast from around the world and the window on the Hudson River through which I saw, for example, the navy hospital ship, the U.S.N.S. Comfort, sail up the Hudson River to make additional medical assistance available. I saw the F-16s flying overhead, securing New York's airspace. I saw Air Force One, as President Bush arrived to address the rescue workers at the disaster site. I saw, day after day, the ghastly plume of smoke rise from the remains of the World Trade Center, while the rest of Lower Manhattan, which was without electricity, remained in darkness.

When the Mayor re-opened Wall Street, I returned to my office from New Jersey, commuting on a new water ferry route that had been established following the destruction of a train station in the financial district. Army vehicles and soldiers patrolled the soot-covered Wall Street. The first few weeks following the disaster, the normally bustling financial district seemed like a ghost town as few people were about. My own office building remained without a central electricity supply, but a large back-up generator erected on the sidewalk provided sufficient electricity for a minimal level of lighting and for computers and office equipment (but not the building elevator). It required some effort to plan for meals—no deliveries of food had been made to Lower Manhattan after the community was closed by the Mayor's office. Grocery stores and restaurants had discarded their food supplies due to spoilage.

I resumed my life, reconnecting with friends and family throughout the world to let them know that I was safe, as telephone service became available, and focusing on my business. That experience was the genesis of the first edition of this book. Prior to starting my business, I was a senior executive at the world's largest reinsurance company. Reinsurance companies deal with major disasters every day and so devote considerable effort to assessing loss exposures to determine how to mitigate risks. This experience proved critical to me in working through 9/11. I was also lucky enough to have Stefan Dietrich's advice on all matters related to information technology. Stefan has a PhD in Engineering and Computer Science and had contributed to the disaster recovery operations of Deutsche Bank in London following the bomb attack on Bishopsgate. My business had its data backed up, online and off-site, which allowed me to work remotely following 9/11. I soon realized that my level of preparedness was unusual.


## CRISIS AND LEVIATHAN

By December 2001, just three months after the terrorist attacks, about two-thirds of the doors in my office building had signs taped on them, usually eviction notices from the marshal or notices from the sheriff. My office building has 12 stories of office suites, ranging in size from about 500 to 3,000 square feet, each one for a small business tenant. The businesses had been viable, but they were not prepared to work through a disruption on the scale of the events surrounding 9/11. They were not unusual. According to the Institute for Business and Home Safety, an estimated 25% of businesses do not reopen following a major disaster.[1]

And so I was unable to stop my tears upon seeing the devastation of the Gulf Coast. Lower Manhattan small business owners, who had worked through 9/11, told me that they had the same reaction to those images. We all felt a mixture of sadness and anger: sadness because we knew how tough it would be for the residents of Louisiana, Mississippi, and Alabama to restore some sense of normalcy to their lives; anger, because we knew that much of what they would experience would be totally unnecessary. Indeed, I can speak from personal experience that most of what is termed "disaster relief" will be more harmful than helpful to small businesses.

The *Battery Park City Broadsheet*[2] expressed this view in perhaps a more concrete way:

> HUD's first allocation towards the recovery effort is $700 million, part of which is earmarked for small businesses. Unfortunately, what most small business owners have found is that receiving a piece of the $700 million is about as likely as holding a winning Powerball ticket. From the Ground Up, an organization comprising more than 100 small businesses in Lower Manhattan, is dedicated to making the distribution of aid fair, adequate and easier to procure.
>
> Kevin Curnin, a lawyer with Stroock, Stroock and Lavan, advised the group. He said agencies allocating financial aid in most cases have defined "small business" as having as many as 500 employees. "Five hundred is not small," Curnin said. "This includes massive firms who have insurance. Put a

---

[1] http://www.sba.gov/services/disasterassistance/disasterpreparedness/index.html.
[2] February 27–March 13, 2002 issue—the *Broadsheet* provides local news to the residents of the Battery Park City Community. HUD is the acronym for "Housing and Urban Development," an agency of the U.S. federal government.

big fish in a small pond and that big fish is going to take a disproportionate share of the resources. It's impractical and wrong. . . ."

Aid is not getting to the businesses that really need it, Mr. Curnin said. Many pizza parlors and shoe repair shops—businesses that Mr. Curnin argues make a neighborhood a neighborhood—did not have adequate insurance or a safety net that would allow them to survive being closed for months.

We included this quote in the first edition of our book, when Lower Manhattan small businesses, including members of From the Ground Up, maintained the optimistic belief that small businesses working together could make government disaster relief programs transparent and equitable. They did not succeed; indeed, their efforts served another purpose. Small businesses in disaster-affected areas are often, in my view, used as visual props to manipulate the sympathies of taxpayers to generously fund disaster relief programs, which rarely serve their stated purposes. Drs. Raghuram G. Rajan and Luigi Zingales described this phenomenon in a much more elegant manner in their book, *Saving Capitalism From the Capitalists*.[3] They describe how the distressed surface in times of an economic downturn, seeking relief through political means, and that their political agenda is subsequently captured by more powerful incumbents. Several years after the 9/11 terrorist attacks, local New York newspapers reported how disaster aid was captured in the form of corporate welfare. Presumably, the politicians who lobbied for this aid were rewarded for their efforts.

I *really* knew what was in store for the Gulf Coast: In the reinsurance industry, we model a range of disaster scenarios and there was little about Hurricanes Katrina and Rita that came as a surprise. In fact, in August 2004, a full 14 months before the hurricanes struck the Gulf Coast, I was in Washington, DC, conducting briefings on the subject of disaster preparedness for small businesses, particularly disadvantaged small businesses. I had reached out to each of the members of the U.S. Senate's Committee of Small Business and Entrepreneurship. On August 30, 2004, I was in the Washington, DC office of Louisiana Senator Mary Landrieu to discuss the threat of hurricanes to the Gulf Coast with her staffer.

We had specifically discussed the vulnerability of low-income entrepreneurs in Louisiana. For many disadvantaged groups, such as first-generation immigrants, entrepreneurship is the first step on the economic ladder. In poor communities, small business is often the *only* business as committed entrepreneurs see opportunity even in areas of economic blight. Yet, notwithstanding the tens of billions of dollars in government aid flowing to the Gulf Coast, small businesses and poor communities see little or no benefit.

So I was not terribly surprised when I received an e-mail in April 2007 from Carmen Sundra, a Katrina survivor and small business advisor:

---

[3]Crown Business, 2003.

The best response I would give and would certainly recommend this in your book—somewhere in BOLD BIG LETTERS—is that you CANNOT depend on the Government or Corporate America. They no more have a plan to handle the disasters than most small businesses. Money does not come quickly, the paperwork is tremendous and your square pegs do not fit their round holes. Bureaucratic organizations are arthritic and move like a bent-up old lady trying to cross a six-lane street. Trying to legislate how you will handle a disaster is a disaster—how can you predict what you will need until you know the disaster's needs? Small businesses have to have plans to protect themselves.

In this edition, we will examine how to put in place a disaster preparedness plan to protect your business and how that effort will yield a positive return on your investment *even if disaster never strikes.* I am still in business, six years after 9/11, because I did not rely upon government aid. In fact, I was able to negotiate a double-digit percentage decrease in my commercial insurance premium by having a simple and sensible disaster plan in place. I was also able to secure uninterrupted insurance coverage after 9/11 because of my disaster preparedness plan. I did not become a "victim" or a "constituent" for big government.

This is my wish for you: that your business is disaster-resilient so that you realize your entrepreneurial dreams and plan for the safety and security of your family and employees. If you do so, you will realize immediate benefits for your business, I promise you. And on that uplifting note, let's begin by debunking some common myths about disasters.

# CRISIS AND LEVIATHAN

# 1

# Yes, You Should Sweat the Small Stuff!

Disasters occur more frequently than we realize. Research consistently shows that for small businesses, the effects of a disaster can be devastating:

- More than one in four businesses will experience a significant crisis in any year.[1]

- Of those businesses that experience a disaster and have no emergency plan, 43% never reopen.[2]

- Of those that reopen, only 29% are operating two years later.[3]

The losses that these figures represent do not appear to have motivated preparedness efforts by small businesses: A recent survey of 2,500 small business owners found that 71% did not have a disaster preparedness plan in place. Nearly two-thirds of them stated that they do not need one. 63% expressed confidence that they would resume business within 72 hours if they were affected by a natural disaster, even though historical experience shows that this is absolutely not the case.[4]

Disasters are, for the most part, manageable. We cannot prevent disasters from occurring, but we can equip small business owners with the knowledge that they will need to mitigate their risks and to recover quickly when disasters do strike. That is the goal of this book.

As small business owners, our resources are limited and we must work our assets smarter, not harder, than the assets of larger companies. We must spend our insurance premium dollars wisely and make cost-effective decisions on establishing backup information technology (IT) support. In the first edition of this book,[5] Stefan Dietrich and I provided our readers the tools to put in place an appropriate contingency and disaster recovery plan. This second edition has been updated with all-new material, drawing on the experiences small business owners around the world have shared with me since the first edition was published. This second edition also features new material about disaster recovery programs, as we were still working through the process with the Federal Emergency Management Agency (FEMA) and other relief agencies when our first edition went to press. Now that time has passed, I can share with you more information about how that recovery process works. If I were ever, heaven forbid, to experience another major disaster, there are certain "assistance" programs that I would avoid. Now that I have fully completed the recovery process, I can share these insights with you.

Before continuing, let's be clear about what we mean by "disaster." A disaster can be defined as an event that disrupts business operations at a given site and results in a temporary or permanent dislocation of the business. A factory fire is, by this definition, a disaster. A product liability crisis, by the same definition, is not. Consider Johnson & Johnson's 1982 experience of tampering with its Tylenol® product. That is a business crisis, one that requires careful management of communications with stakeholders and possibly changes to business (or in this case, packaging) processes. The Tylenol® crisis, while undoubtedly painful for the company, did not disrupt business operations or cause employees to lose access to Johnson & Johnson facilities. Work at Johnson & Johnson continued on-site, even as the company's executives worked to communicate with their customers, the investment community, the distributors of their product, and other stakeholders. I cannot advise you on situations such as the Tylenol® crisis; this is not my expertise. As such, crisis management is beyond the scope of this book and I would refer you to other sources.[6]

Few small business owners have the reach to find themselves in a crisis comparable to that of Johnson & Johnson. However, many of us will, unfortunately, experience natural disasters such as fires, floods, and disruptions in power supply during the course of building our businesses. Carefully crafting an insurance program and ensuring adequate IT capacity can mitigate the consequences of such disasters. Many of the techniques and suggestions in this book are applicable to the nonprofit sector as well. Nonprofit organizations, like small businesses, pursue their missions with limited resources and may benefit from putting in place a disaster preparedness plan.

Of course, each small business (or nonprofit organization) faces unique circumstances and constraints and no one can reasonably anticipate the needs of each and every single reader. It is best to consult experts, such as commercial insurance brokers, where appropriate, and expect that the information in this book will enable you to be a more knowledgeable consumer of such services and to use such services in a cost-effective manner.

I hope that your business never experiences a disaster. Unfortunately, we cannot prevent such tragedies from occurring—and they do occur from time to time. However, I hope to assist you in preparing your small business when disasters happen. I also believe that you will find that contingency and disaster recovery planning improves the efficiencies of your business processes and therefore, the planning process will immediately benefit your business—*irrespective of whether your business ever experiences a disaster*. Now that I have outlined what we hope to accomplish with this book, let us begin by debunking a common myth.

It is commonly believed that preparing for the worst-case scenario automatically subsumes preparation for all lesser risks. This assumption should not form the basis of your contingency planning. Do you really want to initiate a full-blown disaster recovery every time you experience a minor deviation in business operations? That is not a very efficient way to run your business. There are also other reasons why this myth must be exploded:

- **It Induces Planning Paralysis.** If your entire preparedness effort is focused on the catastrophic event, you are likely to do nothing at all. Why? Because you can (quite reasonably) discount the likelihood of the catastrophic event occurring, leaving your business vulnerable to less severe disasters. Imagine sealing your office with duct tape for fear of a dirty bomb and then losing all of your business-critical data because of a power outage. It is ridiculous, isn't it? But that is how disaster preparedness is sold to the public.

- **It Distorts Assessments of Risks.** Have you seen people wearing t-shirts with glib slogans about how everything is going to seed anyway, so you may as well surrender to the flow? By looking at catastrophic scenarios, you are tempted to say to yourself, "Well since I cannot prepare for everything, I guess I will prepare for nothing." This type of feigned helplessness is poison for your business.

- **It Fails to Provide for the Benefits of Responsible Behavior.** Building disaster-resilience into your small business will *provide immediate benefits to your business even* if disaster never strikes. Later, in the section titled "Preparation Pays" I will show you how.

I would like to propose another perspective on risk: the one used by reinsurers and risk management professionals. In this chapter, I will present the model of building increasing organizational resilience and (I hope!) de-bunk the myth that small businesses should prepare for the worst-case scenarios.

## SPECTRUM OF RISK

In the reinsurance industry, we typically evaluate risk across the spectrum from the high-frequency/low-severity events (the "everyday" disasters), such as human errors and computer crashes, to the high-severity/low-frequency events (the "catastrophic" disasters), such as earthquakes and hurricanes.

**Exhibit 1.1**    Risk Spectrum

<table>
<tr><td colspan="3">**Sweat the small stuff**</td></tr>
<tr>
<td>High frequency,<br>Low severity</td>
<td></td>
<td>High severity,<br>Low frequency</td>
</tr>
<tr><td colspan="3">◄—————————————————————————————►</td></tr>
<tr>
<td>*Examples:*<br>Human error<br>Computer crash<br>Power outage</td>
<td>*Examples:*<br>Fire<br>Flood</td>
<td>*Examples:*<br>Natural disasters<br>Sabotage<br>Terrorism</td>
</tr>
<tr>
<td colspan="3">
**Categories:**

1. Human errors         4. Environmental hazards
2. Equipment failures   5. Fires and other disasters
3. Third-party failures 6. Terrorism and sabotage
</td>
</tr>
</table>

Often, small business owners forego contingency planning for disasters, believing disasters to be catastrophic in scope and beyond their control. In fact, the "disasters" your business are most likely to experience are of the mundane human error variety. Although often trivial, human errors may have severe consequences. Consider that the root cause of the 1986 Space Shuttle *Challenger* disaster was human error. More recently, the runways at Los Angeles Airport were closed for several hours due to human error.

There are procedures that you can put in place to mitigate your business losses from such disasters. Those procedures, in turn, will help you build more resilient and robust business processes, better equipped to recover from the larger-scale disasters. Let's examine six categories of disaster in more detail (see Exhibit 1.1).

1. **Human Errors.** Human errors are triggered by actions unintentionally undertaken by managers and employees acting in good faith; actions that are subsequently shown to be mistakes. The most common causes of human errors are inadequate computer-user training, fatigue, and carelessness. These errors can reduce productivity and increase the costs to your small business.

   *Real-world example*: A new employee at a small business client support group wanted to add new phone numbers to the contact information in the company's call tracking system. He thought that instead of entering the telephone numbers manually, he could save time by writing a script that would automatically replace the appropriate numbers. Upon running the script, all phone numbers in the system were replaced with the first phone number in his script. It took hours to retrieve the backup tapes and to rebuild the database. All the updates made to the computer system that day had to be manually corrected—the original task the new employee had sought to avoid became the least time-consuming part of the recovery process.

2. **Equipment Failures.** These are malfunctions or complete failures of any type of office machinery used to store or to process information. Office equipment commonly includes fax machines, personal computers, phone systems, and network components. Equipment is prone to breakage and failure, and so you should anticipate that your business will, at some time, experience equipment failure.

   *Real-world example*: After five years (!) of service, the main disk of an old file server would no longer spin after the machine had been routinely rebooted. Subsequent investigation revealed that none of the remaining computers could read data from that main disk. After comparing the costs of hiring a data recovery service to reestablish the data and the hours required to restore the data from the backup system, it was determined that only about 20% of the most critical business data would be recovered, leading to great frustration among the employees who had lost files.

3. **Third-Party Failures.** These are failures of third parties to deliver services that you need to operate your information storing and processing equipment. Included here are electrical power failures, loss of phone service, or failures of Internet or market data providers. This category also includes financial disasters (e.g., the default of your largest customer).

   *Real-world example*: A telecommunication provider defaults on its debt and seeks bankruptcy protection. Your business telephone system malfunctions. Your service provider informs you that they are using the services of a repair company that also had to temporarily suspend its services because its main creditor was the telecommunications company now in default. You are assured that everything is being done to fix your phone connection as soon as possible, but with other "big" clients on their priority list, you, a small business owner, have to wait a couple of days. When you go home in the evening, your answering machine is full of messages with urgent calls from your clients.

4. **Environmental Hazards.** These are all conditions that do not permit you to enter your regular business offices while your IT infrastructure stays operational. These conditions could include smoke from a nearby fire, hazardous substances discovered in your building, irritants

like fresh paints, pollutants in your building, or contamination of your office with either radioactive, biological, or chemical substances. These hazards prevent you from entering your worksite.

*Real-world example*: Asbestos is discovered during construction work in your neighbor's offices. You share the same air conditioning unit and you have to leave your offices. You are not allowed to take any computer equipment with you as the fans have collected asbestos with the dust and require cleaning that will take days to complete.

5. **Fires and Other Disasters.** Here we consider all events that are destructive to your office and hence, to your IT infrastructure. Although fire poses the most common threat, other disasters include natural events, like earthquakes, floods, storms, and man-made disasters, like gas leaks and subsequent explosions. All of these can be very destructive and would render your office unusable or simply prevent your key employees from coming to work.

   *Real-world example*: A water pipe in the ceiling broke. Water sprayed throughout the office. Eventually, it seeped into some IT equipment and short-circuited the power supply. Fortunately, the water was quickly shut off, the equipment dried, and some parts, including the power supply, replaced. Everything seemed to be fine. Two weeks later, severe mold developed. A hazardous condition existed and the office could no longer be used. The IT equipment was relocated to a temporary office location, but the equipment became unreliable. Water corrosion inside the PC damaged plugs and prevented the central processing unit (CPU) fan from running at full speed. Insufficient cooling of the CPU caused system crashes. This is a good example of how a single event can cause a series of related disasters, in this case, from a water leak to equipment failure.

6. **Terrorism & Sabotage.** A terrorist attack is an intentional, systematic, planned, and organized effort with the goal to cause maximum damage with resulting publicity. Sabotage is also motivated by calculated intent, but rarely attracts the same level of public attention. Unlike the other disaster types, acts of terrorism and sabotage can be the most threatening because they are based on malicious intent; and if the perpetrators have access to sensitive information about your business, very concentrated damage can be done with relatively little effort. For terrorists, all means are considered just to reach the goal. Hence, the spectrum of attacks is unusually large, from hostage situations to large bomb explosions, and, as we saw on September 11, suicide missions using planes as weapons of mass destruction. Saboteurs, however, like the secrecy of underground activities and work with sophisticated tools. They can attack you from the outside (e.g., attacks by computer hackers), or attempt to infiltrate your organization with computer

viruses. You can also be struck from the inside when, for example, a disgruntled system administrator sabotages your backup system.

*Real-world example:* These are rare cases, and unfortunately, practically impossible to be fully protected from. Terrorist acts are usually public and can result in the complete destruction of IT assets. Cases of sabotage seldom reach the public's attention, and it cannot always be determined if the damage was the result of a highly sophisticated act of sabotage or simply a common equipment failure. Since it is not a good idea to make suggestions to those with bad intentions, let's refer to a real-world example from 20 years ago. A company with approximately 40 employees had a so-called minicomputer and a green bar paper printer, both of which were located in an air-conditioned room. The company depended on this one computer system, as the cost to back it up with a second system was simply prohibitive. However, the operating system was very stable, so typically this was a very reliable setup. An employee, possibly by accident, reduced the level of humidity in the air quality control unit resulting in the buildup of high electrostatic voltage in the printer paper. The voltage was discharged through the connection of the computer with the printer, thereby destroying the whole computer.

Each category of disaster requires a unique form of preparation and emergency response. In developing your business contingency plan to protect against these disasters, you should consider that as you cross the spectrum from Human Error toward Terrorism and Sabotage, the frequency of the event decreases but the severity of the resulting damage increases. Human error is by far the most common cause of business disasters on a day-to-day basis. In most cases, it is relatively simple to protect against this risk and it is possible to recover from such errors with minimal impact to your company's business. However, an act of terrorism and sabotage would be a rare event for most businesses, but should such an event occur, it would cause significant damage that could critically affect your company's future. Thus, it is important for you to weigh the likelihood of occurrence with the risks associated with each type of disaster in order to create the type of disaster contingency plan that best meets your needs.

## EVERYDAY DISASTERS CAN HAVE SERIOUS CONSEQUENCES

How many times have you watched in horror as the evening television news shows images of frustrated small business owners dealing with computer-related disasters? I cannot think of one example from my own experience. But if there is a car accident on the highway, it will likely lead the evening news. Television news depends upon highly visual, graphic images of disasters and as such, tends to distort our perception of risks. Let's consider a series of true case studies involving computer-related disasters that small businesses deal with every day.

---

### Online antiques dealer disabled by a virus

FromGlobaltoYou.com is an online antiques business based in Utah that was struck by the Klez e-mail worm. Notwithstanding the fact that the company had installed anti-viral software, the worm flooded employees' e-mail in-boxes and locked up its ten desktop computers, shutting the business down for two days. As a consequence of this disruption, FromGlobaltoYou.com permanently lost about 30 customers who were disappointed with the poor service and e-mail spam caused by the virus. In addition, the Company lost a significant amount of revenue from eBay auctions because it couldn't complete sales before getting back online. As a result, the Company's expansion plans were delayed for nearly two years. The co-owner of the business, Dianne Bingham, said, "small- and medium-sized businesses never think it can happen to them, but it can and the results can be devastating."

---

Now we don't see e-mail worms on the television news, but they can do as much or more economic damage than fires! Let's consider another, related, example.

---

### Newspaper disrupted by server virus

*Providence Business News* serves readers who work for growing businesses in Rhode Island and nearby Massachusetts. The newspaper had carefully backed up its key data and had, on occasion, experienced minor viruses on local workstations. However, around Thanksgiving 2004, a virus infected the e-mail server and disabled the entire system. The backups were infected with the same virus that had disabled the main server. Staff coped by using G-mail and Yahoo e-mail for six weeks until the newspaper was fully back online. According to *Providence Business News* Publisher Roger Bergenheim, "You don't realize how much you depend on e-mail; at this point it is more important to business than the telephone."

---

Imagine that you have your employees running from your office to the local copy center so that they can rent computers by the hour from which to send e-mails across Web services. That is not the type of disaster the media will cover, but it is certainly disruptive and costly. The following is another example.

*Online pet retailer loses a week repairing damage done by a virus*

Kitty's WonderBox® was founded in 1991. The company grew out of a product concept for an easy, convenient, and disposable cat litter box. In 2004, the company's systems were infected with a virus, which required that the management team purge and rebuild many of their files. The company had backups, but getting everything back online took a week of their time. Said company CEO Riza Chase-Gilpin, "I can certainly attest to having a good support IT person or company in place when disaster hits!"

Let's move from viruses to equipment failures.

*Busy restaurant experiences disk crash*

Komegashi is a chain of Japanese restaurants that does an active business serving customers dining in and taking out meals. Each restaurant organizes customer data electronically by telephone number for ease in retrieving information for takeout orders (such as the customers' addresses, directions to their homes, etc.). During one busy dinner shift, the hard disk of one restaurant's computer overheated, causing the disk to crash. The customer data were destroyed. General Manager Carol Hu said, "the computers are powered and in constant use, and our database is enormous as customers who relocate often remain in our system. It is an enormous amount of work to maintain such a database reliably."

Here is another example:

*Seminar interrupted by a defective video card*

Theweleit Consulting is an engineering firm based in Cologne, Germany, focusing on energy-efficient solutions. The consultants often use laptop computers to work on-site with clients. Minutes before an important presentation, the laptop's video card failed.

Although a replacement laptop was quickly found, transferring the presentation files was a challenge. Sending the laptop in for repair could have meant potentially destroying the data, which had not been backed up. Finding an IT expert to repair the laptop while preserving the data without any screen required a great deal of effort and several days of work.

Then, there are the old-fashioned power outages.

---

*Power interruption disrupts physician's office*

---

Dr. Schmidt maintains a medical practice in Kassel, Germany. An overnight interruption in the electrical supply caused the two PCs running physician practice management software to reboot. The following morning, the staff noted that there had been a power interruption that caused the system to reboot, but as they detected no other anomalies, they continued to enter new patient records into the system. Several days later, the staff noted that the database had been corrupted by the unclean system shutdown caused by the power failure. It took several days of work for the staff to manually compare the patient's paper records with the data in the computers, and to merge the old with the new records entered since the power failure.

Let's not forget the basic disaster, human error.

---

*Australian firm loses valuable time and data in upgrading its server*

---

IRC is an independent consultancy in Australia providing risk management and engineering services to the energy industry. The company used two servers, one as a mail server and the other as a file server. Although backup measures were in place, when the company sought to upgrade to an advanced server over one Christmas break, they learned that the installation parameters were not exactly the same on the new system as on the existing system, causing staff to lose four days of valuable time and a small amount of unique information not available on the backup. The system was restored 100% when IRC performed a complete rebuild several months later. "Although from a technical standpoint it sounds like a minor problem, the loss of e-mail data and communications for that period had the potential to delay projects by several days. Many of our projects are short duration with tight deadlines—a four-day delay can have major implications for our clients," said Colin Wright, a cofounder of IRC.

Or, how about a one-two punch?

---

*Filmmaker's studio loses data*

---

Gypsy Heart Productions is the brainchild of Jocelyn Ajami, an artist and independent filmmaker whose recent work debuted at the Museum of Fine Arts in Boston. Jocelyn maintains an extensive digital library of her work and sustained a "one-two" punch when she lost data due to a power outage, and then a subsequent data loss when a new virus, unidentified by the antiviral software she was using, infected her system. "Everyone I know has experienced this," she said. "It is just so frustrating to have this downtime."

Unlike large corporations, small businesses have limited resources. We simply cannot throw more people at the problem or keep enormous stocks of reserve equipment for when the video card or the disk fails. It is the smaller, "under the radar screen" disasters that can be ruinous.

Let's close with one more example before moving on to the next section. Do you recall that emergency officials in Canada had to evacuate a good part of Newfoundland when Hurricane Juan moved up the Atlantic Coast? If you are from Canada, then you likely remember this one. If you are from elsewhere, think of the Asian tsunami or Hurricane Katrina or your local major natural disaster. Now, what if I told you that the economic losses borne by local small businesses were far greater due to over-fishing off the coast of Newfoundland than the economic losses caused by the hurricane? The disruption of the fishing industry had a "domino" effect on the local economy. Imagine that your small business serves a clientele of local fisherman or that your restaurant purchases from the local fishmongers. The consequences of Hurricane Juan were not as devastating. Yet, that is not how we think of risk.

The following are the key takeaways from this section:

- You are, by definition, more likely to experience a high-frequency disaster than a high-severity one.

- High frequency, or "everyday" disasters, can be painful and costly.

## TACKLING RISKS ONE STEP AT A TIME

For these reasons, it is best to begin by preparing for the "everyday" disasters to incrementally build resilience to more serious forms of disaster. Let's consider the example of a power outage. Power outages can occur on a stand-alone basis. In the summer of 2006, thousands of small businesses in Queens, New York, were without electricity for as long as nine days. Some grocers and restaurants were financially ruined as a result of the outage. Perhaps an example that is better known is the power outage during the summer of 2004 that left 50 million residents of the United States and Canada in the dark. Less well-known are the episodic interruptions of power in the affected areas during the weeks following the major blackout, after power was officially restored. So a power outage is a disaster in its own right.

It is also a common occurrence in the aftermath of more serious forms of disaster, such as hurricanes, earthquakes, and terrorist attacks. If you develop a plan for how your business would function with a disruption in the supply of electricity, you are automatically better prepared for coping with the more serious forms of disaster.

For another illustration of this concept, let's return to our case study of the filmmaker who lost her digital files due to a power outage and later a virus. Those files are gone forever and they are her creative work product.

What if she had backed up her digital files off-site? Then she would not only have been better prepared for the power outage and the virus, but she would also have been better prepared for a possible fire.

For the record, my disaster preparedness plan never contemplated anything on the scale and scope of what I experienced on 9/11. When I began thinking about risks to my business, I had two "worst-case scenarios" in mind: a fire in the nearby Wall Street subway station or an event similar to the scaffolding accident that had occurred near Times Square that caused small businesses within a radius of many city blocks to lose access to their premises. Yet the disaster preparedness plan I put in place was sufficient to see me through something far worse.

In Chapter 2, we will consider incrementally building resilience to disaster, starting with addressing the risks of human error and moving on to more serious threats. But before we dive into the specifics of planning, I want to conclude this chapter on a positive note.

## PREPARATION PAYS

Many people mistakenly believe that preparing for disaster is time-consuming and costly. This is another myth that I hope to debunk by the end of this book! You should not think that if you invest time and effort in preparing your business for disaster, and the disaster does not occur, that it was all for naught. Investing in disaster preparedness yields an immediate return, *even if disaster never strikes*:

- **You Can Decrease Your Expenses.** I negotiated double-digit percentage decreases in my commercial insurance premiums by sharing a robust disaster preparedness plan with my insurance company. I demonstrated that I was a better risk than my peers and argued that my improved risk profile should be reflected in a lower premium.

- **You Can Increase Your Opportunities to Grow Revenues.** As part of their own contingency planning, large corporations are increasingly looking at the resilience of their supply chains. As part of their due diligence, they are evaluating how prospective vendors would meet their deliverables in the event of a disaster or severe disruption. To the extent that you can build confidence that you have a methodical disaster preparedness plan, you are more competitive to win the business.

- **You Can Increase Your Operational Efficiency.** The process of developing a thoughtful preparedness plan involves doing process engineering on how your business works. This process will inevitably yield insights into how you can run the business more efficiently. I will highlight specific examples later in this book.

Let's be pragmatic: From time to time, bad things will happen and it is best to prepare for them as well as we can. Then we can sleep soundly at night knowing that we have acted responsibly to ensure the safety of our families and our employees.

## NOTES

1. This was the finding of a January 2005 survey conducted by *Continuity Insights* magazine and KPMG Risk Advisory Services.

2. The Hartford's *Guide to Emergency Preparedness Planning*, The Hartford Financial Services Group, published in 2002.

3. *Ibid.*

4. See www.officedepot.com. This survey was conducted in February 2007 for Office Depot.

5. Donna R. Childs and Stefan Dietrich, *Contingency Planning and Disaster Recovery: A Small Business Guide*, John Wiley & Sons, 2002.

6. During the course of my business career, I participated in excellent crisis management programs offered by the Corporate Response Group in Washington, DC, which I highly recommend.

# 2

# Our Roadmap

This guide is intended to educate you about contingency planning so that you can develop strategies that will protect your small business against a variety of unpredictable disasters. Any company, regardless of its size and financial resources, can take steps to significantly improve the protection of its business in the case of a disaster. This is simple, hands-on advice that does not require expensive external consulting guidance. Throughout this book, we use the symbol next to this paragraph to highlight important steps or unusual ideas for your disaster contingency effort.

## PART ONE: PREPARE

Part One of this guide discusses the steps that should be taken to prepare for a disaster. This preparation effort will mitigate your losses should a disaster strike. We consider the following points:

- Determine assets that are critical for protection
- Establish general protection measurements
- Take precautions to avoid specific disasters (e.g., loss of computer data due to human errors)
- Mitigate potential damages

These precautions are designed to protect your information technology (IT) infrastructure by providing user training, creating additional contingencies by augmenting essential equipment, avoiding concentrations of functionality, determining policies for backing up critical data, and establishing a secondary office location. You should establish "redundant" financial capacity, analogous to redundant information technology capacity, in the form of an insurance program and a financial reserve, so that you will have resources on hand to meet unanticipated expenses following a disaster.

## PART TWO: RESPOND

This part presents advice on how to react once a disaster has struck, with a special emphasis on how to minimize the risks as well as the liabilities to your business. To protect your IT infrastructure, this may require an emergency shutdown of your systems, an isolation of any systems found to be defective, and an effort to contact third parties to begin rebuilding your operational capacity. At the same time, you must document your insured losses and file timely claims with your insurance carrier. Here, you will also find advice on how to go about those processes.

## PART THREE: RECOVER

Part Three discusses how to move your business forward following a disaster, how to assess damage and communicate with all of the stakeholders in your business, and how to begin prioritizing tasks to resume business operations. This part provides information on disaster relief services and advice on coping with the emotions that surface following a disaster. To guide you in resuming operations from your IT assets, we will discuss how to recover data, replace equipment, review the performance of the third parties that have supported your recovery efforts, and reestablish business operations at a new site, if necessary. Since your insurance program will be affected by a disaster, this part presents specific advice on how to reconstruct your insurance policy, resolve disputes, and reinstate your coverage.

By definition, disasters are acts of God that cannot be prevented; but you should be prepared for a disaster, know how to respond to it, and be confident that you will recover and almost certainly learn from the experience. Before you start preparing your disaster contingency plan, you need to identify the critical assets of your business, what you consider to be the "jewels" of your business.

You will likely learn that the most valuable assets of your small business are:

- The proprietary knowledge of your company; and
- The people who understand and work with that knowledge.

Small business managers are typically aware of the risk of loss of proprietary knowledge that resides with human capital. Managers often think of how to respond if a key employee leaves the company. But they have a much lower level of awareness of the risk of loss of proprietary information that is exclusively stored in their IT systems and rarely have in place concrete plans for responding to a major computer failure. Many small businesses simply feel overwhelmed by a technology that is evolving at a frantic pace. Systems become obsolete after two or three years. During their brief lifecycles, systems are inundated with data and must be frequently upgraded. Computer systems in small businesses are often assembled without any structured plans for the storage and retrieval of data.

The first step in preparing a disaster contingency plan is a rigorous assessment of your business. Let's start with a plan of preparation for your critical IT assets and for a program of insurance. I will share with you what I have learned about the need to put in place redundant technology and financial assets so you can recover faster when disaster strikes. This guide begins with some questions for you to keep in mind as you work through this section of the book. The questions are meant to challenge you. The answers, which only you and your employees can provide, will help you to identify areas on which to focus in developing your contingency plan.

You must identify the critical business assets that you wish to protect. Now is the perfect time to assess past events that have affected your business (e.g., Have you had prior experience with natural disasters? Is your business located in a flood zone?), and your business' current status. Consider how you would react to the categories of disasters we have identified and take into consideration how your clients and suppliers would be affected should your business experience a disaster. For example, if your business operations were temporarily disrupted, would your clients seek alternate sources for the products and services you supply to them? Could you mitigate this risk by diversifying your production and operations sites? Would your suppliers have difficulty sending shipments to an alternate business location that you might use on a temporary basis?

Given the existing resources of your small business, define the scope of the endeavor that you think is reasonable. Also define some intermediate goals and estimate the costs of developing your contingency plans relative to the potential benefits. Make some assumptions and identify some risk factors for your business. For example, contingency plans have most often included the provision that only one building will be affected in a disastrous event, but the attacks on the World Trade Center invalidates this assumption in cities with major structures that could be attacked from the air.

You may also have to consider a wider range of disaster-affected areas as you begin to develop your contingency plan. Stefan, my IT expert, knows a small business in Lower Manhattan that backed up its data nightly and placed those backup tapes securely in a bank safe deposit box. Unfortunately, that particular bank branch was located in the shopping concourse of the World Trade Center. I used to bring backup CDs home with me when my contingency plans contemplated worst-case disaster scenarios such as a fire destroying my office building. I had not contemplated a scenario that would simultaneously affect my home and place of work. I have since revised my contingency plan for recovering electronic data.

Developing your contingency plan should not become a large bureaucratic effort. Indeed, to be effective, your small business' contingency plans should be a model of clarity, understood by every employee. It begins with key management leaders and includes all the employees—because in a disaster situation, every person who is knowledgeable and prepared can make a critical difference to a successful outcome. Employee training is key, because each person must understand the importance and necessity of contingency planning and response to a disaster, and know what his or her role will be. In a real emergency, you cannot afford to delay your response because of undefined roles. Indeed, in order to build employee consensus about the need for contingency planning, you should educate your employees and encourage them to develop their own personal and family contingency plans. Such efforts will likely yield extraordinary dividends—small businesses are often wonderful places to work in part because we are like families; not large, impersonal bureaucracies. The sincere care and concern you show for your employees will result in higher productivity, I promise you.

To illustrate this point, I would like to share with you three real and painful stories of families that suffered in disasters. These are examples of suffering that could have been alleviated had the families done some personal contingency or disaster planning. The first concerns a friend who suffered a head injury from the force of falling debris in a burning building. His relatives probably saw the disaster reported on the local television news. Imagine the mental torture they suffered as they worried about what had happened to him. Had he maintained an "in case of emergency" card in his wallet, medical staff would have contacted his relatives and informed them of his status. Until he was able to communicate—he was heavily sedated following major surgery—his relatives were left to frantically call his apartment in the hope that he would answer or return the messages they had left on his answering machine. Several of my aunts are nurses, which is probably why I have a laminated card in my wallet advising whom to contact on my behalf in the event of an emergency. I provide secondary contacts in the event our first contact cannot be reached. Verify this information annually as people do move, change employers, and so forth, and outdated information is of little use.

Consider the second example. I had a neighbor who worked in the World Trade Center and has not been seen since September 11. Her father came to New York City to inquire if anyone had seen her and showed photographs of her to the other tenants of the building. This lady had daycare arrangements for her child but no one, including the child's grandfather, knew what they were. Presumably, the daycare provider had an emergency contact person; but imagine the anxiety that the child's grandfather suffered that might have been mitigated had he been made aware of the childcare arrangements and knew how to directly contact the daycare provider.

Finally, I want to share with you a very personal example that had a happier ending. My mother suffered a traumatic brain injury that required extensive medical intervention. My parents, as part of their contingency planning, had prepared advance healthcare directives and durable powers of attorney in the event that one or both of them should become incapacitated. I was able to sign consent forms authorizing the forms of treatment that were consistent with her wishes. I'm happy to report that she is alive and well.

Most people generally don't give much thought to these matters. I am not by nature ghoulish, but I have nurses in my family and my grandfather was a fireman, so I have a greater awareness of the incidence of disasters. I don't intend that my loved ones should suffer needless worry and you shouldn't either, and neither should your employees. Encourage your employees to bring the methodology of contingency planning and disaster recovery home with them. Advise them of the first aid classes offered by the Red Cross. Ask them if they can remember when they last replaced the batteries in their smoke alarms at home. It is hard to concentrate on the business task at hand if you or your employees are worried about the safety of your families. If your son were missing following a disaster, how productive would you be at work during the time that he is unable to call you and the medical staff treating him have no family contact information? Make careful planning a way of life and of business for everyone in your extended small business family.

You will also discover that you should do some general process engineering on how your company works. If your business has clear lines of responsibility, defined processes that are established and followed, and documents that are properly filed, you will likely be successful in establishing a good disaster recovery scheme. If your normal business day is characterized by managing the *crisis du jour* in an atmosphere of confusion, you will likely have difficulty implementing a disaster recovery plan.

I have visited many companies that were not ready to implement disaster recovery solutions. Many of them had gone through so many computer and system upgrades, using many different "bundled" applications. They are faced not only with a wide collection of similarly-named documents in various locations, but also with documents that can not be assigned to any former activity because it is no longer possible to read them without going through a major deciphering effort. This is much more an issue for small businesses, as large businesses usually have standardized roll-out IT platforms and consolidated user data storage.

Now you understand why any contingency planning effort must be conducted in concert with a major review of your business, not only to identify the critical assets that you need to protect, but also to identify and organize all related items. As you can imagine, although it will be time-consuming at first, your small business will benefit as a result.

Once you have reviewed your business operations, you will be ready to order your priorities and select the areas on which to focus. You may consider some of these areas because they are located in offices that appear to be at high risk. You may consider other offices as candidates for a contingency provision with a remote backup site. An alternate business site is needed if your original site is out of service or inaccessible. An excellent solution for small businesses with multiple sites of operations is to share disaster contingency space or other facilities. So if one business location goes down, the other locations would provide for some key employees space and IT services. You could also consider integrating a telecommuting setup in your temporary disaster recovery provisions whereby key employees would work from home using services provided from an off-site IT setup.

Once you have developed a thorough plan, you must be prepared to revisit it regularly and revise it, if necessary. Take the opportunity to schedule a disaster shutdown of your company's operations, for example, on the weekend following a regularly scheduled fire drill. Once your backup location is ready, you should regularly update and train your key staff on disaster mode operation. As your small business grows, your needs will change and you will need to adapt your disaster contingency plan accordingly. You should also update your inventory of your property, plant, and equipment.

*For IT assets you need to keep a record of:*

**Hardware assets:** Manufacturer, model name and number, quantity, serial numbers, service tags/configuration code, maintenance dates, support phone, location, replacement cost

**Software assets:** Manufacturer, title, version, quantity, serial number/license key, support phone, location, replacement cost

**IT Staff/Human capital:** Employee's name, position, telephone (work, home, cell), responsibility during disaster

**System Data assets:** System name, operating system, location, availability and location of backup unit, where, backup frequency, person responsible

**User Data:** System name, operating system, location, availability of backup unit, location, backup frequency, person responsible

**Third Party:** Service name, provider name, phone (support desk, emergency number)

**Printers, Network, and Other Peripherals:** Manufacturer, model name and number, serial number, maintenance dates, phone (support desk, emergency number), replacement cost.

This will be important in your recovery efforts as you need to know which equipment (and which personnel) can be redeployed and which assets your insurance policy may replace. Now that we have completed our "preparation" overview, we are ready to "drill down" to specific areas on which to focus in developing your contingency plan. In the "Prepare" part of this book, we will discuss topics such as proper handling of office mail, developing an IT infrastructure, and putting together an insurance program.

# PART ONE

# PREPARE

Notice that this part contains two chapters and is longer than the parts that follow it, "Respond" and "Recover." I didn't plan it that way, but that *should* be the result: planning is the most important activity you will undertake. Risk management and disaster recovery specialists have an expression, "To fail to plan is to plan to fail." The time and effort you invest in preparation will expedite your recovery from disaster.

The second point I would like to emphasize is that because successful contingency planning is closely connected to a thorough understanding of your business operations, contingency planning almost always yields benefits to your business—even if disaster never strikes. I know a small financial services company that began considering how to treat mail delivery following the anthrax scares in the Fall of 2001. As the company reviewed its existing procedures for handling mail, it discovered something shocking: It was spending $9,000 annually to send inter-office documents by overnight delivery, when an electronic document delivery system would have done the same work at negligible cost. Now, $9,000 is a lot of money to a small business, and any small business owner can think of better ways to invest that sum. In the process of developing a contingency plan, this small business improved its operating procedures and realized a return on the time and effort invested in contingency planning—even though disaster has, thankfully, not struck. Your small business can, too.

# 3

# Preparing Your IT Strategy

Your information technology (IT) strategy is critical to your disaster prepar-edness and recovery efforts. Most businesses have an in-house IT staff or a relationship with an external consultant that built their systems. Such rela-tionships are valuable and it is not in the interest of a small business to abandon them in frustration. The IT team that built your system knows it in detail and has made decisions based on the specifications that your business had required. They may have been instructed to implement a certain fea-ture "exactly this way." Should you terminate this relationship in haste and replace your existing team with a new IT solutions provider, you will incur additional costs and will likely once again be disappointed with the results.

Remember the expression from the movie *Cool Hand Luke*: "What we have here is a failure to communicate." It can be very frustrating for IT professionals to try to implement a systems solution at the direction of busi-ness people who don't understand the technical constraints or the inherent contradictions or unreasonableness in what they are asking. At the same time, it is very disappointing for business people to invest significant sums of capital in IT capacity only to find that the result is not what they had anticipated. In such situations, what you need to do is to make sensible and powerful changes that will be welcomed as improvements without embar-rassing or blaming the existing IT members for their decisions.

A good IT solution provides contingent capacity, is simple, and easy to operate. Creating or reviewing for contingency includes analyzing the cur-rent infrastructure, determining how the system is used, understanding current and future needs from a high-level perspective, and observing if those needs are being met and if they will be met in the future. The exercise of developing a contingency plan opens the door for a productive dialogue with your IT staff, as well as your customers, suppliers, and business part-ners who should all be a part of your contingency efforts. The result of this dialogue will be, I hope, a simplified and streamlined technical architecture that leads to more cost-effective solutions and additional contingent capacity. This is a far more effective solution to your business than mindlessly importing the solution developed for large corporation XYZ. Generally, a solution developed for a large corporation and then scaled down for use by a small business fails to yield the desired results.

Small business requirements for IT contingency and solutions differ substantially from those of large businesses. We see too often good solutions that have been developed for large customers simply downsized and implemented in small businesses. In most cases, they are not cost-effective, are sufficiently inflexible, and difficult to use in your day-to-day operations. And, I am sorry to report that should you find your small business in disaster recovery mode, the system you imported from a large corporation will become an impediment to your recovery efforts. The good news is that you can learn from the mistakes of other small businesses that imported solutions that were inappropriate for their needs, and develop your own, much simpler solution, at greatly reduced expense.

In developing a disaster recovery plan, businesses often put in place IT systems that anticipate and prepare for the worst case scenarios, such as the total destruction of their business facilities. They assume that all less severe disasters are subsumed and automatically protected by such a system. In fact, I have read such advice in a number of general books about disaster recovery! This assumption generally holds true, but it should not be the basis of your contingency planning. Do you intend to initiate a full-blown disaster recovery action plan each time you experience a small deviation in normal operations? Is it a cost-effective way to run your operations? It is much more sensible for small businesses to have a good solution implemented that deals efficiently with the most common "small" disaster types, such as human error, and therefore provides a swift recovery. Of course, you also want to have some protection in place against the worst case scenarios, such as a severe terrorism attack, but it is unlikely that most of the readers of this book will ever be required to implement such recovery operations. Small businesses typically need a modest, cost-sensitive solution that deals with their specific daily operations issues. This typically means developing a solution that provides for immediate recovery from modest disasters, even at the expense of slightly extending the period of recovery from severe disasters.

It is, of course, a very different approach from the one implemented by large-scale corporations. They need more complex solutions to protect themselves against severe disasters, such as terrorist attacks. In such disasters, their very existence is at stake. Imagine the situation faced by IT teams of the large money-center banks in Manhattan on September 11, 2001. They have an enormous volume of financial transactions to process, and so fast recovery from severe disasters is mandatory for them. You won't be surprised to learn that backup facilities in Jersey City were humming on September 11, taking over the responsibility of processing banking transactions from their Manhattan-based colleagues. At the same time, however, these large corporations don't expend much effort worrying about protecting against human errors, such as the mistaken deletion of a computer file. Should such human errors interfere with their operations, they can simply correct the problem by mobilizing the manpower of their vast IT departments.

To find out what you as a small business really need to feel comfortable, and to make IT infrastructure a cornerstone of your business, start with finding good answers to the questions related to protect yourself against the six disaster types already presented. The following are some sample questions; you will probably have to add your own questions to this outline:

- **Human Error.** How do your employees store their data? Is a standard naming scheme in place? Do you have version control for documents in place? How do you share data between groups? How much do you want to invest in user training versus protecting data through more technology expenses? How quickly must lost data be restored?

- **Equipment Failure.** Which are your most critical systems? What performance do you require from each system? What are acceptable downtimes to your business in case of malfunctions? Which infrastructure elements need special protection? Do you have a dedicated budget for spare parts and equipment replacements?

- **Third-Party Failure.** How essential is e-mail (and reliable Internet connectivity) to your business? How long could you work without your phone? How often do you expect power outages and how long would they last?

- **Environmental Hazards.** Did you check your offices for environmental toxins? Is your lighting system compatible with your computer screens? How did you prepare for office safety against contamination by hazardous materials? Which systems must be available remotely if you were to leave the office right away?

- **Fire and Other Disasters.** Do you have backups at a safe remote location? Do you have special equipment to detect fires and to automatically shutdown your equipment? Is your staff aware of the emergency shutdown operations? Do you have fire protection containers for important or valuable items?

- **Terrorism and Sabotage.** What is your emergency plan? Will it ensure safety of your trade secrets? Are you secured against a targeted hacker or virus attack? How do you protect your business from any disgruntled former employees?

These are the questions you should ask yourself. Did you find some that caught your attention? Are you beginning to think about answers to these questions? As you continue to read, we will ask more questions, and even answer some of them.

This exercise, the process of asking questions, is often an eye-opening one for many small businesses. You will realize for which types of disasters you have adequate protection and to which ones you are vulnerable. As you work through this exercise, you begin to see how your business processes and critical tasks are connected to your IT infrastructure, and how you can achieve a better link between critical tasks and information systems. You will also be able to view your IT infrastructure with more confidence, advising your IT staff or consultants on targeted actions to improve specific processes and to respond in anticipation of certain scenarios.

## HUMAN ERRORS

Human error is, by far, the most common and most frequent cause of business disasters. By definition, human errors are unintentional. Since they occur randomly, I hope that the overall impact on your business operations will be negligible. Each of us has had the experience of developing a new document by revising an older document or by using a template. When we finish our work and hit the "save" button, we immediately realize that we wrote over an old document that we will need again in the future. The same is true when we reorganize our files to reduce clutter and unintentionally delete a whole folder of important documents.

Unfortunately, there is no single, simple solution. We have to expect that human errors will be made, and be able to protect our businesses from ourselves to the extent possible. Managers often hope that their employees will be careful with important files, and when they inadvertently delete a file, they hope a backup file exists. Try to keep track of these events. If you do so, you will realize that these errors occur with greater frequency than you realize. And the corrective action taken is more often less than satisfactory. Frequently, the loss of a file is either not realized, or simply never reported, until someone runs nervously through the company asking if anyone still has a copy of a particular file. By that time, it is usually much too late to recover this file from backup systems and it would require more time to retrieve the deleted file than to create a new one. IT managers often have business people making requests of them such as, "could you see if we still have a backup file of the presentation we gave to our most important client last year? I don't remember the name of the document, but I wrote it in the first quarter of the year." This is not an efficient use of anyone's time, and as a small business owner or manager, you know that experienced IT professionals are too expensive to be used in this manner; you have too many other important tasks for them!

Small businesses need a solution that is a combination of user-training and a backup mechanism from which users can recover unintentionally deleted files themselves. It helps both the users and the IT staff save time because the users no longer have to request the IT staff to recover files for them. And as a small business owner, you do not need to hire someone to operate the backup system in the event your staff needs to retrieve files.

## User Training

It took me some time to develop an archiving system for my business files that allows me to recover work that was done years ago. I am sure you can appreciate the volume of documents and files that a business creates, so you understand the importance of retrieving your data. The future of your business depends on the quality of its information resources and the timely availability of any data needed.

Now imagine you have hired a new employee. Unless you have some guidelines in place, how do you expect this new employee to store documents in a way that other employees can easily retrieve two years later? Training your new and, if necessary, current employees, will not simply be a computer training exercise, but it will also raise the awareness of how your employees should support the contingency plan. You should provide at least some instructions to your staff on:

- Storing data on your computer system (and how NOT to store data)
- Sharing data among work groups
- Naming files in progress and naming of files for archival;
- Using version control for documents
- Creating logical links (e.g., hyperlinks between documents)
- Archiving files and initiating immediate snapshot backups
- Retrieving files from your backup system
- Shutting down your computer system safely
- Deleting files

This project has a cost associated to it as it requires an investment of time. But once you adopt agreed-upon practices for data handling, they will soon become standard procedure and your existing staff will cross-train new employees. I am certain that after a few months, you will realize the benefits of establishing these procedures. When Stefan advised me on how to establish such a system, I found that within two months, my business spent less time retrieving, changing, and filing documents. It was particularly helpful for my business as I work with overseas clients. Differences in languages and practices can result in some creative document naming (and some hair-pulling exercises trying to imagine which keyword would help to locate a document when the author of the document speaks a different language!). Once you adopt these practices, your business will easily identify inconsistencies and correct them much more quickly. Group collaboration will become much easier—and isn't that what your business is all about?—bringing people together to accomplish a shared goal?

**Data Backups: Part I**

You have data that must be stored safely. Most of it is mission-critical. Types of digital information may range from the product documentation created by your employees to the details of key customer accounts, business contacts lists, sales databases, and e-mail correspondences, just to name a few. For yours as well as for many other companies, the competitive advantage resides in these information assets and the trained staff who can work with them. But they are the very same people who make mistakes from time to time. User-training can only do so much, as user errors will continue to occur.

Making data backups regularly is your second line of defense after training your users. But these are not the type of complete system backups that are made as a precaution to equipment failure—we will discuss those later. The backups needed here must address the needs of the users, therefore be more frequently done and initiated by users themselves. Restoration must also be simple and quick. A small business cannot afford long downtimes or call an IT specialist for retrieval of your files, merely when an important file has been mistakenly altered or deleted. The fact that it was important already indicates that it is most likely used and modified frequently.

Tapes as backup medium disqualify for this purpose for the reason that they store data sequentially, meaning data cannot be accessed directly; thus, recovery time is fairly long. It can take hours to find a particular file on a large tape. Other removable media, like USB sticks and CDs, allow the direct access of data. They are very limited in their storage capacity, and as such, usable only for small projects. DVD and HD DVD drives have much higher capacities, but still, you do rely on the user to make backups in a patient, regular, and correct manner. Users can make mistakes here as well. Nothing is more disappointing than finding out that your employee's backup did not store the important files correctly. In any case, users expect automatic backup of their work and will rightfully consider anything short of that a needless annoyance.

In addition, you need to be aware that creating backups on removable media could raise security concerns because employees could take large amounts of confidential data with them without leaving a trace. In fact, if data security is a major concern for you, you should restrict access to all high-capacity media drives and monitor online data traffic in and out of your company.

You will need a backup strategy that allows you to make quick backups with easy retrieval of files by each individual user. There are about 50 companies supplying the backup storage systems market. Most specialize in enterprise-size solutions, but some of them also offer downsized solutions from their larger cousins to small businesses. They are indeed fast and reliable backup solutions, but they come at a steep price that would leave a large dent in your IT budget or they are not intuitive to use. In any case, you should select an adequate backup system that fits your requirements as a small business in several ways. It must:

- Provide the data security that you need, either on-site or off-site

- Be able to handle to handle your typical amount of data within timeframes acceptable to you

- Provide a retrieval time suited for the disaster type case that you are trying to address

- Provide a cost-effective solution for your targeted recovery time

For small businesses, in most cases, you do not need fancy storage area network hardware or the latest gizmo in online storage technology to provide an adequate contingency backup solution with fast retrieval possibilities. Imagine that you would like to make a snapshot backup every hour of all user data files. If the amount of user data that has to be transferred each time is less than about ten gigabytes, and this is true for the wide majority of all small businesses, a simple network-attached storage system with a couple of large hard disks and a basic network configuration will do just fine. If this system is configured for machine input/output (I/O) performance, you essentially have a solution that is otherwise sold for a multiple of the price.

With regards to online storage solutions, you send all your data to a safe data center located off-site. Preferably, your data should be encrypted and secured if you are using the Internet for this purpose. The use of such online storage solutions looks appealing at first glance, and is often an elegant solution, especially if they are directly supported by the operating systems' drag-and-drop windows (e.g., Windows XP Professional/Vista or Mac OS X). Beware that you will pay a monthly or annual fee for the actual amount of storage used; your bottleneck in transferring the data will be your Internet connection, or the Internet itself. And then there are often limits on the amount of data you can transfer in and out of such a facility per month. By the way, similar limits will most likely also apply to your Internet connection, especially if you are using DSL or a cable modem. A small business should consider if online storage solutions really satisfy its needs, and compare them with the alternatives proposed in this book.

There are many different software packages in the market that allow you to create a backup of your data independent of the final storage media, be it another hard disk, a remote location, or a tape drive. A simple backup utility is already included in Windows XP Professional, Vista, or the Macintosh's OS Time Machine, and you may buy other software packages separately. Apple's "time machine" is a good example of an intuitive interface to UNIX built-in backup methods. However, for the amount of data typically handled by a small business and using it to recover from user error, special backup software is not necessary. You want to avoid many of them because they use proprietary backup file formats, and you do not have large business facilities at your disposal to ensure that you will still be able to read your backup file format after five years.

To create backups of user data, first familiarize yourself with any easy-to-use file synchronization tool. There exist a variety of such tools, some commercially available and others integrated in operating systems or simply for download as shareware from the Internet. The way these utilities work is that they simply scan your local files and all your files on the backup system and then determine which files need to be updated because they have been newly created, modified, or deleted. It is similar to a method used by mobile devices synching data with your desktop.

After the initial run (which might take some time if your overall data sets are large), these tools are usually very fast. They scan, for example, 10,000 files with 3 gigabytes total size in less than 10 minutes, and replace 100 altered files on a backup hard disk in less than one minute. The user can trigger the file synchronization anytime. In addition, an automatic update every hour or every night should be scheduled. You can keep as many of these automatically created snapshot backups as you have disk space on your backup system. Note that with hourly, daily, or weekly backups, you should clean up your backups to keep your datasets manageable.

If all users store their data on a file server, run a backup in the same manner between the file server and the backup system. However, be aware that usually no live file server for user data is needed for small businesses until you reach a certain size or data complexity. It is sufficient to keep data locally on each personal computer (PC), and then to consolidate this data by file synchronization, on- or off-site, on a network attached storage server that must be available at certain times. Since the data will be stored at two locations, no further backup of that file server is needed for this disaster scenario. You will be surprised at the cost savings that result from this simple solution.

The backup file system should be configured to provide all backup data with appropriate access rights to the users on the network, to allow everyone access and to rebuild the data at any time. For ease of use, you can even make all backups available through your Web browser, but again, review data access for adequate data security. And by the way, the availability and continuous usage also ensures implicit testing of your backup system, although you want to methodically check it out once in a while.

## EQUIPMENT FAILURES

ner or later a component of your IT equipment will fail. Fortunately, ment failures occur less frequently than human errors. Sometimes, you er an even more frustrating scenario: a computer that periodically malfunctions. This is a fairly common scenario. About half of data losses on desktop computers can be attributed to data corruption on the hard disk, caused in equal measure by physical hard disk surface damage or software glitches. In one-third of the cases, data are lost due to interruptions in power supply. In about 10% of the cases, data are lost from desktop computers due to overheated parts, caused by fans inside the computer clogged by dust or that otherwise malfunctioned. This happens more frequently in dusty or carpeted rooms. The remaining 10% of the cases of data losses from desktop computers can be attributed to other causes, such as processor and board failures.

For our present purposes, let us assume that such an event is localized, meaning that only one system is affected at any given time. As we get further along, we will discuss complete system failures, including the total destruction of the system. We include in this category equipment failures that were originally caused by human error. Imagine that, in the process of repairing a broken lamp, you accidentally pull the computer plug. Afterward, the computer no longer boots because a major data corruption on the hard disk occurred when you mistakenly pulled the plug.

It is possible to create nearly perfect protection against system failures. This can go as far as building so-called high-availability (HA) configurations that call for guaranteed continuous operation and availability in extreme cases. This could be realized with two or more computers that monitor each other, and in the event that one of them malfunctions, the error is automatically detected and corrected and the defective computer is then shut down. These setups are used for critical trading systems, and the space shuttle has five computers in an HA configuration.

However, short of launching a space shuttle or running an expensive  financial trading operation, HA setups for typical continuous availability requirements are not cost-effective. They are expensive to set up and to maintain. It is unlikely that your small business has such requirements. But you may have systems that require 24/7 availability, for example, revenue-producing Web sites and other e-commerce applications. Many companies would consider it desirable to also have 24/7 e-mail systems availability. You should outsource such systems to a large data center that can do the job for you in a much more cost-effective manner than a small business ever could. They are experienced in professionally managing thousands of servers under nearly continuous operating conditions.

The reason why e-mail is often included as a critical functionality is simply the fact that it has become one of the most valuable resources for small businesses. In particular, businesses that have traditionally done most of their communication via regular mail or mail pouch now prefer to use e-mail for daily, informal communication and the exchange of ideas, for example, law offices. A couple of years ago, you would have visited your lawyer to discuss a contract. Today, you discuss these items efficiently via e-mail. If you are not a company that is doing business in the IT arena, like this example of the law office, and you have to call a third-party service to fix your computer system, you should consider outsourcing your e-mail operation to professionals who ensure its proper functioning around the clock.

For any IT systems that you will maintain inside your business, there are methods to improve the contingency against equipment failure. To begin, rank your systems and associated work flows into the categories:

- **Critical.** Systems that directly support your core business operation. As discussed, for a small business, these systems should be out-sourced and operated from a data center, but you might have very specific reasons, such as concerns about data security, why you want to keep them in-house and you are willing to accept the occasional lack of availability to keep costs down. Examples of systems you may prefer to maintain in-house are your client relationship management system, your company shared documents database, and your internal Web server.

  *The goals:* System Availability: close to 24/7; Downtime: less than one hour during business hours; Data Restoration: complete and immediate access on backup server during business hours.

- **Important.** Systems that provide important add-on services to your business operation, such as your meeting, scheduling, and calendar system or payroll and accounting.

  *The goals:* System Availability: expected during regular business hours; Downtime: less than one to two days; Data Restoration: complete with backup data availability on the same or next business day.

- **Optional.** Systems that make your daily activities more efficient, such as scanners with text recognition software or video conferencing systems. However, no vital information is stored on such systems.

  *The goals:* System Availability: usually operational during business hours; Downtime: less than three days or uptime as requested; Data Restoration: not required, but possible on special request.

You probably already have a good idea which category each of your computer systems would fall into. You are now ready to make a direct comparison and assess the tradeoffs between system failure and contingency measures that should give you a clear idea on the required budget and manpower to protect each computer system appropriately.

Note the importance of simple regular maintenance on your equipment. This is an effective measure in avoiding failures that are most often caused by trivial circumstances and therefore create more hassle than actual damage. For example, components like monitors, keyboards, and mice often fail because they are directly exposed to human beings who sometimes spill coffee over them. Fortunately, they are easily exchanged as long as you have replacements available. You also want to open each computer from time to time. Fan inlets that are clogged with dust do not allow sufficient cooling of the internal components. This can quickly lead to overheating. Another warning sign of pending equipment failure is grinding noises from fans or hard disks.

## Data Backups: Part II

The backup strategy for equipment failure will differ from the strategy to deal with human errors. With respect to contingency for human errors, the priority was immediate accessibility of data, preferably by the users themselves, and brief retrieval and restoration times for individual files. For equipment failure contingencies, the goal shifts to minimize the total time needed to restore the full functionality of the affected system.

Creating a system backup will help to protect critical and important business systems. Again, we must select the appropriate backup media for this purpose. In this case, we no longer seek quick retrieval of data, preferably by the user, but a complete backup of a computer system. Depending on the number and average system size of computers, tape can be beneficial because of its low unit cost per megabyte of stored data. If we compare the costs between the different storage media and assume that the cost of storing 1MB on a CD is normalized to one, storing the same megabyte on a DVD drive is about 50% less expensive, on hard disks about 99% less expensive, and on tapes about 99.9% less expensive. However, this picture changes when you take into account the cost of the actual hardware for the media drive. Fast and reliable tape drives are expensive, and unless you measure your data storage requirements in terabytes, which would be unusual for small businesses, high-capacity hard disks are close to an optimum between cost-effectiveness and quick data retrieval.

We often use a backup system with large disks to store complete images of the system partition. The advantage of doing so is the instant availability of this image anywhere in the network should the system ever fail. There are a variety of software tools in the market that provide this disk to image functionality. Note that disk images are only dependent on the file system being used, which means that the data format is not proprietary to specific software.

Since your backup system itself becomes a critical part of your operation, hosting two different backup data sets, you should consider installing a Redundant Array of Inexpensive Disks (RAID) system. You simply add a second hard disk and connect both the old and the new drive to a RAID card that is available at low cost. Configured properly, the operating system will recognize the two drives as one logical drive and any data written to that drive are written to both disks at the same time, effectively mirroring all data.

Actually, if you use one of the free UNIX operating systems, like Linux, on your backup system, you can use the software RAID solution that is included for free as it is done on a commercial network attached storage drives. It is more than sufficient for a backup system.

The mirroring functionality gives you protection against hardware failures. But remember that a mirroring RAID system does not protect you from data lost due to human error or electrical shock failures. If you delete a file, it is deleted on both mirrored hard disks and in case of an electrical shock; both hard drives would be affected. This also applies to externally connected hard drives, so for protection you should always use two alternating external hard drives. If you are concerned about human error as well, you should simply partition the logical hard disk into three areas, one for the operating system, and two partitions of equal size, one for user data and the other as backup of the user data partition. Periodically, or on demand, you can use a file synchronization tool to update the backup data partition. Now you are storing each user file four times on two disks.

It is a low-cost solution that should give you more confidence about storing data on your desktop computer. Of course, the computer could be stolen or destroyed in a severe disaster. We will come back to this topic later in this book when we examine more severe forms of disaster, as in the section for "Fires." For now, you could make the backup hard drive a removable drive and take it home with you each night to provide a readily available backup in the event of severe disaster. It will not be necessary to do anything other than to reinstall a disk should one of the hard disk drives fail as replacing the defective disk with a new one will automatically trigger a copy from the old disk to the new disk until the data on both disks are the same again. This process is easy, but can take hours to complete if the disks are really large.

If this RAID method appears to be overkill with regard to your contingency requirements, another method is to use a single additional disk and copy data from the main disk to that additional backup disk using the same file synchronization or disk-to-disk backup tools as previously described. The advantage to this method is that you would initiate the backup yourself after you are sure that the changes on your main hard disk reflect the changes you wish to make. You can even use these tools to create a backup directly on an external backup medium, such as CDs or DVDs. With these solutions, however, you lose the on-the-spot safety of a RAID strategy. If the main disk fails, you will have lost all changes from the time you ran your last backup to the moment that main disk failed.

Don't forget to periodically back up your system partition. You might think that if it fails it can be easily reloaded from the installation CDs. Think again. Within one year, you probably install numerous patches and updates, software specifically for use by only that particular computer and customized settings with regards to the actual computer usage. Recreating this environment when the goal is to minimize system downtime is simply counterproductive. Reloading the system from scratch could easily become a daunting and time-consuming task.

Always remember, the additional costs of a backup system will pay off handsomely if you have to make use of your backup system only once in its lifetime. Trying to repair parts or recover data from defective hard disks rarely makes economic sense. Replace the faulty part and rely for restoration of data on your backups instead. Interestingly though, manufacturers report that about 70% of the hard disks returned for repair under warranty are still in perfect working order, but their data structure is corrupted. So before you return a hard disk for replacement under warranty, try to reformat the disk first and run a thorough hard disk check.

If you send your disk to a data recovery service, make sure you understand the costs involved. The service typically charges a low fee to take an initial look at your hard disk, but data recovery work on your disk can easily cost hundreds of dollars, even thousands, if data forensic experts have to reconstruct files that have been deleted. Consider not only the cost, but also the inconvenience of not having your data for up to several weeks. Of course, there is also a potential security concern when you send your hard disk to others.

One last piece of advice on this subject: If you have to re-create a system disk from the stored image on the file server, you will need to buy a new disk. Try to purchase the exact same model disk from the same manufacturer. If you choose a hard disk from another manufacturer, you need to be aware that hard disks vary slightly from manufacturer to manufacturer in size, even if the overall given size is the same. Copying the disk image back to a disk that is too small, even if by only a couple of megabytes, will not guarantee success.

## Network Reliability

Network failures, especially for local area networks, are relatively rare. But a network is a good first test on how far contingency planning has progressed. When someone tells you that their network is completely protected and fail-safe, tell them that you would go over to their office and "pull the plug" on any one network cable. Observe their response!

Before you see network failures, you will typically first face network performance issues, like overloads of routers or switches, which clearly illustrate the need for good network capacity planning especially if your network exceeds 100 users. If network reliability and performance issues are both of great concern to you, try a practical approach, simply to "double-up." Every computer is equipped with two network adapters, and you have for each workstation two network cable connections. You double your hubs, switches, and routers as appropriate. You may consider this overkill, and it probably is, but you should look at it this way: If it is done while building your network, the additional costs will be modest. Standard CAT5e/6 cable used for offices can by itself support two network and two phone connections, while building in a performance enhancement and a reliability upgrade at the same time!

With doubled network cabling and routers you are now also able to have the routers automatically reroute your traffic through an alternative network path if the preferred route is down due to a failed connection. You can also use the mechanism for load balancing, but at that point you would probably need the help of an experienced network consultant. In any case, if you just think about this early in the process, such as when setting up a new office infrastructure, the additional cost to your overall bill will be minimum.

Of course, you should always have a carefully chosen inventory of spare networking components available, so that you will be able to quickly replace a faulty part. And if a network does go down, and you still have not outsourced your systems that need near 24/7 availability, you should install a network monitor that would automatically dial the numbers of the people that are assigned to handle the emergency. By the way, most of these units also monitor environmental conditions, such as loss of electrical power or room temperature as an indication of proper air conditioning. Some can even detect smoke or water in the room and they can therefore be of great help in avoiding subsequent damage.

You should purchase stand-alone network components. It is generally not worth shortcutting expenses by not purchasing additional network equipment and instead configuring a computer as a router or print server, for example. You are building network functionality on a complex piece of equipment that is much more likely to fail than a comparatively simple stand-alone solution.

## Equipment Quality

If you are concerned about contingency, you want to have high quality equipment. A few unreliable components can cause lots of trouble. They fail more often, they require frequent repairs, and they will eventually have to be replaced with a more reliable component.

The question often follows, "Which computer should I buy?" This question is easier to answer if you are looking into some special market segment, like the large scale IBM and Sun computing and storage systems or the Apple Macintosh OS X if you have only basic home media functionality needs or work in a specialized design or media business. But when it comes to standard PCs, the answer is not as straightforward as you might think.

To tell you the truth, the differences between computers are marginal. The parts that are inside the box are pretty much the same in all computers. They are produced for the world market from a variety of large manufacturers. If you are in the market to buy a standard office PC or a simple file server, you should look for systems that have been labeled for use by small businesses. Many manufacturers offer these base systems at attractive prices. However, you need to know that they make their money with all the add-ons to that system which you then purchase at a relatively high price. Not unlike purchasing a car from the dealership! If you are looking for something truly specific, like a fanless, super-quiet system, and you are somewhat PC-literate, you are probably better off looking for a "no-name!" Actually, even with good "no-names," reliability of the parts inside of a computer is of little concern, because if you really look inside, you will find that all manufacturers use more or less the same basic parts from worldwide suppliers anyway. And by the way, for the actual parts, you will always find reliability measurements, like mean-time-before-failure (MTBF).

Let's take a different perspective. Think about the elements that you will interact with daily once the computer is on your desk: the screen, keyboard, and mouse. Here you will find quality differences, and if a part is defective, it is easily changed. So make sure that you always have some spare components available. As for the keyboard and mouse, there are big differences in quality between a no-name and a branded product. From most inexpensive to most expensive, prices vary by a factor of ten and more. If you ever experienced a mouse that constantly got stuck while you were trying to finish an important presentation, you will appreciate an optical mouse. It is more reliable, more exact, and works on nearly any surface. For the keyboard, you should defer to the individual preferences of employees. A keyboard, and to some degree a mouse, can make a difference in someone's overall experience with a computer system. In the end, these are inexpensive purchases anyway.

LCD displays with LED backlighting over their lifetime will actually be the more cost-effective choice as they should outlast about two generations of computers without deteriorating color over time. They use 50% less energy and can therefore provide extra time if you run on batteries. But you should be aware that there are differences in quality between LCD displays. The same manufacturer will produce a "consumer" and a "professional" version. The price difference is often marginal, but the professional versions are improved on important parameters, such as the color calibration or contrast ratio that should be at least 1:500 or higher, but in consumer products you will most often find only 1:300.

The optimal amount of memory and disk space, as well as the processor clock speed, will depend on your specific usage of the system. In general, however, most systems benefit from an upgrade of the video card, as often poor video signals from original video cards can ruin your effort to obtain a clear image on your screen. Remember, no monitor will make a good picture from a poor input signal, and upgrading your video card is inexpensive. Since a fast processor can only perform well if it gets the required data from memory or the hard disk fast enough, plan to spend generously on memory (RAM) and a fast hard disk. Also, note that when comparing different systems, it is not simple to compare the processor frequency from one processor to another. Different processors with different architectures can have significant performance differences on certain tasks.

For contingency planning, "equipment quality" as such is of little concern, as most brand name companies build their systems from parts often made by the same original equipment manufacturers. You need to make sure that the three things you work with every day—the monitor, keyboard, and mouse—meet high quality standards. Keep your computer network as consistent as possible. The greater number of identical systems you have, the easier it will be to rebuild your office infrastructure. You always want to try to buy or have at least two to ten PCs that are identical. A greater number of identical PCs is even better, but small businesses typically buy about four PCs at a time. Always buy the latest generation processor. This should extend the lifetime of the PC for an additional year and usually compares favorably to the cost savings of buying last year's processor at a discount.

If you consider using laptops with a docking station at the office, keep in mind that laptops are generally more expensive and slower than comparably priced desktops. They are, however, very well suited for contingency planning, as you can simply take them with you.

For printers, an inexpensive printer will quickly become more expensive with increasing print volumes. Calculate the cost per page by considering the various ink and laser cartridges and then compare the costs with your expected printing volume. You will find amazing results. So carefully review your requirements. If your printing output is mostly black and white copies, we recommend you start with a laser printer because it is generally more reliable than an ink jet printer. There is simply no liquid ink that can dry and clog-up a print head. The laser printer should print at least ten pages per minute and its cartridge should print 5,000 pages. If you like to print color occasionally, or you need a second, inexpensive printer, then buy a separate ink jet printer.

There is a downside to purchasing a system that has many integrated functions. Multifunction machines have become popular among small businesses. They are less expensive than stand-alone machines as they can share the housing, power supply, and so on. But it becomes quite frustrating when such a machine malfunctions and must be sent away for service. You lose all its functionality at once. This is an acceptable risk for home and personal use, but for your business, you need to ensure that you have at least your basic everyday needs covered with simple, but reliable units, like an inexpensive black and white laser printer. Then a multifunction machine with color printing can be a fun addition for tight spaces.

### Software Installation

Computer systems fail more frequently due to software glitches than to hardware problems. It happens all too often; the computer simply freezes and you need to reboot, potentially losing all the data in the documents you were working on. You should use only operating systems that have been proven stable and reliable in deployment for large installations (e.g., Windows XP Professional or Vista). The Mac OS X and many of the UNIX operating systems, either on their native platforms or in their Intel-compatible versions, are also very robust. They have become an economical solution for simple server functions, like file servers, Web servers, and so forth.

In large businesses, PCs are deployed with a standard configuration installed. In small businesses, we often find PCs as they came out of the box, with various different software packages installed, most of them demo or light versions, also known as "bloatware." While this is done for marketing purposes, it is sometimes counterproductive to the reliability of such systems. Don't be surprised when months later you suddenly introduce an incompatibility between new software that you just installed and a package whose name you had never heard of, but that was installed on your PC. Also check the compatibility of the software you are about to install with your operating system. Systems often have to be reinstalled after a failed attempt to install incompatible software, such as installing Windows 2000 software on a Windows XP/Vista machine. Small businesses should also perform a clean installation of the operating system on delivery of the new hardware, and then install the applications that are truly needed, even if this initially requires more effort. But it will be beneficial in the long term, especially for reliability. It will effectively prepare you if you are growing and soon will have a network that would call for a "your-standard" PC configuration; with a standard office package and some standardized network and backup data access features.

I strongly recommend re-installing Windows without the additional "bloatware" software and loading a system maintenance program. Make sure that the software you choose has at least the following features that you should be able to schedule for automatic run one or two nights a week:

- System virus scan and automatic updates over the Internet
- Disk defragmentation
- Thorough system inconsistency check
- File system and hard disk error check.

These preventive functions will help keep your PC in optimal shape, long before larger issues become significant and possibly interrupt the operation of the PC.

## THIRD-PARTY FAILURES

You have made significant efforts to protect your business from human errors and from equipment failures. But you are not alone in this world and your business is highly dependent on third parties providing a variety of services to you. There are direct IT services, such as your Internet connection, e-mail, and Web hosting that are provided via the Internet from a data center if you outsource these services. And of course there are the standard services, like phone lines, electrical power, water, heating, and air conditioning, and so forth.

If you could, you would like to buy each service from two separate vendors, so that you have two companies providing you with phone service, another two providing you with Internet access, and so on. In theory, if one service fails, you would always have the same service from your other provider available. But that is only in theory.

When you buy services for your business, each supplier offers a whole list of service offerings and to make it really attractive, your salesperson will offer a nicely priced packaged deal. So a phone company would offer you Internet access together with their phone service, a cable TV company would offer you Internet access with your cable TV, and so on. Most throw in additional services, like e-mail and Web-hosting. Many people do not know that you can get add-on services by themselves, such as cable Internet access without having to sign-up for cable TV. In fact, you should carefully review if any type of bundling of services from one provider is really worth the savings. Often it is not, and there is more built-in dependency than you would appreciate at first glance. For example, the e-mail accounts that accompany the service subscription are normally accessible only when you have been authenticated and are connected via that particular Internet service. Of course, the vendor will tell you that they are doing it to protect themselves from abuse of their mail services for relaying spam mail. But this is only partially true because there are many other methods, like separate authentication for outgoing e-mail or limiting the number of outgoing mails from one e-mail account, which would have little effect on you, but would deter individuals that would like to send spam mail to thousands of people.

However, what your Internet service provider (ISP) is trying to do is to tie you, their valued customer, as much as possible to their services. This means that if your Internet access goes down, so does your e-mail. Only when you try to change your ISP, will you realize how much they have managed to lock you in. And imagine this happening to you in a disaster situation, your ISP no longer offers services for whatever reason, and suddenly you not only have to work on getting a new ISP, but you need to change your e-mail address as well. When you are in an emergency situation and responding to a disaster, you don't want to have your hands tied this way.

Choose your ISP independently of the other services they provide in their package. You first want to make sure that the Internet service suits your needs. As for the provider's other offerings, like phone service, make them secondary services for your business and obtain a separate primary phone service contract from another provider. This is particularly true for e-mail and Web hosting service through your ISP. Use them for noncritical applications, such as a Web site for internal information that you make available with password authentication. Here you can post the latest marketing information that can be accessed by your sales staff on the road. Purchase critical services, like your e-mail and your sales-generating Web site, through a large independent data center.

When we speak of service that has failed, we do not necessarily mean total blackout of that service. In fact, most third-party services have in their contracts clauses about reliability guarantees, so the service itself rarely goes down. But the quality of the service provided can be so poor that it is practically useless to you. Then you have to fight with the provider to fix trivial problems like noisy telephone lines, slow Internet connections, surges in electrical power, or insufficient heating or air conditioning. Before you sign up with any company, try to meet the people in charge for your technical support when you enroll. They need to give you satisfactory answers to how and how fast they would resolve issues for you and specify those guarantees in the contract. You also want to explore the possibilities of a test connection or visit one of the provider's existing clients and have your IT-savvy person check out important parameters, such as the bandwidth and latency for a planned network connection. You can then determine if it is within the range you need.

Before you start looking for an alternate provider, it makes sense to first meet with a representative of each of the organizations that wishes to provide the service to you. They will sensitize you to issues that you had not appreciated. It is essential that you try to establish a good relationship with your contact at the third-party service provider. Attend any information sessions to which you are invited. They are a good opportunity to meet the senior management of that company in a casual setting. Mention to them that you are working on preparing a contingency plan for your business and would like their recommendation on which provider you should use as a backup if their service fails—not that you assume it will, but just in case. It is a good idea to follow it up with a "thank you" letter expressing your interest in promptly completing your contingency planning.

You will achieve two results:

1. You will receive a letter outlining the contingency plans that your third-party provider has in place that will guarantee your service. The guarantee that you receive is usually somewhere between 99.5% and 99.999%, equivalent to a few minutes per year.

2. Your provider will, reluctantly, recommend one of their competitors as a backup provider. They won't do it in writing, but they will tell you on the phone.

If you do not achieve those two results with your service provider, then switch if you can. It makes no sense to stay with them in the long run. In any case, you need to obtain contingency, meaning at least a second, maybe even a tertiary, service provider. And having personal contact with direct phone numbers is very important. If you are in disaster-recovery mode and need their help, you do not want to log a support request with their customer support desk thousands of miles away and hope for a prompt response by their local emergency team.

Again, if e-mail and Web hosting are essential to your business they should be hosted in a professionally managed data center. Outsourcing is not expensive. You can find simple Web and e-mail services that cost below $10 per month, but you should be aware that at low prices, you are sharing the service with others, which has security implications. However, the advantage is that you definitely do not want to do your own constant network load monitoring, fault detection, and upgrade plans for scalability as your business grows. There are also some inherent advantages because you might get some services at a data center that you cannot build yourself. For example, hosted e-mail services most often provide additional antispam measures that work by comparing e-mail that is sent to hundreds of accounts of different companies at the same time, indicating that it is some sort of mass mailing, most likely spam, that is then automatically blocked if you have requested this service.

In the case of a disaster, you want your staff focused on getting the business up and running. You do not want to think about moving services to get your Web site back up because your ISP has failed. In that sense, good planning and purchasing of services can definitely simplify your own disaster contingency plans. Make sure, however, that your service providers are well equipped to handle their own emergencies and can handle disaster situations at least as well as you can.

## Phone Service

We have become used to reliable phone service. It is still one of the most used methods of communication. Remember that phone lines are not only used for oral communication. They are also used to send faxes, to connect to the Internet via modem, or for credit card authorizations. After the World Trade Center disaster, many businesses suffered further losses of income simply because they could not use their credit card authorization machines when the telephone lines were down. I frequently visit the Strand Bookstore Annex in Lower Manhattan, just a short walk from the World Trade Center site. For many weeks after the disaster, this store, as well as many other businesses as far away as Chinatown (which is about one and a half miles from Wall Street), was unable to accept credit card payments, as their telephone service had not yet been restored. As you well know, customers who must pay in cash typically spend less than when they charge their credit cards. It would be difficult to calculate the revenues lost to such businesses that had already lost revenues when they closed immediately following the disaster. Consider these other uses of phone lines to come up with an effective contingency solution.

In large cities, you can usually choose between several telephone service providers. You need to make sure that you are not buying from two phone companies that are in fact reselling phone services from other parties. Otherwise, if that party has a problem, your service goes down, and your phone companies will simply refer you to the support desk of that third-party provider. It sounds ridiculous, but when you evaluate phone service providers, let the providers show you their own physical phone connections into your building and make sure they are completely separate for the two companies you select.

Phone service failures are rare, but when they occur, you will need a backup solution. If you only have one phone company you can deal with, you protect yourself best if you have phone service through two different offerings of that company, such as analog phone lines combined with Voice Over Internet Protocol (VoIP, your data network). VoIP provides a fully featured backup. Analog lines typically work even if your area is experiencing a power outage as the lines are powered by the phone company.

But in fact, for small businesses, it is rarely cost-effective to implement redundant phone circuits. If telephone service fails, it is most likely due to a service outage, not to the actual hardware. But even if it is the actual hardware, since nearly every business executive has a cellular telephone today, the cellular phone is the natural backup[1] solution for your land-based circuits. You should choose cellular phones as your backup service of choice unless you are in a rural area with little cellular phone coverage.[2]

The question is how to automatically connect land- and cellular phone-based services so the cellular phone service would take over if the landlines fail. The problem is that once the landlines have failed, it is not possible for you to forward landline calls to the cellular phones.

The solution is developed by thinking in reverse. What you want to do is to buy a cellular phone[3] specifically for phone contingency purposes. You give out that number as your general contact business number. You program the phone in such a way that any incoming call is forwarded to your land-based business phone number when the cellular phone is switched off. If your land-based line fails, you simply switch on your cellular phone, and *voilà*.

This scheme can be easily extended to any number of cellular phones and any number of landlines. You would simply configure both the cellular phones and land lines in hunt groups, meaning a call to the first number in the group would—if it is busy—automatically and instantaneously redirect to the second line and so on. The last cellular phone would redirect to the first land line, which in turn rolls over to the second land line if busy, and so forth. If the land line service fails, you just switch on any number of cellular phones that you need. If you like this setup even for use during non-disaster times, remember to give out the number of the cellular phone that you are carrying from the group of contingency cell phones so that people may call you directly, especially if they are used to calling your direct extension on the land-based system.

The last cell phone (or the last cell phone in your cell phone hunt group setup) forwards to a voice mailbox. Again, you do not want to use any voice mailbox that is provided with your land-based lines or your cellular phones. You need one that has a different delivery mechanism than by phone because you also need to be prepared that the cellular phones might stop working. In that case, any call would be forwarded directly into your voice mailbox where you can listen to the messages, assuming, of course, that the forwarding mechanism still works. Therefore it is a good idea to publish your voice and fax service number on your letterhead and your business cards so that people have an alternative voice and fax number to reach you.

 You should sign up with a voice mail provider that delivers your messages over the Internet via e-mail. In fact, you should sign up with an integrated voice and fax service. This service often costs less than a regular phone line. Single providers of only voice mail or fax delivery via the Internet are usually not cost-effective.

Since the Internet has been designed to automatically reroute traffic if one or many paths no longer work, as long as you can connect to the Internet from somewhere, it is likely that you can receive your e-mails and hence, your voice messages and faxes.

In case both your land-based phone service and your cellular phone service fail, your calls or faxes are forwarded to your integrated service number. You could even configure your system in such a way that it automatically sends you a short notification message with a summary of your voice or fax message to your cellular phone or pager. At least, you would know who called or who sent a fax. It is a service you will also enjoy during nondisaster times. It reduces unnecessary calls to your cellular phone.

You might want to use your integrated service number also for other benefits. If you use it as your public phone and fax number, you will prevent telemarketers and other people from calling you directly. They would need to leave you a message and since the message is delivered by e-mail, you can screen it upfront. If it originates from a known junk message or fax source, you simply route it to your junk mail folder.

 Another great thing is that these integrated services give you a local phone number or 800 number in any part of the world, with voice greetings in the local language. So people in Hong Kong can leave you a message as if you were a local business. And if you do not have Internet access, you can listen to your messages by phone. The system's computerized voice can even read you your e-mails over the phone.

## Electrical Power

You probably will not have much choice with respect to utilities. You have to take what your city or county provides to you, although you can choose from which company the electricity should be bought from in the end. That doesn't change the fact that there is only one connection to the building.

Whatever contingency you need in utilities during a disaster, you will need to provide yourself.

Electrical power is usually available at any time. Still, there are also quality issues, like peaks in voltage as well as microoutages, especially in rural areas where you have large users of electrical energy. Since most IT equipment is sensitive, it is best to use a surge protector, even better to use an uninterruptible power supply unit (UPS), which is usually a surge protector, together with a small buffer battery that would supply energy for about ten minutes, enough to finish important work and to shut down the system. Most units support an automatic shutdown before the battery is completely depleted. Think of laptops as computers with built-in UPS!

Some buildings supply self-generated backup power. Note that this power is usually much "dirtier" than power from the outlet. Under these circumstances, you need to have a UPS unit, preferably one that is designed to smooth out rough electricity supply. Most do.

During any power outage, one of the most limiting factors will be the fact that simultaneous failure of the air conditioning can lead to insufficient cooling of equipment, especially if it operates in a small space. It is therefore a good idea to keep track of the inside temperature of key equipment, to ensure that the environmental conditions are adequate. If the air conditioning for a machine room fails, all nonessential computers should be shut down. The essential equipment will be monitored and, in due course, will be shut down as well.

### Internet Access

In general, a small business will most likely consider the following options to connect to an ISP:

- Dial-up via an analog or digital phone line

- Connection via DSL or Cable

- Connection via a data circuit, usually a T1 line, either dedicated solely to the business or shared with other users

Before we can talk about how to use these different services to establish good redundancy, we will go a little deeper into some specific technical details that you do not find advertised as such. Each vendor will tell you only the benefits of his solution and not how it compares with competing services.

The dial-up method through a regular phone line is the most basic means to connect to the Internet. The immediate advantage is that phone lines are readily available and can immediately transfer data. The drawback is the limited bandwidth. In general, consider a "56 kbps (kilo bits per second)" modem as the bandwidth that you will probably never reach.

Depending on the quality of the phone line, the actual connection speed is much less; in this case, typically around 50 kbps.

Phone companies use digital circuits with digital compression methods to optimize their usage of available bandwidth. With ISDN (Integrated Services Digital Network) a direct connection to the digital phone line is established. Two data channels of 64 kbps provide a total usable bandwidth of 128 kbps. Like an analog modem connection, ISDN is still a dial-up to a service provider and thus it usually comes with per-minute usage charges if you exceed your monthly allotment. ISDN has been quickly superseded by higher bandwidth solutions, such as fiber, but this might be a cost-effective solution in rural areas where other data line services are expensive.

Most residential high-speed Internet connections are based on either cable modems or DSL (Digital Subscriber Line). The data signals are overlaid through your cable TV or phone line without interfering with the primary signals. The main difference between the two is that TV cables are highly interconnected within the same building; thus, you share your high-speed connection with everyone else who is connected. In contrast, DSL lines are dedicated connections. However, this does not guarantee that your data are not eventually routed into a shared data network at your ISP. In fact, this is most often the case, and your ISP might hand the data to another ISP, which hands it on to another ISP, and so forth. Of course, that can also happen with a cable modem ISP, but we have seen it more often with DSL service.

The bottom line is that both DSL and cable modems provide fast Internet connections, although they do not guarantee data throughput. Performance will vary greatly depending on the load of the network segment to which your service is connected. You will often see service disruptions especially during peak usage hours. Often, ISPs will even limit the maximum amount of data you are allowed to put through your DSL or cable modem Internet connection, simply to discourage users who are misusing the connection to host Internet services. While both services are generally reliable, there are occasional short outages and not the same uptime guarantee you get with true data connections. If the service goes down, Murphy's Law states that it is just at the moment that you are sending your most important e-mail ever.

Dedicated data connections, often labeled "business grade," such as T1 circuits or fiber-based offerings, are best if you rely heavily on your Internet connection. They have been around for a long time, and they provide solid data connections. You can obtain data service with a variety of up-time guarantees, but it is usually significantly better than DSL or Cable. Of course, this comes at a price about five times higher than for DSL or cable connections at a comparable bandwidth. In rural areas, unfortunately, you also have to pay a charge per mile to the next data connection point of the telephone company. Sometimes you have the option to share a T1 connection with several of your neighboring businesses, which could be a cost-effective option.

Even if you obtain a dedicated data connection with a high availability guarantee, if you really depend on the Internet for your business, as many small businesses do, you still need at least one more alternate connection.

Data lines, like telephone lines, are susceptible to equipment failure due to ordinary events such as disruption by construction work. It has happened that data lines have been mistakenly cut by construction work on the street, leaving you vulnerable if no other third-party provider has its own independent cabling in place.

You need at least two methods for connection to create additional redundancy. In principal, you could use any two methods, but for practical purposes, you would always choose two comparable bandwidth solutions. As a third backup, it is always a good idea to have one or more analog phone lines reserved. A word of caution: You do not want to connect your PC directly to an analog phone line and dial-up your ISP. You would create the risk of a security breach. Instead, you should use a separate dial-up modem, router, and firewall integrated unit that will protect your network and automatically share the access to all computers in the network.

DSL and cable modems are a good pairing for redundancy. In most cases, these services are delivered through two different access points in the building. The drawback is that cable modems are usually not available in commercial areas. For a small business it could be sufficient to have the DSL connection at work, and the cable access at home, if it is feasible for you to drive to your home if the DSL connection goes down.

I recommend most often a (shared) T1 connection as primary Internet service with a DSL as backup. You need to ensure that both services come through two different sources, meaning, physical access points in the building and different network paths to the Internet backbone. In urban areas, it is often the case that DSL service is routed somewhere at the phone company through the same connection points as T1 lines. If there is a major disaster, both services are lost. If in doubt, add some analog lines from a different phone company or through your cellular phone, just to be safe.

In any case, to ensure adequate Internet service at any time, suggest that your Internet providers configure your line to ensure minimum throughput to certain sites, especially during peak usage of the system. All other less important traffic is routed through your backup connection. Or you can reserve the bandwidth on your main connection for certain types of traffic, and restrict other traffic (e.g., music files, to a maximum of 10% of the available bandwidth). This would also be a precaution against a denial of service "attack" provoked consciously or unconsciously by an employee. You might also consider using a system that would page your IT person if the Internet connection becomes slow or gets lost.

## ENVIRONMENTAL HAZARDS

Imagine you arrive at your office in the morning and the building is closed. Or you are already in your office, an alarm sounds, and you are asked to leave your office immediately. This occurs when a hazardous substance has been detected or if the building is to be closed for police action. In any case, you are standing outside the building and you do not know when you will be able to reenter your office. And the worst part was that you had no warning that this was coming.

If you think that this scenario is highly unlikely, well, think again. There are many possible scenarios and many have already happened to thousands of small businesses. Whenever air pollutants reach an intolerably high level and government-set limits are exceeded, you may no longer be able to reach your office. Possible causes include nearby accidents, fires with dangerous chemicals and toxic smoke, asbestos fibers in the air, and foul odors. We have also seen the worst scenario with regard to hazardous material: Chernobyl. The widespread radioactive pollutants will remain for centuries.

For a certain period of time, you will need to maintain critical business functions remotely. The environmental hazard may have affected the health of your employees, so you may need to operate with fewer staff.

You can prepare for such an event by having all important documents online for remote access and training your staff appropriately in using a telecommuting infrastructure (which can also be convenient even when no disaster has occurred!). Of course, there are costs associated with the development of a telecommuting infrastructure and you need to assess if the potential benefits justify those costs. You may conclude that the hazardous conditions will not likely last for more than several days, a length of business interruption that small businesses can tolerate.

## Remote Operation: Stage I

In remote operation at Stage I, you and your employees cannot physically access your worksite or business office, but the office is still intact and some core systems continue to function properly. You need to prepare in advance so that you can remotely access all important company data and e-mail. The provision for this disaster scenario will have the benefit that it will also allow your employees to telecommute even in nondisaster situations or allow your salespeople to access your company's data when they are traveling. It will permit the sharing of your data with other company offices.

It is a good idea to scan and electronically archive most important documents. You can access them remotely if you are forced to do so under hazardous environmental conditions and they will be secure. If your building site is compromised in a disaster, you have little control over who will enter your offices and have access to your files. I remember a recent story in the news of teenagers finding boxes of confidential company salary data in a dumpster when they were skateboarding in the corporate parking lot! If you need to store original documents, you should store them in a safe that cannot be opened or easily removed. Remember that your business has a legal requirement to maintain certain documents, such as tax records, for a specified period of time. Your legal counsel can advise you as to which documents you must safeguard and over what period of time they must be preserved.

You also want to offer evacuation training to your staff, so that they know how to shut down all nonessential office computers, how they can warn all employees using a paging feature on the phone system and how they may shut down electricity or gas services.

If the hazardous conditions are expected to continue, you may be escorted into your business premises by civil authorities for a brief period to retrieve key items. Therefore, it is a good idea to label all equipment according to your earlier ranking as "critical," "important," or "optional" with large color-coded stickers and larger numbers, so you can, if necessary, ask someone to retrieve item RED#4 for you.

With regard to your phone system, if you used the setup recommended in the last section, turn on your company's cellular phone to continue receiving company phone calls.

You need to agree with your staff on a meeting place where you can convene after your building has been evacuated. If you are a really small company, you can simply meet at someone's home, but if your company has more than 20 employees, have a separate office site where you can meet. It is unlikely that you will need dedicated recovery sites such as large companies have built. It is sufficient if you have a good relationship with a partner company that can give you some temporary place to work, such as their meeting rooms. If you plan in advance, you should make sure that this company is using different third-party providers than your own company so that you are less likely to be negatively impacted by the providers having difficulty keeping their operations up and running for other customers not affected by the disaster. And you should have a good stock of spare parts and PCs that are stored off-site and that you can use temporarily.

If you are looking into a secondary site, such as rented office space that you would normally use for client meetings or training seminars, but plan to use as a disaster recovery site, review carefully if that site could function under disastrous conditions. Does it have sufficient electrical power and air conditioning? Is there enough space to store spare equipment? Note that your disaster recovery facility requires full third-party services. And of course, your disaster recovery facility's phone, Internet, and utility providers should be as different from your main office as possible. You also need to make sure that you have software licenses for all of your IT systems and determine if any additional computer systems and software licenses have to be acquired.

To reach the main office, you need to establish a secure connection, because you will transfer sensitive information, such as human resources (HR) records, budgets, competitive, and strategic documents. If you are working at your secondary site, you might consider a dedicated data line back to your main office, if this is cost-effective. Usually, however, you will connect to your office network by direct dial-up or over the Internet using a secured virtual private network (VPN) connection with strong 128-bit encryption. A VPN connection creates a "tunnel" on the Internet through which your data are passed safely, thus acting exactly as a private network, and the same security, management and bandwidth policies can be applied. VPN is a cost-effective network solution that is sufficient in most cases. However, you will want to look into a private leased-line connection between offices if you require a minimum bandwidth guarantee, or if the office locations constantly require exchanging large amounts of data.

There are two solutions to build a VPN network. Software VPN solutions are available and are already part of the Windows XP Professional/Vista or Mac OS X operating systems. A VPN connection can be configured from any client running those operating systems, to a server machine, independently if they are on the same network or halfway around the world. The second and preferred solution are VPN appliances, such as routers. This is especially useful if you like to provide a permanent VPN connection, for example, to connect your main office with your training center offices. If a remote user on the road likes to dial in, he requires additional VPN client software. You may also want to investigate the use of "thin client" terminals, which require a network connection to work but retain the data within the company's infrastructure.

### System Security

For a small business you want to have at least a classification for document accessibility that translates directly into security measurements on your system. There are at least three categories to consider:

1. Public data, like brochures, annual reports, your Web site. These data are available to all users without special restrictions.

2. Restricted access documents, like communication with clients or data in your bug tracking system. This information is generally available internally, but has not been reviewed. It might contain embarrassing information if released to the general public.

3. Confidential documents, like expense reports, strategy documents and so forth. These data must be protected because they reveal specific business practices or future plans that should remain confidential.

These three examples represent a basic classification scheme. It is important that security measures are followed to safeguard your business information assets.

In addition to organizing a classification scheme for safeguarding documents, you need to specifically address system security in your business. With a majority of your proprietary information now stored electronically, you are vulnerable to intentional or unintentional misuse by your own employees. Therefore, to integrate these technologies securely and successfully, you must deal with them on an organizational level. The loss or corruption of mission-critical information may have serious financial and legal consequences for your business.

Consider the value of your company's knowledge and information databases. You will need to safeguard this information by an effective and proven security mechanism. These high security measures are necessary because of the ease with which digital information can be assessed, modified, or deleted without leaving behind traces of intervention. For this reason, you need to include file access and intrusion detection monitoring with your security efforts. Strong password authentication is also required combined with data encryption whenever data leave the company's network.

Each user account should be protected by a password. Users must choose passwords with a minimum length of eight characters, nondictionary words or names, and a mixed use of upper and lower case and special characters and numbers, like "BGsRGr8t!." Ideally, passwords should be changed every 90 days or so. But from experience in small companies, people don't like to change passwords too often and dislike complicated passwords. Sometimes, they even share their passwords with colleagues. This practice should be discouraged as it almost always indicates that the file structure setup is not congruent with the requirements. Did you know that many people use as passwords their first and last names, or the names of their children, friends, dogs, or cities and landmarks? You would be amazed how quickly hacker programs available on the Internet can decipher such passwords by simply guessing combinations of these items. It hardly takes a couple of minutes to obtain the passwords of at least 10% of average users.

The bottom line is that small businesses do not need complex security measures, but they need *some* measures. Of course, the security measures should be periodically reviewed so that the implemented guidelines meet the requirements and to ensure that they are generally accepted and used. All security safeguards should be periodically assessed and adjusted to meet the latest developments.

## FIRES AND OTHER DISASTERS

We now consider disaster types that are destructive to the worksite, be it an office, a manufacturing plant, a retail establishment, or any other type of construction (here the generic word "office" refers to all worksites). Among all of the scenarios, fire is by far the most common hazard that also creates a secondary hazardous condition due to toxic smoke. Natural disasters, like severe weather, earthquakes, and floods, may also damage or destroy your office or at least render the office unusable for some time. In the case of severe weather, however, you often have advance warning of the disaster and can begin an evacuation from the premises.

Whatever the cause, you need a disaster recovery site, even if it is only a meeting room at another company's premises. It will take you some time to assess your losses, but you should strive in good faith to provide basic services to your employees and customers and honor your contractual obligations, even though conditions will be challenging. Try to mitigate your losses by maintaining whatever level of operations you can sustain until your business has fully recovered. Your employees and customers will appreciate the effort.

In addition to assessing which services and products your company is obligated to provide, you should also inquire as to which services and products you will need from third parties to operate your business in the aftermath of a fire. Determine who will provide you with temporary services at the disaster recovery site in the event that the permanent provider is also affected by the fire or natural disaster. Identify a priority ranking of systems that must be operational and which data will be needed to operate your business even at a minimum level of functioning.

**Fire Protection**

Plan and discuss with your local fire department the precautions you should take to protect valuable documents or IT equipment from fire. Special fire safes for documents are affordable, and larger safes would also protect against theft and survive substantial mechanical abuse and water damage. You should have an up-to-date, detailed, off-site inventory list of all IT equipment. Labeling your valuable assets with easy to read, fire- and water-resistant stickers facilitates subsequent identification and should be used in nondisaster times as an asset control mechanism.

You will find that many traditional businesses, such as law firms, have begun to conduct more and more business electronically. But you will not need all documents online at your alternate site. You need to identify which ones you will need before the disaster strikes. It will be sufficient if you have the documents you need for an emergency operation. It is, however, a good idea to plan to store paper copies of all important original documents at a secondary location and determine which documents to make available online.

It is important that you have regular fire drills with the help of your fire department. This should include instructions on how to initiate an emergency shutdown of all systems. It would warn every user that the emergency shutdown is in progress and that all systems will be automatically shutdown in about five minutes. The emergency shutdown can be stopped by anyone, unless system administrators force the shutdown. To expedite this process, you can install a "Panic" button that would be pushed at the same time as the fire alarm in the event of a fire or an immediate threat, and would shut down all IT equipment within minutes.

**Data Backups: Part III**

This scenario assumes that the main worksite will be destroyed. Business will continue at an alternate secure location. An emergency replacement IT infrastructure must be ready at that location.

To prepare for this case, if you are using a backup system at your original office location, use a VPN connection to copy all data from your main office location to your alternate office location. Again, a file synchronization tool is easy to use and efficient as it will transfer only the changes that made to files during that particular workday. Since the data will be available at the disaster recovery location, a small and simple network can be configured to start disaster recovery operations. You would have the same benefit if you use an online data backup service. In both cases, you will need a fast Internet connection at your disaster recovery site. If you have used traditional methods to back up your data, such as tapes or CDs/DVDs, you have to retrieve them first from your storage location and then re-build a file system at the alternate site. Obviously, this is a much more time-consuming task, especially if your data sets are so large that they do not fit the selected medium, and incremental or partial backups have been made and the originals must be restored. Some people also use their e-mail systems as an effective storage repository of documents.

For most small businesses, some form of online storage, like your Web server or special online backup space, will suffice. If you have many gigabytes of data that you need during disaster operations, use a file server with large disks at the disaster recovery location. These solutions are more cost-effective and less time-consuming. But there are reasons why you would also want to have backups on removable media as we shall see in the section dealing with sabotage.

If you used a removable backup medium, store it in a safe place that tracks incoming and outgoing items. Please note that many armored car services offer this service and they may also pick up and store your backup tapes. Employees should create backups of their own data on the backup system.

The important issue is how much downtime your business can afford until you are up and running at your alternate location. If your marketing and sales tools fail, you can probably estimate the direct costs of lost sales opportunities. If your client support tools fail, you have additional intangible costs like blemishes on your public and client relations. And for other systems, you will most likely find variable factors, such as your downtime costs, changing over time. For example, if you own a tax accounting business, you are faced with downtime requirements that change with time. If your system goes down just before the tax reporting deadline, the impact on your business is definitely more severe than a failure later in the calendar year. You can make a rough estimate of the cost of your downtime that should correlate with your disaster recovery budget.

## Remote Operation: Stage II

In Stage II, we assume that the computers at your office location no longer function, the communication lines have been cut, and you will not have access to your office premises for some time. The data backup is available at the remote location either from online storage, your own large disk file system, or from removable media. A small office can be built where an emergency operations team handles the most important business functions. You already contracted data lines into that alternate site and you use cell phones temporarily until you can return to your old site or you have to find a new office altogether.

The question at this point is how to prepare for other services, such as mail delivery. Here, the first step is to establish a secondary location in advance; a virtual office that would handle all your mail even during non-disaster times. If you consider the older scares about anthrax in letters sent through regular post office mail, you may consider outsourcing mail handling to a third-party. As a small business, you cannot afford to buy expensive x-ray machines, or to spend time investigating each piece of mail. There are various providers of such services. Not only will they accept your mail, but you can also direct them to open your mail, scan it, and send it to you immediately by e-mail. Of course, you can also use them to establish an office presence somewhere else in the world. But the main advantage is that they will receive all mail for you, open it, pre-sort, and forward it to you quickly and efficiently. And if you live in an urban area, it is possible to receive the most critical mail via messenger on the same business day. Some service bureaus also offer additional add-on services, such as an assumption of payroll and accounting functions. Choose these services based on your budget and your assessment of your likely circumstances, should you temporarily lose access to your permanent worksite.

You may consider a bill payment service that will receive your bills for you, scan them, set up money transfers via wire or check, and let you decide when and how much you want to pay simply by a pre-established "auto-pay" function or by selecting the bill online. These services are provided by various companies, and are much more advanced than the bill payment services most financial institutions provide with their online systems. Keep a directory of your service providers with your business account numbers, so that in the event of a disaster, you have that information conveniently available to notify your creditors of your circumstances.

## TERRORISM AND SABOTAGE

Terrorism strikes without warning and is of particular concern as its goal is to inflict maximum damage, including the loss of human life. Deliberately orchestrated violence, such as terrorism, has a profound psychological impact on those who experience it, quite unlike the psychological response to natural disasters. Your first concern is the safety of your employees. There will never be complete protection from terrorist attacks and acts of sabotage. Terrorists will use any means for their cause, including suicide missions, bombs, and contamination with biological, chemical, or even radioactive agents, if they manage to acquire the material to build such weapons. Terrorists are also becoming increasingly skilled in the use of highly sophisticated IT equipment, trying to "hack" their way into government agencies and into commercial computer systems to steal secret data or to cause considerable damage by altering or deleting data. Because the potential damage is so severe, you need to take protective measures. Similar precautions apply for destruction of your office by fire or hazardous substances.

## Hacker Attacks

As soon as your single home office computer or your small business computer network is continuously connected to an outside network, such as the Internet, some method of protecting your data on the computer or the internal network is required. Any computer system that is directly connected to the Internet will sooner or later be the target of hackers trying either to penetrate your network or making it unusable by, for example, flooding your system with data requests. Also, you have to be aware that the traffic from your network can be watched from the outside, as it is often not encrypted. This is even easier when you are connected via a cable modem because everyone on your cable segment can monitor your data traffic.

You need to protect yourself by using firewall software on the stand-alone PC, or even better, building an internal network and use a network router that separates your internal network from the Internet. There are many router products on the market, and the ones marketed for home offices or small businesses often include a firewall where you specify which data traffic you allow through your firewall and which outside parties are allowed access to your network. Usually, you will want to allow all traffic that was initiated from inside your network to pass the firewall to the outside. Traffic initiated from the outside should only pass the firewall if it is in response to a former request from the inside, or if you have specific machines and applications that you would allow access into your network. But for the general public you would either refuse the data packages or route this traffic to a separate network called the Demilitarized Zone (DMZ). Here you would place, for example, a testing Web server, or a place where you make the latest information available for salespeople connected to the Internet.

Although this might appear complex, the configuration of these routers for home offices and small businesses has become fairly simple. Most routers now provide Web-based interfaces with good online help. But that alone is not a guarantee that it will be simple. Some products come with Web-interfaces that are poorly designed or require firmware upgrades before they work with your ISP.

The advantage of a network router is that the connection to the Internet is simplified because all ISP-related network information is configured only once in the router, and communicated to all internal machines automatically if the dynamic host configuration protocol is supported.

However, if your ISP is charging you based on the number of computers connected to the network, and you use a router, you have only one connection point to the ISP's network. The ISP can detect a router from its hardware Ethernet address. Most off-the-shelf routers have a built-in function that allows spoofing the address of the router by substituting an address from an internal computer, so the router will appear as a computer from your internal network. Check with your ISP first.

Do not use the built-in firewalls of a computer to act as a firewall or a router for connection sharing or both. Stand-alone network appliances are much easier to set up, are inexpensive, and provide a much higher guarantee that you have not created any kind of loophole in your setup that would compromise network security. You may want to investigate using "managed" security devices where the provider is managing the security updates.

Note that a firewall is only one step in a larger network security scheme that must include a security policy, automatic intrusion detection and monitoring for viruses and Trojan horses that can sneak in with regular traffic. There are also various solutions that you can run on a PC that will allow it to be accessed from the outside, even if a firewall is in place. These software packages mimic the same traffic as Web browsing would, but instead of Web site information, they send data about your PC and the files on it. With some software packages, you can remotely take control of your PC although your firewall does not allow any traffic initiated from the outside. This is possible because in this case, the traffic is initiated from a small application running on your PC and therefore for the firewall, the traffic appears to be legitimate because it was initiated internally. You can use it to your advantage, but you also need to be aware that certain security risks accompany it.

Make certain that virus protection is current to avoid compromising your security by viruses and Trojan horses entering your system. Update your operating system on a regular basis. Updates are provided nearly every week. It is important that you train your users how to handle suspicious e-mail attachments and how to detect virus-like activities. Your ISP or e-mail provider can often provide additional security measures.

Be aware that even cell phones can become the target of virus activities, particularly if they are in the league of the new phones that allow you to browse the Internet.

Your overall attention to security issues and the technical expertise that you obtain will determine the effectiveness of your security precautions. Do you always remember to remove accounts for employees who have left the company? Special care should be taken if a system administrator leaves, as he usually knows back doors into your systems.

## Internal Sabotage

Good system administrators build their reputations on trust that has been earned throughout their careers. But even with the best system administrator in the service of your small business, you are obligated to protect your company against attacks by internal sabotage. These measures are not too difficult to implement and should be welcomed by your systems administrator as being in the best interest of the company. There are some basic auditing methods that you can apply and review periodically, such as identifying who accessed which files, who generated which external network traffic, and who sent a large number of e-mails or large attachments to which addressee. You should, of course, inform your staff that you are monitoring activities on the company's network and the results of these activities are not matched with personal information unless there is a compelling reason to do so. Ask staff to refrain from storing personal information on company computers. These guidelines should be formalized in company policy.

While it is practical to make backups from one disk to another, it is also important to occasionally make a backup on a removable medium and to store it in a bank safe that is not accessible by the system administrator. The system administrator would probably also want a bank safe to store his backups, but he should have a separate one, preferably at a different bank.

Having outsourced your e-mail to a third-party provider, you already took an important step to be independent of internal systems staff for your e-mail service, thereby reducing both the work burden on the staff and the opportunities for internal sabotage.

Insist that the passwords for all equipment, particularly for network equipment, are given to you in a closed envelope. You want to keep it closed, unless there is a big emergency or your system administrator leaves the company. Then it is best to have another system administrator come in and change the entire list of passwords. In fact, do not use any built-in "Administrator" accounts, but instead, give two user accounts administrative rights on the system. This way each week, those two people can independently monitor and audit suspicious activities on your network and system administrator tasks can be traced to their user identifications.

Even so, your business could be the target of a saboteur who "infects" your network with a virus. Usually, with good protection in place, this should not be an issue; but in small businesses passwords are often not safeguarded, users' permissions are not set, everyone can have system administrative access, and files are open for everyone to read and to delete. You have to be aware of this and take the necessary precautions. Review your protection scheme regularly.

## NOTES

1. Even during the World Trade Center tragedy, cell phone services continued with little interruption. But you might expect that the cell phone

network is quite easily overloaded when land-based phone service fails. It is therefore a good idea to have several cell phones from different providers available as part of your contingency planning.

2. I found services on the Web site for this purpose, www.getconnected .com and www.lowermybills.com. You enter your telephone area code or ZIP code and the service generates charts of available services in your area—long distance, wireless, Internet, gas and electricity, sorted by price.

3. Of course, if you plan to use it only for contingency purposes, choose a calling plan that has the lowest monthly fixed costs.

# 4

# Ensuring Financial Liquidity

The information covered to this point will enable you to prepare for a disaster and to develop a contingency plan with respect to the IT infrastructure of your small business. Special emphasis is placed on developing redundant capacity; that is, having additional sources of computing power and backups of all data for your small business readily available in the event of a disaster. It is now time to apply the same concept to the financial elements of your contingency plan, in effect developing redundant financial capacity by means of various tools, such as insurance. Should a disaster strike your business, you may need additional funds to replace lost or damaged assets and to cover additional operating expenses during the recovery period following the disaster. Let's begin by examining the role insurance plays in contingency planning.

## ROLE OF INSURANCE

When you made the decision to start or join a small business, you assumed certain risks. You almost certainly did so because you believed that the rewards you would receive were commensurate with, or disproportionately generous to, the risks you would assume. These rewards may include the freedom to chart your own course, the ability to own your own life, to balance work and family, the joy of realizing a creative vision, and the financial rewards that come with entrepreneurship. You almost certainly took steps to mitigate your risks. Entrepreneurs are, by nature, resilient and resourceful. We are optimists, and believe we can create a better future for ourselves. We are also reluctant to jeopardize our small business vision and our future by taking needless or reckless risks. All successful entrepreneurs take prudent risks, most likely beginning with the formation of your company!

When you started your business, your legal counsel certainly advised you about the need to incorporate in order to minimize your personal liability, among other reasons. Your insurance program is the next step in the process of mitigating risks to enable your small business to succeed. A carefully crafted insurance program protects your business assets against the risk of *unanticipated* losses. You should not insure against *anticipated* losses—it is not cost-effective to do so. Consider the example of extended warranty programs for office equipment that are analogous to insurance on single pieces of equipment. I decline to purchase such coverage because we expect that office equipment depreciates and must be replaced from time to time. As such, I can budget for it. I did not pay $150 for an extended three-year warranty for the $600 laser printer that sits in my office. It has functioned adequately for the four years that I have owned it. It shows the signs of normal wear and tear and I will likely replace the printer within the year. Newer models with features comparable to my existing printer can be purchased for $450. Clearly, the extended warranty plan—which covered anticipated costs to repair the equipment due to normal wear and tear—would not have been a sensible investment.

I did, however, have my printers covered under a business owner's policy. When an unexpected disaster occurred, the insurance benefit mitigated my loss. The business insurance policy provided for each of the printers and fax machines that were damaged by ash and soot from the collapse of the World Trade Center towers to be removed from the office, professionally cleaned, and serviced. In some cases, drums and cartridges were replaced. The insurance policy paid for the repair of those machines as a consequent of an *unanticipated* event—certainly no one expected a disaster of the nature that had occurred on September 11. Those losses were not inconsequential—the cost to repair a single printer or fax machine was $250. The insurance premium I paid for this benefit was a sensible investment for my business.

This is the first take-home lesson of crafting your insurance program: It is not cost-effective to insure against anticipated losses. Consider the losses you can predict and for which you can budget. They can be self-insured; or paid for out of your cash and short-term cash equivalents account. The extension of this lesson is the insurance deductible. The deductible is the amount of losses that your business must bear before your insurance policy pays a benefit. Generally, the higher the deductible, or the greater the amount of losses that you will bear before your insurance policy is obligated to pay a claim, the lower the premium. Discuss with your insurance agent the options available to you so that you may select the deductible that is appropriate for your business.

You likely see how this lesson applies to your personal insurance program. It bears repeating: It is not cost-effective to insure against anticipated losses. I see many small business owners who pay premiums to cover losses that they could afford to bear themselves, but they fail to insure against risks that would be catastrophic. The same is true of individual policyholders who often don't transfer risks to the insurance markets in a cost-effective manner. For example, consumer advocates report that many credit life insurance programs (i.e., insurance that pays the installment debts of the insured upon his death) are not cost-effective. They argue that consumers would be better served by purchasing other forms of life insurance where the cash benefit would be available for a broader range of uses. Those very consumers may be uninsured for other types of risks that could be covered by a broader life insurance policy. Spend your insurance premium dollars wisely; purchase coverage for unanticipated losses, not expected and predictable ones.

Now that I have persuaded you (I hope!) that your insurance program should be crafted to cover unanticipated losses, let us consider some of the risks you should insure. Many insurance companies bundle property and liability coverage into a product known as a "business owner's policy," that is sometimes referred to as a "package policy." It allows the business owner to obtain broad coverage with affordable premiums. Since each business is unique (and each business owner's level of risk tolerance is unique!), insurance coverage can be customized to suit the particular needs of the business. A retail sales operation has different insurance needs from a restaurant or a dentist's office. As it is not possible to anticipate the individual circumstances of each reader, I will try in this chapter to give you the tools you need to enter into an informed discussion with your insurance broker. Additional information on insurance issues can be found at www.preparedsmallbusiness.com.

Your insurance broker may begin a meeting with you by discussing mono-line policies, or policies that cover against the risk of a single peril, such as fire or auto theft. Business owners' policies and package (or multiline) policies are the sum of two or more mono-line covers, except the premiums for the whole package policy are generally less than the sum of the parts of constituent mono-line policies under a property-casualty insurance program.

I find it helpful to prepare an inventory of business assets to be insured prior to meeting with a broker. Many software packages for small businesses provide an inventory of property, plant, and equipment. You can record the date of purchase, the model number of the equipment, the manufacturer's name, and the purchase price. Many of these programs interface with your accounting ledgers to update your depreciation expense. I also take digital photographs of key equipment, such as office furniture and other items to keep with my records, item-by-item. Obviously such records are helpful in documenting losses should a disaster damage the assets of your business.

These records are also helpful in assessing the amount of property you need to insure. I was quite surprised when I calculated the replacement cost of all of my business assets and was relieved to have that figure available when selecting the appropriate insurance coverage. The reason many small businesses are underinsured for property losses may be that the business owners underestimate the value of their assets. When you include everything that would have to be replaced in the event of a fire or similar catastrophe, it adds up. Make multiple copies of these records and store one or more off-site. Your receipts and photographs of business property are of little use if they are destroyed in a disaster.

## PROPERTY-CASUALTY INSURANCE

Property insurance protects the assets of your business against losses arising from perils such as fire and theft. Basic form commercial property coverage typically protects your small businesses against the following perils:

1. Fire, plus extended coverage, such as:
2. Lightning
3. Explosion
4. Windstorm/hail
5. Smoke
6. Aircraft or vehicles
7. Riot or civil commotion
8. Vandalism
9. Sprinkler leakage
10. Sinkhole collapse
11. Volcanic activity

Broad form commercial coverage includes basic coverage for fire (1), extended coverage (2–11), in addition to:

12. Breakage of glass
13. Falling objects
14. Weight of snow, ice, or sleet
15. Water damage

Special form coverage provides so-called all-risk protection. The term "all-risk" is misleading, because it doesn't necessarily cover all risks, it typically covers basic form risks, broad form coverage (named perils 1–15) and other causes of loss, such as earthquakes, unless the peril is specifically excluded from coverage. Read your insurance policy carefully to understand

**Exhibit 4.1**    Possible Endorsements to a Commercial Insurance Policy

| | | | | |
|---|---|---|---|---|
| Accounts receivable | Additional insured endorsement | Automatic annual increase in building limit of insurance | Automatic annual increases in business personal property | Boiler and machinery |
| Civil authority | Consequential loss | Crime | Data processing and hacker's insurance | Debris removal |
| Earthquake | Electronic media and records | Fine arts | Fire protective equipment discharge | Improvements to the property |
| Increased cost of construction | Inland marine | Intangible property, such as trademarks | Loss of rents | Mechanical breakdown |
| Mobile property | Personal property of your employees and/or customers | Personal property off premises | Property of others under your care, custody, and control | Refrigerated food spoilage coverage |
| Signage and other outdoor property | Trees, shrubs, and other landscaping | Transportation | Utility services | Valuable papers and records—cost of research |

which perils are excluded from coverage. Property coverage options may include endorsements or additional risks covered. Exhibit 4.1 lists some of the endorsements that may be available for coverage under your insurance policy. It does not present an exhaustive list of perils for which endorsements may be obtained, but it is sufficient to start you thinking about the types of risks you should discuss with your insurance broker. The design of your insurance program will be highly customized to suit the unique needs of your small business. For example, like many small businesses, I maintain a refrigerator in my office stocked with fruits and other perishable foods for consumption by visitors to the office. When our office building lost electricity, the food was spoiled and I had to throw it out. I was not reimbursed for this loss as I had not included such an endorsement in the insurance policy because I believed that it was a loss I could afford to bear. However, if my small business were a restaurant, it would be a different matter. Imagine if the supply of electricity to a restaurant were disrupted. The business could easily lose $50,000 or more due to spoilage of food. For a food-service business, a policy endorsement for refrigerated food spoilage coverage may be critical.

Perhaps the best way to think of endorsements is to imagine a restaurant menu in which your choices are made *á la carte*. You order the main course (the business owner's policy) and then choose additional courses, such as the salad or dessert for an additional incremental cost. A Manhattan restaurant, Steamer's Landing, presents an excellent example of the importance of understanding endorsements. The restaurant was used as a staging area for emergency response in the aftermath of a major disaster. Emergency personnel removed furniture from the restaurant for their use. The restaurant filed an insurance claim for the furniture and received payment for the fair value of the items. The problem arose when the restaurant, which had a consistent nautical theme, attempted to purchase replacement pieces. The manufacturer of the furniture no longer produced this particular line, so the restaurant had a choice of either purchasing new pieces that would not match the tables, chairs, and other furnishings that remained, or discarding the remaining furniture to acquire a whole new matched set. The latter choice was very costly, as the insurance company would not pay to replace the entire matched set; it would only pay the claim for the value of the pieces that were taken. The restaurant would have avoided this by electing an endorsement to the insurance policy called "set and match" so that the full claim would be covered.

I share this example to illustrate just how complicated endorsements would be, because the owner of Steamer's Landing had never considered the idea of "set and match." Space limitations for this book prevent an exhaustive treatment of the insurance issues with respect to endorsements, but it is such an important topic that I am posting supplementary materials for readers to download at www.preparedsmallbusiness.com.

Steamer's Landing was paid for the replacement cost of the individual tables and chairs that were taken. It is important to understand the means of calculating insurance settlements. To ensure a prompt and fair settlement at the time of loss, your insurance policy will likely specify the valuation method used to determine the value of your assets covered under the policy. Your policy may provide for replacement cost, or the actual cost of replacing an asset, without deducting depreciation. It may provide for an actual cash valuation, that is, the replacement cost of the asset less the accumulated depreciation.

Finally, the policy may specify that the valuation method is an agreed amount or functional replacement cost. This is the method most commonly used for works of art and other unique items for which it can be difficult to obtain an objective valuation.

By the way, items such as plants and fish in the office aquarium are generally not insurable, but the aquarium itself and its equipment are insurable. Property insurers won't underwrite the cost of replacing living organisms, such as plants and fish. They consider aquarium fish as pets. But the aquarium, filter, plant pots, and so forth are property that can be insured. I share this with you because I have a soothing 25-gallon aquarium in my office. The technician who comes to service the tank related an anecdote of another of his clients who had a large salt-water aquarium gracing the reception area of his small business, a commercial real estate brokerage. He had not thought to obtain insurance for it as he considered it a decorative item. It was damaged in a disaster and the cost of replacing it was $50,000. He could have insured it for several hundred dollars. Photographs and receipts can be helpful in documenting the loss, as obviously there is no standard replacement cost for such items—an aquarium can be a modest desktop unit with ten gallons and a few goldfish, or it can be a custom-built floor-to-ceiling decorative piece with exotic fish, as this gentleman apparently had in his office. Receipts and photographs will help you to come up with a fair assessment of the replacement cost.

I generally recommend electing to value assets on the basis of replacement cost. It facilitates settlement of your insurance claim by avoiding a discussion of accumulated depreciation on each damaged asset. It also immediately provides you with the funds you need to replace damaged assets. Exercise particular care in insuring IT equipment. The PC you bought five years ago may no longer be available and you and your insurance company will have to identify a model available on the market with comparable features to your old PC in order to establish a fair replacement cost. I recommend that you keep records of the functional specifications of your IT equipment for that reason. If you know the memory, disk size, and other functional specs of your machine, you can easily identify a comparable model. If you record that information now, it will save you time and aggravation should disaster strike. In disaster-recovery mode, you don't want to waste time searching through old sales literature to determine the processing speed of your damaged computer for the purposes of identifying a comparable model.

Before concluding the discussion of property insurance, I would like to call your attention to a specific insurance policy endorsement that is rarely considered by small businesses: disruption of electrical supply. I know of many small business owners in Lower Manhattan who elected to forego coverage for this peril, believing that the surge protector equipment that they had in place was adequate to protect their computer equipment from anticipated fluctuations in electricity supply delivered to their offices. The attack on the World Trade Center changed that assumption. Much of Lower Manhattan was left in the dark for days following the disaster and businesses cannot operate in the dark. Consider carefully whether you wish to purchase coverage of additional perils and if so, at what cost.

This section of the chapter is titled "Property-Casualty Insurance" and "casualty insurance" is insurance-speak for "liability insurance." Liability insurance protects the assets of your business in the event that you or one of your employees is accused of an act that causes injury or damage to another person or property, or that such injury or damage is the result of your failure or the failure of one of your employees to take action to prevent such injury (also known as "negligence"). Liability insurance typically covers not only the costs of the damages, but also legal and other expenses associated with resolving the issue of liability. In the context of this discussion, remember that we are considering liability insurance with respect to contingency planning for a disaster—an event that disrupts operations at one or more of your business sites. The needs of your small business for liability insurance (and property insurance) are much broader than what is presented in this book. For example, I would recommend that your business carry employment practices liability insurance to protect your business against claims of sexual harassment, wrongful termination, or other types of employment-related lawsuits. However, based on the definition of disaster set forth earlier in this book, this is unrelated to contingency planning. Similarly, professional liability insurance is a coverage recommended for professionals such as physicians, dentists, architects, engineers, or attorneys to protect them against liability for negligence or malpractice. Yet, this is a topic for a general primer on business insurance, not for contingency planning and disaster recovery.

Liability insurance policies might include endorsements for personal injury (arising from claims made for libel, slander, etc.), host liquor liability, fiduciary liability, or fire legal liability. With respect to disaster planning, there is a risk that your business could be held liable for injury or damages should you have inadequate contingency plans in place. For example, imagine that a fire occurs on your premises. The main entrance to the office is burning and so you must seek an alternate means of egress. The only other exit is by means of a back door that is boarded up and blocked by storage boxes and crates that cannot be removed in a timely manner. Your business could be held liable for the loss of life that could have been prevented had there been a second, safe means of exiting your business premises.

There are certain types of liability coverage that you should discuss with your insurance broker as you design your insurance program and your overall contingency plan. The first is business interruption insurance, a form of insurance that pays a benefit to your small business when your business is unable to continue operations during a disaster or immediately resume operations following a disaster. Because this form of coverage is so important to your contingency plan, I devote a separate section of this chapter entirely to business interruption insurance. Next, I want to call your attention to commercial auto insurance. I expect that your business has its vehicles insured for physical damage and liability. But what you may not have appreciated is that you may also need insurance known as "non-owned automobile coverage," if you or your employees use personal vehicles when on company business. Imagine that one of your employees offers to drop a package off at a client's office on her way home. If she is in an auto accident during the course of that trip, your business could be sued for damages even though your company does not own the employee's car! Consider carefully whether you should include nonowned automobile coverage in your overall insurance program. Such a policy may also cover rental cars when you travel on business. Hired and nonowned automobile coverage is relatively inexpensive and may be an important part of your insurance program. Should a disaster require you to operate from an alternate location, you may rent cars and commingle personal commutes with business tasks; nonowned auto coverage will protect your business against the additional risks assumed.

When thinking of operating your business from an alternate location, consider insurance coverage for your home office. If you work from home, either in the normal course of affairs or in response to a disaster limiting access to your customary business premises, update your homeowner's policy to include coverage for office equipment in your home, and business liability coverage for the business activities conducted in your home. This coverage *is not* automatically included in a standard homeowner's policy. If you rent your home, you may want to include your home office equipment in your tenant's insurance policy. If your business has issued equipment to employees for use at home, such as laptops or cellular telephones, insure those assets through your commercial policy. It is an easy mistake to omit assets from your inventory of property, plant, and equipment when they are off the premises.

Next, workers' compensation and disability benefits insurance are typically mandatory coverage for businesses, depending on your state's requirements. Should a disaster cause injury to an employee on the job, these components of your insurance program will be very important to the recovery of your employee and your business. Workers' compensation insurance protects employees against the risk of sustaining a job-related injury. Workers' compensation insurance covers medical expenses, disability income benefits, and death benefits to dependents of an employee whose injury or death is job related. Premiums are assessed according to payroll and depend on the industry classification of your business. An advertising firm would pay lower workers' compensation premiums than a construction company, reflecting the relative risks of injury to employees of those two businesses. That is why it is important that you classify employees accurately for their job descriptions and wages. If you are adding new employees to your payroll, be certain to update your workers' compensation coverage to avoid incurring an additional year-end charge.

Obviously, the risk of incurring workers' compensation-related claims increases with the occurrence of a disaster: Employees may incur injuries themselves while evacuating the business premises, stress-related injuries and depression and other types of disorders may occur as a result. Be certain that your workers' compensation coverage is up to date. Similarly, employees injured in disasters while on the job may require disability benefits. Certain states mandate coverage for short-term disability for all employees. Check the Web site of your state's insurance commissioner or consult with your insurance broker to learn the requirements of your state.

I have three suggestions that may help to reduce your workers' compensation premiums, and possibly enable you to pay for nonowned automobile coverage or other insurance coverage that your business may need. First, ask your insurance company about merit-rating credits. In most states, small businesses that have favorable claims experiences may be entitled to credits toward their premiums. Second, consider adding a deductible to your workers' compensation policy. Workers' compensation typically covers from the first dollar of losses, but most states allow deductibles that will reduce your costs. Finally, consider foregoing coverage for yourself or for other officers or directors of the company. Many states let small business owners and certain officers and directors opt out of their workers' compensation policy. This would lower costs, but would leave you without workers' compensation benefits should you be injured on the job. This may make sense if you have medical insurance to pay for medical expenses incurred in an on-the-job injury or other means of financial support, such as a disability income policy, if you or any of your directors and officers were medically unable to work.

Director's and officer's liability insurance (commonly known as D & O) is an executive protection policy that covers directors and officers who may become personally liable for their actions on behalf of the company. With respect to contingency planning and disaster recovery, any corporate action that increased the company's loss may give rise to a D & O claim. An employee injury on the job or a fire at the company plant, for example, may result in a suit against the officers and directors of the company for their alleged failure to take steps on behalf of the company to mitigate the risk of fire, such as installing smoke detectors or training employees in basic safety practices.

Stefan, my IT guru, worked at a site in which regularly-scheduled fire drills provoked concern from the firefighters when the doors to the exit stairways were found locked, thereby blocking a safe evacuation by that route. Should a fire occur, the insurance company may deny parts of the claims for damages, on the ground that the building management failed to mitigate potential losses by ensuring that the exits were not locked.

It is important to involve all of your directors and officers in developing contingency plans and to ensure that the directors and officers are adequately protected against the liabilities that may be incurred in serving the company. Your contingency and disaster recovery plans may one day be reviewed and, with 20/20 hindsight, found to be insufficient by some measure. Limit your liability with the purchase of D & O insurance.

Indeed, the need for insurance expertise may be a consideration when assembling your company's board of directors or advisors. I was asked to serve on the advisory board of a high-tech start-up company, in part because of my reinsurance experience. Each member of the board of advisors was recruited because he or she possessed some specific expertise, be it marketing, public relations, or regulatory experience that augmented the talent available to the management team of this particular company. The advisors were compensated with stock options, thereby conserving start-up's resources. You might consider a similar arrangement for your company.

Along with D & O coverage, consider a "key person" insurance policy. If you or any other individual are so critical to the operation of your business that it would not continue in the same manner without you, you should consider "key person" insurance to finance the continuity of operations during a period of transition following death or disability of an owner or "key employee" of your small business. Government loan programs, venture capitalists, and banks frequently require this type of insurance policy. If the financial performance of the business is dependent on a key employee, the bank, or other lender, will want some type of protection should the key person become incapacitated.

In addition to key person and D & O coverage, consider purchasing excess liability coverage, also known as an "umbrella policy." This type of policy provides benefits when the limits of the basic, underlying policy are exhausted. Umbrella coverage allows you to substantially increase your insured coverage for a relatively modest incremental cost. The amount of coverage your business needs depends on the size of the business and what I call the "p-o-m" factor—what you require to have peace of mind.

In determining your insurance needs for contingency planning, take into consideration other requirements of your business to ensure that you do not omit or duplicate required coverage. For example, if you rent your office facility, your lease probably specifies that you are required to maintain insurance on the space you lease and to name your landlord as a beneficiary. In the event an employee or visitor to the office causes damage to the property, the landlord wants to be certain that you can reimburse that loss. Your type of business may require specific insurance coverage, such as surety, to provide a guarantee to your customers. Look at your insurance program in total, not in parts, to ensure that your business is adequately covered.

Business interruption, workers' compensation, key person, disability benefits, directors and officers' liability, nonowned automobile liability, and home office insurance are some of the types of coverage you should consider including in your insurance program as part of your overall contingency plan. As stated at the beginning of this section, business owner policies often offer a relative bargain, bundling different types of insurance covers for a single premium that may be less expensive than the costs of purchasing each additional cover in a separate mono-line policy. One final suggestion before concluding this section: industry-specific covers. Many insurance companies have developed insurance programs specific to certain industries. A visit to the Web site of a property-casualty insurer, for example, may list a menu of options of coverage for businesses in the financial services industry, or businesses in a certain profession, such as dentistry. These insurance programs include specialty coverage that is advantageous to the businesses in those designated industries. They may also give you free or low-cost access to consultants who can advise you on how to reduce your risk of loss. These specialized industry coverages are often well worth the premium. They may also include business interruption protection customized for your unique needs.

## BUSINESS INTERRUPTION INSURANCE

A disaster, such as a fire or flood, may interrupt your business. Until your business recovers from the disaster, it may experience a loss of income while at the same time paying fixed obligations such as rent and payroll. Property insurance may pay the cost of replacing assets damaged by the fire or flood, but your business may have difficulty meeting its obligations until the damaged assets are replaced and the business is once again fully operational. Business interruption insurance is designed to mitigate that loss.

Let's consider an example. I know a dentist whose premises were damaged in a storm that shattered windows and left debris throughout the office. Property insurance covered the costs of replacing the broken windows and removing the debris from the dentist's office. Three weeks were required to assess the damage and to make the necessary repairs, during which the dentist was unable to see patients in his office. He was liable for his office rent, payroll, leased equipment, and other ordinary business expenses during that time, but he received no revenues. If he had been covered by business interruption insurance, he would have demonstrated what his average daily revenues had been prior to the disaster, and sought reimbursement of that sum per day for the number of days that his office remained closed for disaster repair.

Business interruption insurance was generally not well known within the small business community until Hurricane Floyd struck the United States and the recent storms in Europe resulted in longer-than-expected recovery times for small businesses to resume operations. Frequently, it was the loss of income rather than property (which was often insured), that caused small businesses to file for bankruptcy protection. I have found many small business owners in Lower Manhattan, and more recently, the Gulf Coast, did not have business interruption insurance because they were not aware of it. Imagine if your restaurant, printing press, or barbershop is closed by civil authorities for several weeks. Could you afford to forego that income, given that you still have obligations to meet?

Business interruption insurance is typically sold as an endorsement to property insurance policies. It indemnifies policyholders for losses associated with insured interruptions of their businesses. It is designed to pay you what the business would have earned had a disaster not disrupted the business operations. Because business interruption insurance is an endorsement to a property insurance policy, it cannot be purchased separately. That is, your business must first sustain an insured property loss before the business interruption coverage is "triggered."

Let's consider a real-world example. A husband and wife own a sandwich shop and close the business for three weeks when the husband is hospitalized for a major surgery. The wife stays home to care for him during his recuperation. During this period, no income is earned, as the shop remains closed. Can they claim a benefit under their business interruption coverage? The answer is no, because their business did not sustain an insured property loss. The husband's absence from work was independent of the conditions of his business.

Many small businesses will derive limited benefit from certain disaster recovery recommendations in this book, owing to the fact that their businesses are immobile. For those businesses, the business interruption coverage is particularly important. Consider a restaurant. As a restaurant owner, you can (and should) back up your data, such as tax records, employee wage records, customer accounts, and other information. The IT contingency plan recommended in this book will prepare you for the first three (and the most common) disaster types: human errors, equipment failures, and service failures. But an event that displaces you from the worksite (caused by environmental hazards, fires, and terrorism and sabotage) leaves you with few options. You cannot operate a restaurant or a retail store from a remote location, even on a temporary basis! The business interruption insurance is particularly important to cover the lost revenues for businesses that cannot relocate. By the way, if your business is dependent on a key supplier or customer that sustains a disaster-related loss that affects your ability to stay in business, you will need contingent business interruption or dependent-properties coverage.

I interviewed small business owners in Lower Manhattan and in Florida who were affected by unrelated disasters and the findings were the same: Small business owners were frequently unaware of the possibility of business interruption insurance. Since the endorsement is an incremental expense to your property coverage, I strongly recommend it. Should your business sustain such a loss, you must be prepared to present a reasonable case for "pro forma" business income; that is, what you would have earned during the time that your business had not resumed operations. The accountants for your insurance company will request documentation of your fixed expenses, such as your office lease and payroll records. They will also request documentation of prior income, such as business contracts and prior period tax returns. To the extent that you can produce this information quickly, you can expedite processing of your claim—another reason why you should prepare for a disaster and keep a second set of business records off-site.

## SELECTING AN INSURER

Designing an insurance program suitable for the unique needs and limited resources of your small business is an important project. There are three types of insurance professionals who can advise you with respect to your insurance program:

1. Agents are licensed representatives of insurance companies responsible for marketing their products. They typically earn commissions based on sales volume. An agent may represent only a single company (a captive agent) or several companies (an independent agent).

2. Brokers are licensed representatives who work with more than one insurance company, but represent the interests of the buyer of insurance and recommend the insurance program in the best interests of the buyer. Like agents, brokers earn commissions based on sales.

3. Consultants may help to assess the needs of the business, design an appropriate insurance program, and recommend a suitable insurance company. The consultant is paid a fee for his service by the business. For large global corporations, consultants may earn their fees by offering specialized expertise with respect to insurance requirements in different locales and, therefore, their fees may be considered a wise investment. For small businesses, however, agents and brokers can generally provide the same advice without incurring fee obligations to consultants.

I would like to suggest that you consider another resource that is free to small businesses: Service Corps of Retired Executives (SCORE). SCORE is a program of the Small Business Administration that is staffed by volunteers, retired executives who seek to share their experience and provide guidance to help small businesses grow and prosper. To find the location of the SCORE office nearest to you, visit www.sba.gov. Your local SCORE office will match you with a SCORE volunteer whose experience is appropriate for your needs. I know of several savvy small business owners who sought to be matched with SCORE volunteers who were retired insurance executives, and so benefited from their experience at no cost.

Once you have selected an advisor to guide you through the process of developing an insurance program, you will need to select an insurance company carrier. As small business owners, we must husband our resources carefully, but do not select your insurance carrier solely on the basis of premium. Cost should be only one of several criteria that influence your purchase decision. Claims-paying ability, or the financial strength of the insurance carrier, is another of the criteria you must consider. Rating agencies, such as Standard & Poor's and A.M. Best, assess the financial strength of insurance companies, based on the quality of their balance sheets, their financial reserves and other criteria that determine their ability to pay policyholders' claims. A strong claims-paying rating is evidence of financial strength and the insurer's ability to pay policyholder claims. A weak claims-paying rating may be cause for concern; as a small business owner you would not wish to pay premiums to an insurance company that may become insolvent and unable to pay your claim.

You may obtain the financial rating of the insurance company from the agent, the broker, or the company itself. You may also go to your public library and read the reports from A.M. Best or Standard & Poor's to learn more about the financial strength of the insurance carriers you are considering. Do some research about the insurance company's quality of service and record in the small business market. Consult with other small business owners to learn of their level of satisfaction with their insurance carriers. Your state's department of insurance, which licenses insurance companies to operate within the state's borders, is also a good source of information about insurance companies and consumer complaints.

I encourage you to consider working with an insurance company partner of an association that represents the interests of small business owners. As an association member, you are likely to have some assurance of superior service from the insurer than you would have as a single insured. I can suggest a few associations for you to look into, such as the National Association of Women Business Owners (NAWBO), and the National Federation of Independent Business (NFIB). Dues-paying members of NAWBO have access to a range of resources that are helpful in contingency planning and disaster recovery. The NAWBO speaker's bureau, for example, may help you to identify fellow members with expertise in insurance and risk management with whom you can network. Fellow members can share with you their experiences with insurance carriers and make recommendations. Finally, corporate partners of NAWBO include insurance companies that are eager to serve NAWBO members and offer specialized services.

NFIB represents the interests of its member small businesses. It also offers its members discounted property-liability insurance programs. NFIB's publication, *Smart Business*, frequently covers insurance and risk management topics and presents its member's case studies that are very helpful. I am a member of both organizations and I find that the benefits to my business far exceed what I pay in membership dues; including high-quality service from outstanding insurance carriers affiliated with these associations.

Some small businesses will find that they are not insurable as risks in the "standard" marketplace and may have to turn to special insurance facilities that serve the residual, or nonstandard, market. These special facilities include the excess and surplus lines market, the national flood insurance program, and the state insurance underwriting associations.

The excess and surplus lines market consists of insurance companies that underwrite special risks. These companies are often nonadmitted carriers; that is, the state insurance departments do not license them, so care must be exercised in purchasing such coverage. An ordinary commercial insurance broker can refer you to an excess and surplus lines broker if he or she is unable to obtain coverage for your risks in the standard market. One engineering firm with which I had spoken obtained its excess liability coverage in the excess and surplus lines market when it was unable to obtain coverage in the standard market. Such coverage is relatively expensive, so your broker should make every effort to place your insurance program in the standard market.

The standard market will typically not provide flood insurance in mono-line or business owner's policies. You may purchase insurance coverage against losses arising from floods through the National Flood Insurance Program if your business property is in a community designated as a special flood hazard area, and if that community enforces measures designed to reduce future flood risks. This program is administered by the government's Federal Emergency Management Agency and provides nearly all the flood coverage in the United States. As Congress is considering proposed changes to the program, any information I might provide here could soon be out of date, so I suggest that you obtain current information from www.fema.gov, the Web site of the Federal Emergency Management Agency.

Finally, states sponsor pools of insurance companies that underwrite nonstandard risks to businesses operating within the state borders. For example, the New York Property Insurance Underwriting Association is a pool of insurance companies that underwrite fire insurance in New York State. The Association offers fire and extended coverage as well as coverage for vandalism and sprinkler leakage to small businesses that are unable to purchase this type of insurance from commercial insurers. The Association also provides business interruption insurance to companies based in New York. However, the Association assesses premiums that are substantially higher than premiums assessed in the standard market. Special insurance facilities in each of the states offer coverage to those unable to obtain coverage in the standard market; for further information, visit the Web site of your state insurance commissioner. However, premiums in the nonstandard market are generally more expensive than premiums in the standard market, so you should adopt risk management practices to facilitate the placement of your risks in the standard market.

## RISK MANAGEMENT

Risk management is a set of practices that will enable you to identify and minimize the risks that your small business assumes. Generally, a risk management program consists of four sets of practices:

1. **Risk Avoidance Practices.** Your small business should avoid risky activities whenever possible. Many readers will chuckle upon reading this, as you say, "of course, no sensible business owner would undertake risk unless it was necessary to the business operations and commensurate with reward," and you may wonder why state the obvious. Yet, we read of businesses that sponsor company outings at which employees burn the soles of their feet walking across hot coals

in an effort to build camaraderie. Isn't that a risk the business could painlessly shed? What arrangements do you make for liquor service at the annual company holiday party? Do you arrange transportation home for those who consume alcohol to avoid the risk of a tragic accident? Consider risks that you can remove from your business without diminishing your business operations.

2. **Risk Reduction Practices.** Seek to reduce risks you cannot avoid. For example, you can install a security camera in your retail store to reduce theft. You can place smoke alarms throughout your office to detect smoke and fire. You can provide your workers with specialized equipment to reduce the risk of workplace injury. You might adopt a policy of not allowing key officers of the company to travel together on the same airline flights.

3. **Risk Retention Practices.** You will retain some risks and insure others. You may choose to increase the risks you retain by raising the deductible. Higher insurance deductibles generally mean lower insurance premiums. Higher insurance deductibles generally also reduce the frequency and likelihood that your business will file claims, and a favorable claims experience also reduces premiums. Be certain that you have set aside sufficient cash in a reserve fund to pay the losses until the deductible is reached and to cover your essential business expenses until at least part of your insurance claim is paid.

4. **Risk Transfer Practices.** Some of your risks may be transferred by insurance and by other means. For example, if you provide advisory or consulting services, you may require your clients to sign an indemnification agreement, in which they hold you harmless from liability for the advice you provide.

A sensible risk management program, one that reduces your risks, may make your business more desirable to insurance companies in the standard market and reduce the risk that you will have to pay more expensive premiums in the nonstandard market. I conducted an informal survey of 20 commercial insurance brokers and asked if they could identify the mistakes most commonly made in risk management and insurance programs by small businesses. Here are the three most commonly cited mistakes they cited:

1. Failure to obtain adequate insurance on vehicles used for business purposes.

2. Failure to cover family members who work for the business under workers' compensation and disability insurance programs.

3. Failure to review the insurance program on a regular basis to ensure that it remained suitable and appropriate to the business as the business grew and changed.

Running a small business involves the assumption of risk. Don't assume more risk than is necessary; make certain you have an appropriate insurance program in place to cover losses.

## OTHER MEASURES

Should disaster strike your small business, you will need extra funds to cover uninsured losses until your deductible is reached, and you may incur additional expenses in activating alternate business sites and paying expenses until your insurance company pays your claim. We learned an unusual variant of this lesson on September 11. Many people carry little cash on their person to minimize the risk of loss due to theft and perhaps to impose spending discipline. On September 11, when workers and residents of Lower Manhattan had to evacuate their work premises, many found that they could not obtain cash from ATM machines and their normal commute home was disrupted. My banker, who lives in New Jersey, had to walk on foot across the Brooklyn Bridge and then needed funds to get home to New Jersey. It took some time before she could find her way home because she had no cash on her. I now keep some petty cash in the office for emergency use. It seems trivial to consider this, with the easy availability of electronic funds, but when you experience the inconvenience of being stranded, you want to ensure that it doesn't happen again.

Take steps to ensure access to capital while your business is running smoothly in the normal operating environment. You may wish to put in place bank lines of credit or obtain higher limits on your credit cards while business is functioning smoothly. You may have greater difficulty obtaining credit after a disaster strikes. Your customers may be slower in paying their obligations to you, and that may, in turn, hinder your ability to pay your obligations, which may create blemishes on your credit report. Having pristine credit will help you obtain disaster-relief financing that is typically offered in the form of loans.

Having access to capital may give you the funds you need to keep your business operational during the time required to complete a disaster loan package and await disbursement of funds. The old adage "the best time to apply for a loan is when you don't need one" applies here. Apply for credit lines in the course of your normal operating environment that will be available to you when disaster strikes. Finally, do what you can to build cash reserves sufficient to meet three to six months of operating expenses. It is difficult when you are launching a business to accumulate savings. In my case, I budgeted for business savings just as I planned for ordinary capital expenses, until I reached a cash reserve figure that gave me peace of mind. Even if disaster never strikes your business, the discipline of risk management and financial planning will improve your business processes.

# 5

# Basic Safety Practices

This and the following chapters are organized around several "key theme topics," including information that is important for you to have but does not easily fit within the more strategic framework of this book. The first deals with basic safety practices. The first edition of this book included summary information on basic safety practices in the Appendix to refresh the reader's memory of information that we learned as children, either in school, from our families, or both. Safety information was almost a *non sequitur* to a strategic handbook for small businesses, because it is common to everyone, but I thought we would be remiss for leaving it out. Since the publishing of the first edition of this book five years ago, I have taught seminars to small businesses across the United States, Canada, and Asia and I discovered not everyone has learned basic safety information! I recently spoke at an event for the San Antonio Small Business Development Center (SBDC) and was discussing this observation with one of the SBDC counselors. She told me that her father was in the military and before she could apply for a learner's permit for her driver's license, she had to demonstrate, to his satisfaction, that she knew what belonged in an emergency "Go kit"—and how to change a flat tire. My grandfather was a firefighter, so I had similar training. It was just unthinkable back then that you would not have a battery-operated radio with spare batteries in the home, along with bottled water and other essentials.

But in my travels, I have noticed that the only people who consistently follow safety practices are the Swiss! (I used to live in Zürich and have great affection for the Swiss and their civic-mindedness.) So I moved this chapter to the front of the book to give it more prominence. I have also included some updated information. Share this chapter, in particular, with your family members, employees and their families, and friends and neighbors. To the extent we are all better prepared, we can reduce unnecessary demands on first responders and enhance the safety of our communities.

Indeed, there are people in your local community who would be delighted to assist you with basic safety training. Your local Red Cross chapter most likely offers training in basic first aid practices. I participated in an on-site training session facilitated by a Red Cross instructor. The Red Cross will come to your place of work for a nominal fee if you have a group for training, with a required minimum of six or ten people. The instructor informed us of the Red Cross's goal to have at least one member of each household certified in cardiopulmonary resuscitation (CPR) and to be familiar with basic first aid practices. The standard first aid with automated external defibrillator course can be completed in eight hours and is also offered at low cost. The course teaches the latest emergency cardiac care: how to use the automated external defibrillator for sudden cardiac arrest. It also covers handling emergencies, adult CPR, and first aid for injuries and sudden illnesses. Those who complete the course will learn how to identify and care for a variety of medical emergencies, including severe bleeding, shock, muscular skeletal injuries, and other sudden illnesses, as well as how to reduce the risk of disease transmission while providing care.

In addition, the Red Cross also offers separate courses in CPR for infants/children and community CPR for those whose work may involve being called on to assist others in an emergency. There is a special course, CPR for the professional rescuer, developed for medical professionals, lifeguards, aerobic/fitness/sports instructors, and public and private safety and security employees. Those who complete the Red Cross training are certified for their skills. We all need refresher training from time to time, particularly when we do not frequently call upon such skills. Accordingly, the standard first aid certificate is valid for three years; thereafter, participants should take a refresher course to update their training and certification. For adult cardiopulmonary and automated external defibrillator training, the certification is valid for one year. Be certain to have a first aid kit on-site. If you operate a business such as a restaurant, you are required to have certain first aid equipment on-site and to be trained in administering some procedures, such as the Heimlich maneuver (abdominal thrusts recommended for a choking person).

The director of the Red Cross Chapter of San Antonio, Texas, told me that she wishes more small businesses would participate in this training and she and her colleagues are more than happy to make it available to you. I have completed such training because it is a small investment in building skills that could someday save someone's life. I encourage you to do the same. I hope it never happens, but should an employee, a visitor to your office, or a member of your family sustain an emergency, you need to be trained to help the situation while more experienced medical personnel are dispatched to the scene. The Red Cross is one of many organizations that offer training relevant to your contingency planning efforts. Other organizations you should consult include your local fire department, your police department, insurance company, building management, and local hospital.

I have consulted such organizations in the preparation of our contingency plans and I would like to share this information with you. As the designated fire marshal for the floor of the office building in which my business is head-quartered, I underwent special training for responding to fires. Since fire is a common form of disaster, let's review some basic safety practices to prevent and respond to fires.

Generally, high-rise buildings are required to have in place building information plans, including a fire evacuation plan, available to residents and tenants. I live in a high-rise apartment building. The building management furnished each of the residents with a fire safety plan approved by the local fire department. The plan includes information such as the identification of exits, the location of the building sprinklers and alarms, the telephone numbers to call in the event of emergency, and basic fire precautions. Regularly scheduled drills verify the functioning of the alarm systems. It is also helpful to place photo-luminescent way-finding markings and signage in your stairwells and hallways. In fact, in some cities, it is a legal require-ment. If you do not live or work in a high-rise that requires such a plan, produce one anyway. Should the need arise, the preparation will expedite the evacuation effort.

I have another tip for you in connection to disaster-related evacuation. I keep a supply of long-feed fish tablets that when placed in the aquarium, will dissolve and feed the fish for up to two weeks. I originally kept a supply of such tablets in my office (and in my home) for use in advance of sched-uled business travel. Now, dropping a tablet in the aquarium is part of my evacuation plan, time and human safety permitting. Another component of our office evacuation plan involves restroom searches. Each floor has two men—one with primary responsibility and one as a backup—and two women assigned to search the men's and women's restrooms in the event of fire. The idea is to ensure that anyone who is in the restroom is aware of the call to evacuate.

Remember that one precaution common to all disasters involves the maintenance of a disaster supplies kit, often referred to as a "Go kit." The kit might consist of bottled water, a first aid kit, flashlights, battery-operated radios, or other items you might need to cope if a disaster interrupts your operations. I have a battery-operated radio in my home and office. That is the means by which I learned that Battery Park City residents had been ordered to evacuate the neighborhood on September 11, 2001. I passed this information on to my neighbors who, like me, were without electricity. I also had on hand a flashlight to guide us down the stairwells. The flashlight wasn't necessary as our building's emergency generator provided a very low level of light in the stairwells that was adequate to get us out safely. But it is always better to be prepared.

Another tip for you: This one comes from the Global Security Team at Lehman Brothers, a major investment bank. (I will provide more details about this team in a separate chapter.) First, they have packaged "Go kits" for each and every employee for emergency use. In addition to the usual items included in such kits, such as a flashlight, they include items many of us would not necessarily have considered, such as goggles for the eyes to protect against irritation caused by smoke. They also include, for example, a mask with aloe vera beads used by professional firefighters to ensure that the lungs stay moist, as breathing can be very difficult in a smoke-filled room. The "Go kits" are not only provided to individual employees, they are also attached to the walls of the stairwells using double-sided Velcro tape. So in an emergency, let's say, when a group of employees are meeting in a conference room, you would not want them to put themselves in harm's way by returning to their offices to retrieve their "Go kits." So they follow the evacuation order by exiting the building via the stairwells and peel one of the "Go kits" from the wall. They are also on there for the use of visitors to the office. I liked this idea so much that I reached out to the vendor for these "Go kits" to see if we could negotiate a volume discount for our readers. (See the Web site www.preparedsmallbusiness.com for more details.)

For many of us, it has been years since we were schoolchildren and received fire safety instruction from the visiting firefighters. I would like to share with you fire safety tips that I learned as part of my training and once again, I encourage you to share this information with your employees as part of your contingency planning. Of course, these safety precautions apply to your home and family practices as well.

## FIRE

In the event a fire occurs in your office or business premises, the following is a suggested evacuation procedure:

- Close the door to the room where the fire is located and leave the office. Close doors behind you as you leave.

- Make certain everyone leaves the workplace with you (remember to search the restrooms and other facilities where workers may not be aware of the fire).

- Take your keys with you. Close, but do not lock, the door.

- Alert the workers on your floor to the fire as you exit your premises.

- Use the nearest stairwell to exit the building. *Do not use the elevator.*

- Call 911 once you reach a safe location. Do not assume the fire has been reported unless you see firefighters on the scene.

- Meet your employees at a predetermined location outside the building. Notify the responding firefighters if there are any employees who have not been accounted for.

If the fire is not in your facility, but is adjacent to your facility, the following is a suggested evacuation procedure:

- Remain in your office and listen for instructions from firefighters unless conditions become dangerous.

- If you must exit your facility, first touch the door and doorknob to detect heat. If they are not hot, open the door slightly and check the hallway for smoke, heat, or fire. Because fire, heat, and smoke generally rise, a fire on the floor below your office or worksite poses a greater threat to your safety than a fire on a floor above you.

- If you can safely leave your work premises, follow the evacuation procedure for premises in which a fire has been detected.

- If you cannot safely exit the premises, call 911 and give the operator your address, floor, and number of people with you. Seal the windows with wet towels or sheets, and seal air ducts or other openings where smoke may enter. Open windows a few inches at the top and bottom unless flames and smoke are coming from below. Do not break any windows. If the conditions appear life threatening, open a window and wave a towel or sheet to attract the attention of firefighters.

- If smoke conditions worsen before help arrives, get down on the floor and take short breaths through your nose. If possible move to a balcony or terrace away from the source of the smoke, heat, or fire. If your clothes catch fire, do not run. Stop, drop to the ground, cover your face with your hands, and roll over to smother the flames.

I emphasize that these evacuation procedures are suggested for you to discuss with your local fire department and emergency response team to adapt them to your own needs. I cannot anticipate every particular circumstance you may encounter, but these suggested evacuation procedures might serve as a starting point for your own customized contingency plan. Don't forget the procedures for shutting down your computer systems and other necessary precautions presented earlier in this book. Of course, I expect you will take steps to prevent fires such as:

- Each room should have at least one smoke detector. Check them periodically to ensure that they are in working order by pressing the test button. Replace the batteries in the Spring and Fall when you move the clocks forward and back one hour. If you follow this practice, you should never hear the detector chirp to signal that the battery reserve is low.

- Maintain a no-smoking policy.

- If you have cooking facilities, do not leave your cooking unattended. Keep the stovetops clean and free of items that could catch fire. Before you leave work for the evening, make certain that all cooking appliances are turned off and any coffee or teapots are unplugged.

- Make sure that you post the telephone number of your local fire dispatcher where it is visible. Keep fire extinguishers on hand and make certain that you and your employees know how to use them.

- Never overload electrical outlets. Replace any cracked or frayed electrical cords. Never run extension cords under rugs or carpets. Use only power strips with circuit breakers.

- Always ensure proper grounding of electric appliances. Usually they will have a three-pin power plug. Do not use the three-pin adapters to plug into a two-hole outlet without having an extra grounded cable connected.

- Keep all doorways and windows leading to fire escapes free of obstructions and report to your building management or landlord any obstructions in the hallways, stairwells, or other exits. Make sure each of your employees is familiar with the locations of all stairwells and means of safely exiting the premises.

- Identify a meeting place a safe distance away from your worksite where you and your employees can convene after evacuating the building.

- Be careful with greens or other holiday decorations. Do not keep them for an extended period, as they become flammable as they dry out. Keep them planted or in water and away from building and office exits.

- Determine if your facility is, or could be, equipped with fire sprinklers, and ensure that the sprinklers are in working order.

- Ensure that each employee understands basic fire safety information, including how to prevent fires, how to report fires, and how to evacuate the premises in the event of a fire. Conduct periodic drills to avoid creeping complacency.

- Ensure that your company is in compliance with local fire codes and regulations.

- Locate utility shutoffs so that electrical power, gas, or water can be turned off quickly.

- Seek guidance from your local fire department and your insurance company to recommend fire prevention and protection measures that are suitable for your business.

## FLOOD

Now, let's consider another peril, a flood or flash flood. Whether you are in a flood-prone area or not, read this section for safety information! Did you know that each year, 30% of floods occur in regions that have never been flooded before? Remember the advice earlier in this book: If you live in a flood-prone area, contact the National Flood Insurance Program to secure insurance protection. If you are not certain of your area's risk of flood, contact your local government's planning and zoning commission for more information. If you are in a flood-prone area, make certain that you keep your IT assets and other electrical powered appliances on the higher floors of your premises. Property that you place in the lower floors of your premises is at particular risk.

Except in the case of flash floods, you will generally have advance warning of a flood. If your local news reports of a flood watch in the area, it means that a flood is possible. A flood warning, however, means that a flood is in progress or will commence very soon. In the event of a flood watch, try to move your valuables to the higher floors of your building. In the event of a flood warning, listen to your local news reports for information. When an evacuation is ordered, shut down your essential systems as described earlier. If a flash flood watch is issued, you may have to evacuate on a moment's notice. I recommend that you err on the side of caution and shut down your systems on the issuance of a flash flood watch. Make certain that your employees understand that in the event of flood, they should evacuate to higher ground away from bodies of water.

When you evacuate, be respectful of barriers erected for your protection. Barriers are put in place to block vehicles from entering flooded areas. Be careful to stay on solid ground. You are at risk of electrocution if you walk in a flooded area in which water could be electrically charged from power lines. And, if possible, prior to evacuation, shut off the electricity at the main breaker or fuse box. After you return to your premises, you can determine if it is sufficiently dry to safely turn the power back on. Following a major disaster such as a flood, your local emergency authorities will advise you on precautions to take when you return to your premises.

## HURRICANE

If your business is located along the coastline, you may be in a hurricane-prone area, but remember that such storms can work their way inland for many hundred miles. The accompanying heavy rain, floods, and tornadoes often compound the damage wrought by hurricanes. When a hurricane watch is issued, it means that hurricane conditions are possible within 36 hours. A hurricane warning means that hurricane conditions are expected within 24 hours. When a hurricane warning or watch is issued, you should prepare for high winds and rain. I remember when Hurricane Gloria struck the New England states. I was a college student and the then dean advised us to criss-cross our windows with masking tape. My roommates and I quickly obliged. Today, emergency preparedness organizations advise against taping windows, as this does not prevent breakage. We, in fact, taped our windows in the hope that if the glass did break, fragments would not scatter about the room, causing more damage. We hoped that the tape would hold fragments together. Fortunately, we did not have to learn the effectiveness of this method. The campus gardeners cut away the branches of certain trees so that the wind blew through, thereby avoiding the risk of a powerful wind blowing away a weaker branch that could cause injury.

If possible, prepare for high winds by installing hurricane shutters or precut plywood for each window of your home. You should also bring indoors any furniture you have outside, such as decorations, plants, or anything else that can be carried away by the wind. Check the signage of your business. It may be wise to remove signs and bring them indoors as well, until the risk of the hurricane has passed. Remain attentive to the advice of civil authorities by listening to the news for orders of evacuation. If you will not evacuate your premises, remain indoors, away from the windows. Remember not to be deceived by the calm "eye" of a hurricane; the worst is not yet over. Don't go outdoors unless you are advised to evacuate by the emergency authorities.

## HEAT WAVE

Did you know that heat waves cause more deaths than any other type of weather-related disaster? A heat wave is an extended period of extreme heat and humidity. The meteorologist of your local news organization will warn you of an impending heat wave. I always anticipate heat waves in the summer, when warnings of brownouts or disruption of electricity are expected to leave much of the city without air conditioning. You won't have to evacuate your premises in the event of a heat wave, but you should take specific steps to protect your employees and your IT assets, as excessive heat is harmful to both. The following are some recommendations to protect people from harm during a heat wave:

- Refrain from engaging in strenuous physical activity.

- Remain indoors to the extent possible. If air conditioning is not available, move personnel to the lowest floor of the building, away from the windows where sunshine will heat the area. Fans won't lower the room temperature but they can cool your body by helping the sweat to evaporate, so turn the fans on if you don't have air conditioning.

- Drink copious amounts of water throughout the day, even if you are not thirsty. Water will help to cool your body and avoid dehydration. Avoid alcohol and caffeinated beverages; they will exacerbate dehydration.

- Eat smaller meals more frequently during the day. Heavier meals will raise metabolic heat as they are digested. Don't consume salt tablets, except on medical advice.

- Wear lightweight, light-colored clothing. Light colors reflect the sunlight and heat; darker colors absorb light and heat.

The consequences of heat exposure are severe, ranging from heat cramps to heat stroke. The latter, also known as sun stroke, can be fatal, as the body can no longer cool itself. Brain damage and death can result if the body is not cooled quickly. In the case of suspected heat stroke, call emergency medical personnel immediately and move the person away from the heat into a cooler room. Remove or loosen clothing and apply cool, wet cloths to the skin. If the person is conscious, he or she should *slowly* drink cool water. Let the person rest comfortably until medical help arrives.

Less severe symptoms of heat exposure include heat cramps and heat exhaustion. Heat cramps are muscular pains that result from heavy exertion in intense heat. They are an indication that the body is having difficulty cooling itself. In the case of suspected heat cramps, move to a cooler place where you can rest comfortably. Drink cool water to replenish fluids that have been lost during exercise. Heat exhaustion can strike people who work in hot, humid places. Those affected often sweat excessively, and, as blood flow to the skin increases, blood flow to vital organs decreases. Hot skin and rapid breathing are symptoms of heat exhaustion. Left untreated, the condition may worsen to heat stroke. The recommended treatment is the same as for heat stroke.

Some of your employees may be at greater risk than others. Young children and the elderly are more vulnerable to heat exhaustion, as are those who take medications, known as diuretics, which flush water from the body. Be particularly concerned about the risk of heat exhaustion if your business processes result in the generation of heat. Do employees work with equipment such as commercial printers or pizza ovens, which raise the temperature of the space in which they are located? Do you have adequate air conditioning in your workspace? Take all steps necessary to protect your employees.

In the event of a heat wave, you may want to consider giving people the day off or encourage telecommuting. Although your work facilities may be air conditioned and you have plenty of water available, your employees still have to commute to and from work. A car that breaks down on the way to work, or a delayed and crowded subway train, may put a vulnerable employee at risk. I used to contract some work to a consultant who had a serious kidney ailment. The medication she took to control her condition was a diuretic and she made it a practice to carry bottled water with her, as she often felt light-headed when she was in hot, crowded spaces. Whenever the weather was excessively hot, I would schedule another time to meet with her or encourage her to work from home until weather conditions improved. I would encourage you to extend to your suppliers the same courtesy, if it is possible. On days in which extreme heat is forecast, ask your suppliers if they would like to reschedule their appointments with you so that they can avoid traveling to your premises on humid, sticky days. If it is not possible to reschedule appointments scheduled with visitors to your premises, be sure to greet them with cool water to drink.

Once you have attended to human safety, give some thought to your IT assets. I advised you earlier in this book to attend to the risks of an over-heated central processing unit (CPU), caused by a malfunctioning fan, in order to avoid a possible systems crash. Presumably, you have done so. Now, when you are confronted with a heat wave and inadequate air conditioning, consider "quarantining" any computers you believe to be "suspect" until you can verify that their fans are functioning properly. If you have air conditioning in some rooms, but not others, move the computers to the air conditioned rooms for the duration of the heat wave or turn them off if possible.

## EARTHQUAKE

I am familiar with measures to prepare for an earthquake as I used to travel to Japan frequently. When you enter a hotel room in Tokyo, you will see an earthquake warning, printed in both Japanese and English, as you close your door to the hallway. The warning is typically affixed to the back of the door to your room. It advises guests that earthquakes and seismic activity are common in Japan, and tells them what to do if they should feel the ground shaking at their feet. It is quite an experience to be in a high-rise in Tokyo during a period of active seismic activity!

Although Japan, California, and other locations along seismically active zones (where plates of the earth's crust come together) are recognized as earthquake-prone areas, earthquakes can happen in many other locales, anytime, and without warning.

You can reduce the hazards of earthquakes by bolting heavy furniture to the walls using wall studs and ensuring that cabinets close securely, so that during an earthquake, their contents will not spill out and injure someone. I have beautiful, but very heavy, office furniture, and for safety, the wall unit, shelving, and chests of drawers are bolted to the walls. Although this makes moving in and out more difficult, it is much safer. Even in the absence of an earthquake, heavy furniture filled with files or other items can become unsteady and collapse. If your business is located in an earthquake-prone area, you should consult with a structural engineer to determine what you can do to protect the facility or minimize damage in the event of an earthquake. I recently attended an exhibit at a museum that featured models of taller buildings in San Francisco and the various features that the architects designed into the buildings, such as more flexible frames and counterweights on the roofs, to minimize risk. There are many innovative building technologies that you might investigate if you live in an earthquake-prone area.

Should you feel the ground move beneath you, remember the phrase "drop, cover, and hold on." Drop to the ground, hold on to something sturdy, cover your eyes by pressing your face into your arm, and hold on until the shaking stops. Stay away from windows that could shatter glass on you, or heavy furniture that could fall on you. If you are outside when the earthquake strikes, try to find a clearing away from buildings, trees, and power lines and then drop to the ground. If you are in a car, drive to a clearing and remain in the car until the shaking has stopped.

Once the shaking subsides, check yourself for injuries. There may be aftershocks following the earthquake, so be prepared to drop, cover, and hold on again. Inspect the property for damage. Turn off the gas, if you smell gas or think there is a risk of a gas leak. Don't turn it back on yourself, leave this job to a professional—call your utility company and arrange to have the gas switched back on. You may detect a small fire following an earthquake; if you are unable to extinguish it yourself, call the fire department. I have friends who attended school in California and they practiced drills in school for earthquake response. As such, they are better prepared. We recently experienced relatively minor seismic events in Connecticut and then in Switzerland, and because we typically do not associate these parts of the world with earthquake risk, many people did not know what to do. Be sure to share this information with your employees so that they will be familiar with the "drop, cover, and hold on" drill.

## TORNADO

Although tornadoes are more common in the Midwestern states, the fact is that they have been reported in each of the 50 states in America and in countries throughout the world. Even if you think you do not live in a tornado-prone area, read this section for the safety information. On April 24, 2007, a tornado tore through Eagle Pass, Texas, causing at least ten fatalities and injuring more than 80 people. Two elementary schools were demolished and almost 300 people were evacuated to shelters. This was an area that is not associated with tornado activity!

Tornadoes are known as "twisters" because tornado winds gust at speeds in excess of 200 miles per hour, destroying everything in their path. Spring and Summer are considered the tornado "seasons," but they can happen at any time of the year. A tornado watch means that a tornado is possible in your area; a tornado warning means that a tornado has already been sighted. An approaching tornado sounds like a speeding train. Remain indoors, away from the windows that could be shattered by the high-speed winds. If you are in a high-rise building, try to make it to the basement safely. Avoid the elevators and take the stairs as fallen power lines could disrupt the supply of electricity to your building without warning. If you don't have sufficient time to go to the basement or the ground floor, move to the center of the building, which is as far removed from windows on either side of the building as possible. If you are outside, go to the basement of the nearest sturdy building or lie flat in a ditch or a low-lying area. If you are in a car or a mobile home, get out immediately.

As is the case with a hurricane or a flood, remember to bring any equipment that is outside indoors. I have two friends, a husband and wife team, who own and operate a charming inn in New England. The inn caters to vacationing families, and, as such, has outdoor toys, swing sets, picnic tables, barbecues, and other items that could get swept in high winds and cause injuries. Their contingency plan calls for the husband to ensure that the items on the northern and eastern side of the inn are brought indoors when a storm warning is in effect, while the wife is responsible for the lower-weight items on the southern and western side of the inn. By assigning responsibilities, they ensure that nothing will be overlooked.

Once the tornado has passed, check your premises for damage. Be careful when you leave your premises, as fallen power lines pose a particular hazard. Don't light matches or use candles, as there may be gas leaks of which you are unaware. Listen to the news reports to determine if it is safe to go home and which areas you should avoid on your commute home.

## THUNDERSTORM

Darkening skies, flashes of light, and increased wind signal an approaching thunderstorm. If you hear thunder, the storm is close to you and lightning is a risk. Take shelter indoors. If you are in a car, roll up the windows. Be careful of conductors of electricity if lightning strikes. You want to avoid damages to electrical appliances, such as your air conditioner, by power surges caused by lightning and avoid the risk of electrocution. Use a surge protector for both power and phone lines. Unplug appliances, turn off the air conditioner, and avoid using the appliances or the telephone. Shut down your computer systems and switch off the printers. Don't run water or take a bath or shower until the storm is over. Protect yourself from injuries caused by shattered glass if flying objects break your windows by closing the blinds and the shades.

For those outdoors when the storm strikes, you must take special precautions. If you are waterborne, swimming, or boating, for example, get to land immediately. If you are in a wooded area, take refuge under shorter trees. Try to go to an open place, away from trees, and drop to the ground, curling into your body. The idea is to make the smallest amount of area to reduce the surface that could be struck by lightning. Remember that if you are in a hospitality business, you need to take precautions to protect your customers. I have friends who own a small motel in New Hampshire that has an in-ground pool. When a thunderstorm approaches, they ensure that the guests leave the pool and they padlock the pool to ensure that no one reenters. They had a scare when children, seeking the thrill of swimming in the rain, entered the pool after it had been closed. Apparently, their parents were not watching them closely and the children were not aware of the risks of being struck by lightning while swimming in a pool. Fortunately, no one was harmed, but they revised their contingency plan accordingly. They also keep on hand a supply of movie videos and games to keep the children entertained until weather conditions permit them to go outside again.

If someone is struck by lightning, seek medical help immediately. Administer CPR (assuming that you are trained to do so), if the injured person's heart has stopped beating. Administer first aid, if necessary, until emergency medical personnel arrive on the scene.

## TERRORISM

Should an act of terrorism occur, you may or may not be called upon to evacuate. Sometimes, terrorists stage acts timed to occur minutes apart to inflict the maximum damage possible on emergency workers arriving at the scene. For this reason, New York City does not make its terrorism evacuation plan publicly available. However, civic leaders are aware of the plan and can act when called to do so. Such acts are unpredictable, so you should follow the instructions of your local civil authority with respect to evacuation. Communicate with your employees in the manner agreed upon in your contingency plan. Follow the procedures outlined for evacuation: Shut down your computer system, turn off utilities, and so on.

Here are a few lessons I learned on September 11, 2001 that may assist you in developing your evacuation procedures should disaster strike:

- I used to travel frequently on short notice for business and so got into the habit of always having an overnight bag ready to go. You may consider setting aside a small bag of items that you would need to take with you in the event you were evacuated from your premises: your telephone contact information, eyeglasses, contacts lenses, prescriptions, and so on. If you have a small trousse packed and set aside, it is one less thing for you to think about when disaster strikes.

- I was able to send an e-mail to my parents after the World Trade Center was attacked, but before we lost our telephone service. I sent the e-mail after being unable to contact them by telephone as their line remained busy, which meant that they were on the Internet. My parents have since switched to an Internet connection via TV cable, and I will do the same. It provides an additional contingency in the event our telephone service is interrupted in the future.

Our September 11, 2001 experience was an extraordinary event, but you can appreciate the frequency with which major disasters strike by looking at the Federal Emergency Management Agency (FEMA) data for that year. Your only disaster-safe places in 2001 would have been: Delaware, Hawaii, Idaho, Maryland, Minnesota, North Carolina, Rhode Island, Utah, and Vermont. And that is just for major disasters declared by the federal government. Like everyone else, those states had their share of localized disasters, such as fires and power outages. So it is well worth it to become familiar with basic safety practices.

# 6

# Business Mail Procedures

Since letters tainted with the deadly bacteria anthrax were delivered through the U.S. Postal Service in October 2001, safety concerns prompted many businesses to reconsider their procedures for handling incoming mail. As time passes and threats recede into memory, complacency creeps in. The purpose of this chapter is not to revisit old fears,[1] but to reinforce a pragmatic approach to processing business mail, an essential part of your preparedness strategy. Let's begin by considering efficient mail handling to reduce the flow of junk mail to your workplace.

## REDUCING JUNK MAIL

Reducing the volume of mail to your business site reduces the number of letters and packages that must be screened by your mailroom. But, apart from concerns about mail safety, there are other pragmatic reasons for filtering junk mail to your business site. If you feel overwhelmed by the amount of messages reaching you, you are not alone. Two out of three workers surveyed reported that they felt "overwhelmed" by the quantity of information they must process each day.[2] As a member of the small business community, your resources and time are precious. Filtering out unnecessary messages frees your time for other more productive work. I remember receiving a deluge of mail solicitations (and telephone calls) after registering my business with the county clerk's office. The volume was excessive and I resented the unwanted intrusions. It resumed when I obtained telephone service for our business. I find it particularly irksome to return from a business trip and waste time sorting through junk mail.

Actions that you take in the ordinary course of work can invite junk mail to your business. These include completing warranty cards for your office equipment; subscribing to newspapers, magazines, or professional journals; filing a change of address form with the post office; listing your business telephone number; or ordering products from the mail or Internet. I don't wish to exaggerate the risk: None of the reported incidents of anthrax exposure that occurred following the terrorist attacks of September 11 involved mail solicitations from direct response marketers. However, as such marketers seek to avoid having their solicitations discarded before being read, they disguise the origin of their letters, thereby increasing mail you may have to treat as suspicious. I recommend that you filter it out as best you can.

Your first step is to contact your local direct marketing association. Send a letter to them indicating that you do not wish to receive any direct mail from its members. In the United States, contact the Mail Preference Service at their Web site, www.the-dma.org. Be advised that the Direct Marketing Association has recently started assessing a $1 fee to remove names from their database. In Canada, the address is www.the-cma.org; in the United Kingdom, www.dma.org.uk; in Australia, www.adma.com.au; and in New Zealand, www.dma.co.nz. For readers in other countries, visit your favorite Internet search engine and enter "Direct Marketing Association" and your country's name to find the site relevant to you.

You may also visit the same sites to address your inquiry to their telephone preference service and request that your business telephone numbers be removed from their telemarketers' lists. Be certain to include your business name and addresses of all of your offices or facilities in your letter.

I have also observed that many direct marketers include free gifts in their mailings, such as personalized pens, notepads, and other inexpensive items. These gifts increase the bulk of the mailings that may appear as "suspicious." Accordingly, your next step is to write to the major sellers of mailing lists. These agencies collect data, such as business names and addresses, and resell them, over and over again, to their clients. Write a letter, include your business name and address(es) and request to be removed from their databases. Unfortunately, the contact information for mail resellers changes so rapidly that the information would be irrelevant by the time this book is in your hands, so I suggest you visit your favorite search engine and enter the term "metro mail" to identify a good place to start.

One ancillary benefit of having your business removed from the marketing databases is the reduced embarrassment of inappropriate mail being sent to your workplace. I will never understand why one well-known company sent me lingerie catalogs at the office, having obtained my business address from a marketing database! How many women business owners wish to receive such catalogs at the office in the presence of their clients and employees?

Your next step to reducing unnecessary mail is to write to each of the major credit bureaus and advise them of your wish not to be contacted. You may need to include your taxpayer identification number in your letter. The three major credit bureaus are Equifax, Experian, and Trans Union. Visit their Web sites for current guidelines on how to put your name on their "Do Not Contact" lists.

Finally, you should contact each of the companies with which you do business and advise them not to sell or rent your business name or address. I have written to publishers of each of the trade journals to which my company subscribes and requested that they not make our names and addresses available to other parties. This has decreased the volume of our junk mail dramatically. You must be vigilant as this is an ongoing process. When you, or any of your employees, complete a warranty card or order a product through the mail, you must be certain to include a note advising the vendor not to sell or distribute your name and address. These steps should reduce the volume of mail to your place of business.

Now, as a small business owner or employee, you may face the opposite problem—how do you ensure that your direct mailings to potential customers are not discarded by the recipient's screening process? In 2006, commercial and nonprofit marketers received $1.93 trillion from direct mail solicitation in the United States alone.[3] The following are some suggestions you can use to assure the recipients of your mailings that your letters are secure:

- Identify your business as the source of the mailing through the return address. Present a professional appearance with appropriate typeface on your mailings. Include your company logo on the envelope.

- Consider using a postal meter to stamp your mailings. In addition to avoiding unnecessary trips to the post office, and the occasion to overpay your postal charges, metered mail is more likely to be opened and reviewed than stamped mail. This is because metered mail is more easily traced and therefore, less likely to be used to deliver tainted mail.

- Eliminate anything from your mailings that could produce bulk or an uneven appearance. A flat letter is less likely to arouse suspicion in the recipient than an uneven, bulky envelope.

- Use clear window envelopes showing the recipient's address. A transparent envelope is less likely to contain an unwanted substance. Or you may use postcards to contact potential customers. You may also choose to notify potential customers by advance postcard that a product sample is coming, for example, so that they expect a bulky package from you.

- You may wish to apply a seal across your envelope flaps to assure the recipient that the envelope has not been tampered with since it left your place of business.

Finally, to protect the reputation of your business, ensure that your outgoing mail facility is secure. Conduct careful pre-employment reference and criminal background checks to ensure that your employees will be of good character and unlikely to misuse your company's mail facilities. Make certain that only your employees have access to your mailroom. I once visited a Manhattan law firm that propped open the door to its mailroom after hours, as the personnel who received courier packages at all hours of the evening did not wish to miss a delivery whenever they stepped away! The mailroom opened onto a public corridor near the elevator bank of a large Wall Street office building. Don't do this. Be certain that your business facilities are secure.

## HANDLING INCOMING MAIL

Make certain that you and your employees are alert for suspicious packages and letters delivered at your place of business. The U.S. Postal Service advises us that suspicious mail includes mail that:

- Displays a powdery substance

- Is unexpected or sent by someone unknown to you

- Has incorrect postage, a handwritten or inaccurately typed address, incorrect titles, or a business title without a name, and misspellings of common words

- Is addressed to someone who is no longer with your company or is otherwise out of date

- Has an unusual amount of tape sealing the mailing

- Gives off an unusual odor or displays stains

- Has no return address or one that cannot be verified as legitimate

- Is of an unusual weight or shape, possibly lopsided

- Is marked with restrictive endorsements, such as "personal" or "confidential"

Do not open, shake, or empty the contents of any suspicious envelope or package. Contain the suspicious piece of mail by placing it in a container, such as a plastic bag, to prevent its contents from leaking. Leave the area where the suspicious mail is contained and advise others, perhaps by posting a sign, not to enter that area. Next, wash your hands with soap and water to prevent spreading any noxious substances to your face. Be careful not to rub your eyes or touch your skin until after you have washed your hands. Contact the police and your building security team and advise them of the suspicious package for their further investigation. Give the police the names of the other people who were present when you came into contact with the suspicious mail. Should the mail be tainted with a toxic substance, all individuals in the area when the mail was delivered will likely have to be tested for possible exposure. You should follow this procedure in the event that a suspicious piece of mail is delivered to your place of business. Be certain that all of your staff members are instructed in the identification and response to suspicious mail.

If a piece of mail escapes your screening procedures and you open it, what should you do if the mail contains powder or some other substance? First: *do not panic.* The substance need not be toxic. Unfortunately, following the events of September 11, the occasional prankster has sent baby powder in the mail to provoke fear and anxiety in the recipient. I was once evacuated from a New York City subway when a powdered substance was found in the subway station. The powder was, thankfully, not anthrax.

Once you have collected yourself, do not attempt to clean up the powder. Immediately contain the spilled contents with any available covers, such as a waste basket, or paper, or a piece of clothing; and turn off any fans or ventilation units in the area. The idea is to limit the amount of powder that can become airborne. Leave the area and advise others not to enter the area. Wash your hands with soap and water, again exercising care not to touch your skin or rub your eyes. Immediately contact the police and your building security team. Remove any contaminated items (e.g., your clothing, items on the desk where the mail was opened) and place them in a sealed plastic bag. This bag should be given to emergency personnel for proper testing and subsequent disposal. Shower with soap and water and remember to give the names of those individuals who were present when the powder was released from the mail. Should the powder be identified as something toxic, those individuals will likely have to be tested for possible exposure. This is what happened as recently as June 2007 when the chief meteorologist of ABC News in New York received an envelope filled with a white powder—which turned out to be a nontoxic substance sent by a former employee of the news network.

I once worked at an investment bank where all incoming mail was subject to x-ray screening. I read that post offices that deliver mail to government offices are also irradiating their mail. Such costly technology is likely beyond the reach of most small businesses, but technological innovation has made other screening techniques feasible. Many companies now offer electronic document delivery. These businesses accept and open your mail—and, with many customers for whom they screen mail, it is presumably cost-effective for them to irradiate the mail—and then electronically scan your mail. Junk mail is discarded. All other mail is delivered to you electronically—you never touch the mail! Stefan Dietrich, my coauthor for the first edition of this book, used this type of service long before anthrax-tainted letters were delivered to victims in the fall of 2001. As he travels to

Europe frequently, he finds it convenient to have access to his mail while on the road. It also helps him pay his bills online, so bill payments are not delayed until his return, and his credit rating remains unblemished. You can find companies offering such services through the Internet search engines.

## INTERNAL COMMUNICATION

Ongoing communication within your business is vital. As time passes, staff may become less vigilant about mail security. Occasional reminders are essential to ensure the safety of your staff. Make certain that your staff understand proper mail handling procedures and provide them periodic reminders. The most important aspect of communicating the proper procedures for handling mail is to address any fear and anxiety that may linger about infection through postal mail exposures.

## NOTES

1. The chance of contracting anthrax from cross-contaminated mail is, according to the former Director of the Centers for Disease Control and Prevention, "very low, the mail is, by and large, very safe."

2. Nucleus Research Inc., October 24, 2006.

3. www.the-dma.org.

# 7

# Special Needs of the Disabled and the Elderly

In the first edition of this book, we wrote,

> You and your employees, as part of your personal contingency planning, should give some thought to the needs of the elderly in your family and in your neighborhood. If an evacuation is ordered in response to a disaster, they may require special assistance. I have elderly neighbors who had seen on television the planes crashing into the World Trade Center, but failed to appreciate the consequences for the rest of the community. When I offered to assist them in gathering some belongings, walking down many flights of stairs and walking through the ash to the boats, they were adamant in their belief that leaving their home for a day or two was not worth the inconvenience. I alerted a police officer to their presence and he explained to them that it would likely be more than a few days before they could safely return, that there was no assurance of when the utilities would be restored and that there were other reasons why they should leave. They did, and got out safely. As part of your disaster response, you and your employees should consider the needs of your elderly relatives and neighbors.

This paragraph provoked a particularly strong response from our readers! In particular, I was contacted by The Center for the Independence of the Disabled, New York (CIDNY), a nonprofit organization that was overwhelmed by requests for assistance in the aftermath of a major disaster. CIDNY published a brief report, "Lessons Learned from the World Trade Center Disaster: Emergency Preparedness for People with Disabilities in New York." The title is a bit misleading, because, in fact, the report deals with the experiences of the disabled in the aftermath of other major disasters, such as the Kobe earthquake in Japan and the 2004 blackout in the United States and Canada.

The report was painful to read. The greatest risk to the disabled, and the reason that so many of them suffer such awful outcomes, is that many disabled people are socially isolated. Presumably, that is why my story of reaching out to my elderly neighbors resonated with so many people. Download the free report at CIDNY's Web site, www.cidny.org. It is about an hour's read and it is important that you do so: It will sensitize you to issues that you had not previously considered. Give careful thought to the needs of your disabled and elderly employees, customers, suppliers, and other visitors to your place of work. Encourage your employees to do the same for their family members and neighbors. It is not only the right thing to do; it will also create a better workplace.

Along those lines, I had the opportunity to visit Lehman Brothers, an investment bank that consistently ranks as one of the top workplaces in the U.S. In the aftermath of 9/11, many investment banks hired top talent from federal law enforcement and security agencies to improve their security procedures in the face of new and emerging threats. Ted Price is the Managing Director of Global Security, Ken Damstrom is the Senior Vice President and Global Head of Security Operations, and James Lapidera is the Vice President of Corporate Security. Together, they represent more than 75 years of professional security experience in law enforcement, national security, and the private sector. These gentlemen were kind enough to invite me to Lehman Brothers for a half-day, where I learned tips for enhanced human security to share with you. In fact, they showed me the stairwells with the "peel and go" kits and put me in touch with the vendor to make these kits available to our readers.

What impressed me most about their approach to corporate security was their deep and sincere concern for the safety of each and every employee. Lehman Brothers has a Human Resources (HR) database where the global security operations team knows, for example, that John Doe has a cast on his leg and his physician will remove that cast on such and such a date. So, during the period that John Doe has limited physical mobility, an employee is explicitly assigned responsibility for helping John Doe to safely exit the premises should an evacuation be ordered. A second employee is assigned as backup should the first employee be out of the office for whatever reason. The global security team knows of employees in the last trimester of pregnancy, elderly and frail employees, and others with disabilities that might need additional help to safely exit the building in an evacuation. Each and every one of them is assigned support from specific colleagues to ensure that they will not be forgotten or left behind in an emergency, the fate of many disabled people so painfully described in CIDNY's report. They also have special chairs to help physically disabled people safely exit through the staircases.

I left Lehman Brothers deeply impressed with the care and concern that they show for their employees. I have no doubt why they earned their spot on the top workplaces. Because of their management practices, they surely have an advantage in the competition for talented employees. I have adopted certain of their practices for my own business.

The following are tips to address other personal and medical needs as part of your disaster preparedness plan:

• Anticipate needs for medications and encourage your employees to do the same. I was in a pharmacy in the World Trade Center to get a prescription refilled on the morning of September 11, 2001. When I returned to Lower Manhattan, I had hoped that another pharmacy in the chain could provide the refills remaining on my prescription since they share databanks. Their policies prohibit transferring prescriptions from one pharmacy to another, but with my label from the remaining amount of my last prescription, they gave me an emergency 30-day supply. My physician's return from vacation was delayed, and because we were without telephone service, it took some time to contact my physician to get a new prescription. The lesson I learned, and would like to share with you, is that if you have a chronic medical condition, don't postpone getting your prescription refilled until your existing supply of medication is nearly exhausted. In an emergency situation, you could be at risk. Insurance companies generally won't authorize payment for more than a 30-day supply at a time, but now I refill my prescription one week before my existing supply is exhausted.

• Along the same lines, many people have their prescriptions delivered by mail. It is a great convenience, except following an evacuation. I followed the instructions by our postmaster to visit the post office nearest my home to present identification and pick up mail for my home and to the central post office in Midtown Manhattan to pick up business mail that had been held there. Still, it took about two months for mail delivery to catch up with us. If the health insurance company that provides coverage to your business offers mail order prescription delivery, you and your employees need to have a backup plan in place should mail delivery be interrupted. A visit to the local emergency room is not a good backup plan, because in the event of a major disaster, there will be victims in urgent need of medical treatment.

• I have all of my medical records scanned for digital storage off-site where I can access them remotely. I did the same for each of my family members, as I am not relying on the adequacy of backup plans of physicians and hospitals where I have been treated in the past.

- As part of your contingency plans, encourage your employees to consider the needs of their children in the event of a disaster. You should discuss emergency planning with your local school and inform your child's teachers of who is authorized to pick your child up from school in the event of an emergency. If your children are not in school, you need to agree in advance with your spouse what to do in the event of a disaster.

Give careful thought to how you might implement these suggestions. We can and should make our workplaces and our homes as safe as possible for our employees and our families. If you have your own tips for creative ways you have applied to enhance safety, share them at www.preparedsmallbusiness.com. I am always eager to improve my business and have benefited so much from the wisdom of my readers. We can learn a great deal from one another.

# 8

# Give Some Thought To Your Pets

On October 15, 2007, the American Humane Society released the results of its survey under the headline "Nearly Half of Americans Won't Flee Without Fido."[1] They found that 47% of Americans surveyed would refuse rescue assistance if it meant leaving without their family pets. Presumably, you don't bring your dogs and cats to work with you, but remind your employees who have pets at home to consider their needs when developing personal contingency plans. Perhaps you have a neighbor with whom you can leave a key to your home for the express purpose of taking your pet if an evacuation is ordered when you are at work. You may have seen television footage of animal rescue workers trying to enter homes in disaster areas to feed animals left behind. The safety of your pets is one less thing for you and your employees to worry about when operating your business from a remote location. The following are tips to help you develop a pet evacuation plan:

- Just as you put together a "Go kit" for evacuation for human needs (e.g., a flashlight, batteries, bottled water), you should also prepare an emergency "Go kit" for your pet. It might include an ID tag, leash, collar, the pet's medical records, a first aid kit, your veterinarian's contact information, medications, food, and water. You may need a current record of your pet's vaccinations to be allowed access to a pet shelter or pet-friendly hotels.

- Locate possible pet shelters and pet-friendly hotels in the event you need to use their services following an evacuation order.

- You might choose to include your cell phone number and the name and cell phone number of an out-of-state relative for your pet's ID tag. This could be very valuable in locating your pet if you become separated. Also be sure to have a photograph of your pet for identification purposes.

- Make sure that you have a pet carrier for each pet.

- Consult experts for additional tips, such as your veterinarian or your local chapter of the Humane Society.

By the way, if you own and operate a pet service business, you could provide a valuable service to your customers by sharing these tips with them. When I was speaking at an *Entrepreneur* magazine conference, I met Bonnie Hayslett, the owner of Bubbles and Clips Mobile Pet Grooming. She shared with me details of her work on pet evacuation and rescue in the aftermath of the riots in Los Angeles. She pays $19 monthly for online backup of all digitized medical records for pets that are in her care. She also put tips on her Web site for her customers to help them develop their own pet evacuation plan (see www.mobilepetgroomers.com).

Provide these tips to your family members and employees and you may reduce the risk that they will disobey an evacuation order out of concern for their pets. You also help to ensure the safety of those animals and the peace of mind of your employees, as this should be one less thing for you to worry about in an emergency.

## NOTE

1. www.americanhumane.org.

# 9

# Take Five

The most valuable information I can share with you is to improve your business processes from lessons learned by our peers in the small business community. I have set up a Web site for that purpose, www.preparedsmallbusiness.com. Another important lesson is that you must test your disaster preparedness plan. There are some risks that you cannot reasonably anticipate without performing a drill. Let me share two stories with you to reinforce this point. When speaking at an event of the National Association of Women Business Owners, I met a business owner who told me how she had backed up all of her business critical data online and off-site. Brilliant—she had her tax records, customer information, and all critical data secured. Then she made a secondary backup in the event that the first one would fail. Also brilliant—in my case, I have backups stored at locations removed from one another by more than 500 miles such that in the event one has a problem, I have redundancy. But she did not test her backups. When disaster struck, she found, to her horror, that her primary backup was defective because it did not capture all of her data; only a random sample of some business data. Then she turned to her secondary backup and learned that it was not an independent backup of the original data, but rather a copy of the defective primary backup. She did not have two independent backup sets of data, she had duplicates of a single defective set. With advance testing, this could be avoided. I do a spot check on my backup data sets monthly to make sure that what I need is safe and secure.

Now after digesting all of the information presented in the book thus far, you may feel overwhelmed. Don't feel that way. This is intended to be a strategic handbook to guide small business owners as you develop contingency plans that will improve your business processes in case you ever experience a disaster. You need to involve your employees, their families, your

# PART TWO

# RESPOND

A disaster strikes. Most often it is something relatively minor; for instance, someone accidentally pulls the plug of an important piece of equipment or a hard disk crashes. But at first, you do not know. Normal operations are interrupted and you have to determine what has happened. Your priorities are to ensure the safety of your employees, customers, and visitors; to minimize the interruption of your business and to limit possible damage from the interruption.

In an actual emergency, you will have little time to execute an elaborate and detailed formal plan, unless you run a large corporation and need this type of administrative coordination to ensure that nothing is overlooked. You also want to be certain not to overreact to a minor incident or false alarm.

With the exception of severe weather, where you often receive an advance warning, disaster can strike at any time. Chaos will ensue. Organizational authority becomes essential even for a small business. Who is responsible for what? Who takes the lead if a manager is not available? There is no time for debate; everyone must understand this and it should be made very clear in the disaster preparation training. For a small business, you do not need a lengthy disaster plan. What you need are simple checklists of specific items that must be done and of who is responsible for seeing that they are done. Such checklists will help you react quickly because they will reduce indecision.

Your main role is to remain composed and to present a calm demeanor to your employees. You have invested the time and effort in preparing for a disaster and now your planning should guide your actions. Your main concern should be the safety of your employees. Assess the apparent danger and determine if you need to evacuate the premises. In most cases, this will not be necessary, as you will most likely be dealing with a technology crisis like the unintentional deletion of a file, a hard disk crash, a network failure, or simply a false alarm. But if the cause remains unclear, and some secondary events occur, like smoke, it is simply prudent to evacuate, and to reconvene at the disaster recovery site.

You have done some work in preparing for contingency and so can meet the challenges the disaster presents with a greater degree of confidence. Because you know that you have backup systems and appropriate insurance, you can stay calm. Your decision process will be rapid because you already know exactly what you have to do to minimize damage and potential liabilities. So you can stay focused on ensuring continuous vital business operations, like customer service, and protecting company assets and shareholders' interests. You will also know that good public relations work is now required to ensure a positive perception and understanding of your efforts by your clients and creditors.

At the beginning of this book, I said that you would soon realize that your efforts in disaster preparation will be beneficial for your overall business. You are able to respond quickly, take necessary corrective actions, and know that your data are safe. Be confident: Most businesses recover from disasters and even learn from them.

# 10

# IT Strategy

If you followed the advice in the earlier chapters of this book, and developed a disaster strategy for your business, your IT infrastructure should be in good shape and allow quick and effective response to the events unfolding. You have routine contingency issues caused by human error and equipment or third-party failure, events that over 90% of all small businesses will ever experience. Only a very small percentage of us will have to deal with more serious disasters.

Imagine that a disaster just struck. It was unexpected and quick. You will soon face demands from different parties. Everyone will want some assurance, to feel cared for, and to be recognized. Sometimes this need presents itself in difficult ways: Everyone wants their particular issue addressed right here and now, and each action taken will be scrutinized. When the disaster struck, everyone was occupied with the ongoing events. In the immediate aftermath, as you are trying to implement an organized response, it may seem as though everyone has forgotten the earlier agreements on priorities and timeframes. Instead of recognizing the damages that were limited, employees may focus their attention on the inconveniences of the disruption (assuming that you were so fortunate as to avoid the more serious consequences of a disaster, such as loss of human life).

Expectations may become unrealistic; employees may fail to appreciate that downtime has been minimized relative to what could have happened had a contingency plan not been put in place. Instead, they are resentful of any inconvenience at all. Any lack of compliance with your contingency plans will become obvious. There will also be the odd person who failed to observe backup procedures. Try to contain your frustration with the situation. The important thing is the safety of your people. With the passage of time, the disruptions in your operations will be viewed as relatively minor events. Remember the saying, "This, too, shall pass."

You may expect that compliance with the contingency plan will not be exactly 100%. So prepare standard announcements to post throughout the company to inform everyone, as the disaster unfolds, about steps that will be taken. Have these announcements on your internal Web site before a disaster so that everyone is clear about what action will be taken for which underlying business reason. Also, keep statistics about any type of unplanned interruption of your operations. Soon, you will get some valuable feedback on how certain processes can be improved when it becomes clear how many more user errors versus actual hardware failures occur.

In most cases, when a disaster happens and people ask for help, your role should be to stay calm in the middle of the storm and keep a high-level view to ensure that everyone can make it through this unpleasant experience as painlessly as possible. But if you have to deal with serious, life-threatening disasters that are beyond the ordinary, your focus should immediately shift to protecting your employees. You might even have to call for an evacuation of the office or building. In that case, you have to decide how to protect your IT equipment. If you expect that the IT equipment will not be affected, shut down all nonessential systems and services. If you expect that you will no longer be able to access your equipment remotely, start the automatic emergency shutdown.

Before examining in more detail the response to specific disaster categories, I want to once more emphasize that you will be dealing with the emotional responses of stress, both your own "hot buttons" and those of the people around you. Let me share with you an example related to me by the managing director responsible for global security at a commercial bank. He was overseeing a disaster simulation that called for employees who ordinarily work in Manhattan to convene at the recovery site in New Jersey. One of the members of his management team got stuck in traffic. With each passing minute, her stress levels rose such that by the time she arrived to join the simulation, she was in "emotional meltdown," the term the director used in relating this story. He immediately picked up his mobile phone and called his Human Resources (HR) manager to deal with it. When the HR person protested that his department was not participating in this drill, the director replied, "If this is what happens in a simulation of a particular scenario, what do you expect will occur if we ever experience the real event? You better learn how to deal with it now." The HR person grudgingly complied. The lesson learned is that just being aware that you will have to deal with the unpleasant responses that emerge from stressed human beings makes you better prepared. So expect some unpleasant behaviors from others and try to contain your own.

## HUMAN ERRORS

Most instances of human error involve the mistaken deletion of a computer file. It may be a localized event that can be recovered from your nightly backups, and therefore of little worry.

But this is not always the case. Imagine, for example, the following common scenario. A work group is rushing to finish a presentation to give to a key client later in the day. Just before the meeting starts, an employee, when trying to incorporate changes, accidentally overwrites this document with large sections of text from an older version of the same document. If you are lucky, the error is discovered before you give your presentation.

Now imagine how this scenario typically plays out. You are upset because the document was not ready on time and are disappointed about visiting a client with presentation materials that are, in part, obsolete. In such situations, there is always the tendency to play the "blame game," which makes people defensive and reluctant to comply with the contingency plan, as they feel embarrassed.

This example highlights the need of the requirements outlined in the preparation part of this book. Nightly backups alone are not enough. They need to be preceded with a campaign of user-training and hourly or on-demand snapshot backups to keep copies of the most recent versions of documents.

The same scenario with the suggested combined effort would have resulted in a different outcome. The group of people writing the document would establish guidelines on where to store documents, how to name them, and which version control methods they would use. They would also agree on how to merge changes into one final document. While writing the document, each person checks his version into the version control system, or at least makes regular copies of the document with an agreed naming convention that would trace the creation of the document (e.g., "presentation-11AM.doc"). In addition, each user would manually copy the files, such as to a remote online backup system, or launch a file synchronization tool to initiate a snapshot backup on his progress, such as on an on-site backup system. This would automatically store all changes to his documents on the backup system.

An accidental deletion of a document would mean that only the work of this one user from his last backup is lost. If a version control tool was used, you would roll back to the last saved version. With this more efficient process, there should be sufficient time to redo changes and incorporate them into the final document.

Note, however, that with this "disaster-safe" operation mode, you would not eliminate the possibility that a document would contain wrong or obsolete information. After all, people also make mistakes in the content itself, but user-training reduces the possibility of confusing documents.

I would like to discourage contingency plans using data recovery tools that would allow recovering deleted documents from a hard disk. In the small business environment, it is a rare occasion that you would have the time to process this recovery, and rarer still that it would be worthwhile to invest the time to do the detective work that these tools require.

You should pay close attention to any events involving human error. These events highlight where your organization may continue to have issues that need your attention and it also shows you which employees can handle the size and scope of the overall project. Initiate corrective action as soon as possible, and if data are retrieved from the backup system, communicate this promptly. Otherwise, you may find that someone has picked up your recovered version and is unknowingly working with obsolete data files.

---

### HUMAN ERROR AT WORK

Let me share with you a specific example involving a jewelry designer in Manhattan whose work is featured in weekly celebrity magazines (which is why I don't have permission to use her name!). Her business captures customer information in a database for the production of sales catalog mailing labels and order processing. Certain individual fields; (first name, last name, address line 1, city, state, and zip code), are mandatory, but "address line 2," referring to an apartment number, office suite number, floor number, or corporate mail stop number, was not required, because most residential addresses do not have a second line after the street address. She had about 250,000 individual customer records in her system and had taken our advice from the first edition of this book and backed up her customer records off-site. Her experience taught her that about 20% of the individuals who request the catalog will make a purchase within a year's time. To reduce postal mailing costs, she eliminates from her mailing list any name that has not made a purchase over the past four seasons. About three-quarters of the individuals in her customer records were those that had not yet made a purchase, but had requested a catalog. This means that about 50,000 of those individuals would likely convert to paying customers within a year's time. Here is what went wrong.

A new employee began entering customer records into the new database: first name, last name, address line 1, and so forth. She did not scroll down to the bottom of the screen to see the fields for the city, state and zip code, and so entered this information in a single line in the "address line 2" field. When the mailing labels were printed for the season's catalogs, everything looked fine so the errors went undetected. The error was noticed when a systems crash forced the business owner to go to the backup tape. The database software randomly pulled information from other customer records to fill in the missing required fields of city, state, and zip code, such that Mary Smith's customer record was filled with the city, state, and zip code from Jane Doe. In other words, the customer records retrieved from the backup were useless. The customer prospects, people who had requested the catalog, but had not yet made a purchase, were permanently lost. The customer records for those who had made purchases were recovered from her shipping service (she is a *very good* customer), but it was extremely time-consuming to eliminate duplicates, as many customers place multiple orders, and reenter all of this information manually.

There are two key lessons here: First, human error is costly, and second, test your backups. We will return to the example of this jewelry designer in another context: terrorism and sabotage. But before concluding discussion of this example, I want to address an issue that is often raised when I speak at small business events around the world. Someone will invariably contest my definition of an "everyday disaster" as an event that is not a disaster at all and counter that it is really a nuisance. The point is not to argue about terminology, but I want to reinforce a broader lesson: What if the jewelry designer's facility had burned down or been flooded? She would have recourse to her backup tapes and face the same situation, but she did so under the circumstances of the statistically more probable event: human error. So she should not take comfort (and neither should you) that major disasters are unlikely to strike her. That may be true, but the "everyday disaster" is the one she should worry about and preparing for that would make her better prepared for a more serious disaster.

## EQUIPMENT FAILURES

For some reason, equipment failure seems to follow Murphy's Law. It is always the most important part that breaks whenever it is most urgently needed. On our last day of work with the manuscript for the first edition of this book, our two main printers ran out of toner and none of the suppliers in New York had the correct toner cartridge in stock! Fortunately, I have a printer at home with which I could swap parts.

Particularly stressful are network interruptions because they affect many people at the same time. Networks are usually very reliable when properly set up. It is much more likely that you encounter issues with network congestion because of poor network design, but the components themselves, such as hubs, switches, and routers, are usually very stable. If your network traffic stops abruptly, you should first suspect a simple cabling problem. Did someone pull a cable? Are all the cables still there? Are they all plugged in properly? Are the uplink switches on the hubs properly pressed? Also make sure you know your cables.

My company's IT leader once had to deal with a case where someone had switched a red cable with a yellow cable from the equipment room because he thought a red cable would be more pleasing aesthetically. As there were no spare red cables left, he took one from the patch panel and replaced it with a yellow cable he found in a colleague's office. Most of the patching cables were yellow; we used red cables only to indicate special connections, such as between the network switches, so everything appeared fine. The next morning the network was down. We needed a network tester. It took us some time to find out that this cable that appeared to be like all other yellow cables was actually a special cross-over cable that our colleague had used at home to connect his laptop directly to his home desktop computer, but it was indistinguishable from the other yellow cables in our equipment room.

If your error does not seem to be located with your cabling, take a closer look at your network components. Do they all have power? Reboot your routers if you are cut off from the network. If you suspect that a network component has failed, it makes sense to replace it. You want to take the error investigation "off-line" in its true sense. You should always have spare network parts on hand, unless you took my advice for the "double-up" network configuration where any network component is already available twice. But even then, you should immediately replace faulty equipment.

The next thing that could happen is an equipment failure of some centralized server. If you followed my advice, you are aware that it is generally not a good idea to put many services on the same platform. If you absolutely had to bundle them on the platform, you have to deal with the fact that several services will be down at the same time. Hopefully, you installed a secondary backup server. Depending on the circumstances, it might be necessary to temporarily switch over to this server to provide network functionality until the primary unit is back online.

The most important issue when dealing with an equipment failure is to stay calm. Users will scream and managers will ask for updates and status reports. Suddenly, everyone will seem to have forgotten the previously agreed-upon system recovery procedures and timeframes, and you will need to handle it. You could offer a continuous briefing by e-mail or have standard pre-formulated disaster recovery updates available and simply modify them from time to time as needed. It is also important to have checklists ready for certain type of events, in particular, apparent equipment failures. Even the most experienced airplane pilots need checklists in case of an emergency because under stress, they can simply oversee a small, but important, detail.

Complete system failures can raise the pressure and stress level for everyone involved in fixing the problem. You need to give your IT staff as much support as possible for their efforts and keep distractions out of their way. Any minute spent without coming closer to a solution increases the stress level. You probably know from your own experience that you are much more likely to locate the error within the first ten minutes or it really takes a while until you can figure out what went wrong.

Here is the recommendation from the first edition of this book, word-for-word:

> So I strongly recommend that when you respond to a case of equipment failure that you limit your error search to about ten minutes. If you have a valid hypothesis on the cause of the malfunction, you can increase the time somewhat, but set a limit. After that limit is exceeded, replace the equipment. Otherwise, your IT consultant or other labor costs will soon exceed the cost of replacing the failed equipment.

Five years after I wrote those words, I was on-site with a client when the computer that I had been assigned failed. The client's compliance procedures explicitly prohibited vendors from connecting their own external devices, such as laptops, to the client's network, so I had to use the desktop computer they had assigned me. Four of their IT support staff spent two days repairing the computer, during which time my productivity was limited. It would have been far less expensive to immediately replace the computer after the first ten minutes of investigation had failed to identify the cause of the failure. The irony was that at this time, I was in touch with Peg Callahan and Deirdre Patillo of the Texas Small Business Development Centers who were likely wondering why I didn't follow my own advice! I am sorry, but my clients are typically large development agencies that believe that they know more than a small business owner!

Now that I have made my editorial comment, let me add that for defective computer drives you will most likely download a backup image from the backup system onto a new hard disk, but your system will again be up and running as it was in the morning or at your last snapshot, and any further data recovery—if it is really necessary and makes sense—can be taken off-line.

Sometimes, a system simply becomes unreliable. It fails without a specific cause, but there is no apparent defect. And it happens again just a couple of days later. An unreliable system is not acceptable to any user, but error searching is most often a time-consuming process. So I recommend that you replace the system first, and look at it quietly off-line without pressure from the users.

## THIRD-PARTY SERVICE FAILURES

If one of your third-party services fails, the first thing you want to do is to switch over to the secondary provider you had in place. Maybe you have specialized equipment that will automatically do the cut-over for you or you may do it yourself by manually patching network cables. Then call your primary provider and report the problem and ask for the timeframe until it will be fixed and request that they send you continuous updates.

Electricity rarely fails, but there are other dangers, like spikes in the voltage, so it is a good idea to have both a surge protector and a Uninterruptible Power Supply (UPS) unit in place that should automatically kick in if the voltage drops below a threshold value. Systems can only run for a limited time on battery power. In most cases, you have just ten minutes or so. You need to quickly investigate the cause of the electricity failure. Maybe it was just a blown fuse or it indicates an electrical defect somewhere else. If you have not reestablished electricity and the battery is close to depletion, the system connected to that UPS should shut down automatically to avoid any loss of data.

Also think about that when you have your own phone system, it should have its own UPS unit. If you subscribe to Centrex service from your provider and have all analog phone lines, the phone company itself supplies the power.

## ENVIRONMENTAL HAZARDS

You need to identify the source of the hazard and determine if the substance is toxic or merely an irritant. In any case, if the substance is released outside the building, a simple effective short-term measure is to keep all windows closed. If the substance is released inside the building, evacuate the premises immediately. Your staff should know where and when to reconvene, either at the site or at an alternate location. However, you want to make sure that you trigger an automatic shutdown of all nonessential systems and that you lock your room with the essential IT equipment and important documents. If you have chosen to use the Redundant Array of Independent Disks (RAID) solution with one removable drive, take it with you now. You have to take these steps because you are preparing for remote operation—Stage I conditions, and you will not know when you can go back into the building and who might have access to the systems in your absence. Decide if conditions warrant reconvening at an alternate location at a later time.

## FIRES AND OTHER DISASTERS

In the event of fire or a natural disaster, like a tornado or flood, your employees and your physical assets are at risk. Treat advance warnings of disasters seriously and initiate an emergency backup of essential equipment, shut down all nonessential computers, and immediately evacuate the building. If you happen to have sufficient advance warning, such as in the case of approaching severe weather, you have to decide which level of backup you would be able to run safely before evacuation becomes mandatory. Before leaving the building, initiate an orderly shutdown of all IT equipment. With fires, the immediate danger is from toxic smoke that spreads quickly. So the precautions for environmental hazards also apply. In any case, you need to prepare your alternate site for remote operation—Stage II, assuming that it will take some time to resume business at your main office.

Let me add one more point on evacuations: I had not attributed any significance to the fact that I had called my office and asked everyone to go home before Lower Manhattan was evacuated on 9/11. I simply thought that was the prudent thing to do and if the event at the World Trade Center turned out not to be as serious as I thought it might be (there was a lot of confusion when I left the World Trade Center on 9/11 and I did not learn until nearly an hour later that planes had struck the towers!), the worst case would be that people work from home for the remainder of the day and avoid the usual rush hour commute. But at an event for the Small Business Development Center at the University of Texas–Pan American, Edinburg's Deputy Fire Chief Ubaldo D. Pérez, commended me for that decision. He said that most businesses would delay an evacuation, thinking it might not be absolutely necessary. I had not thought my response was so unusual, but if Chief Pérez is correct in saying that it is unusual, let me reinforce the message: err on the side of caution whenever you are in doubt. Don't worry that you are overreacting: Employees will not protest having to go home early to be with their families.[1] In my case, sending people home before the City ordered the evacuation spared some people from walking across a crowded Brooklyn Bridge under uncomfortable and scary conditions. So I am glad that I did not delay.

## TERRORISM AND SABOTAGE

Generally, there will not be any advance warning of a terrorist attack. In this case you can only do one thing: Safeguard your employees and try to find a way to escape. This is not the time to worry about backups; leave the area as soon as possible. Nothing under your control could have prevented this disaster. This type of attack is unpredictable.

You should know that you can rely on your remote backup system, and that you have an alternate site from which you can establish an emergency operation.

## NOTE

1. But also remember that in some cases, shelter-in-place is the appropriate response, which is what I did when I remained in my apartment until an evacuation was ordered. With so much debris being scattered about, the risk of an injury warranted my remaining in place.

# 11

# Financial Liquidity

If you have followed the advice set forth in Part One, Prepare, of this book, you have put in place an insurance program for your small business. In this chapter, I will guide you through the process of dealing with insured property losses. I begin with an overview of the steps to follow in preparing your claim. Next, I offer some suggestions to identify insurance policies implicated in your business's property loss and to reconstruct insurance policies. I give some specific information concerning disaster relief programs that your business might qualify for and, as your ongoing business success is dependent of your disaster recovery efforts, I will offer some practical advice to communicate your efforts to all of the stakeholders in your small business. Let's begin with the most time-critical element of securing insurance coverage: mitigating losses.

## MITIGATING INSURED LOSSES

One of the most important activities you will undertake in respect to securing property insurance coverage is loss mitigation. You must demonstrate to your insurer that you acted in good faith to mitigate the losses to your business arising from a disaster. Let us develop an example. Imagine that an intruder gained access to your office over the weekend by means of forced entry and stole laptops and some petty cash. On Monday morning, you arrived at the office to find that a window was broken and there were fragments of glass inside the office. Of course, you will notify the police and the insurance company of this incident. But you must also take steps to mitigate your losses.

Your business must repair the window as soon as possible. The broken glass should be safely removed as it could cause injury to an employee or visitor to the office. Failure to promptly repair the window could give rise to other types of losses, such as property damage. Imagine that a rainstorm is expected later in the evening. If the window is not repaired by that time, your office could be soaked and computer equipment damaged by the exposure. Your insurance company expects you to take reasonable steps to prevent that from happening. If it is not possible for a repair person to immediately replace the window, do what you can to rectify the situation.

Perhaps you could remove the pieces of glass yourself and cover the broken window with material to keep the interior of the office as dry as possible. You could remove sensitive electronic equipment from the vicinity of the broken window such that the equipment won't be exposed to the elements. You could have someone remain in the office, after hours if necessary; to ensure that no one else enters the office by means of that window until it can be replaced. There are various ways of responding to the situation to show good faith in limiting your insured losses to the original loss event of theft. Insurance companies are intolerant of passive policyholders who fail to act in their interests to limit losses.

In connection to your loss mitigation efforts, you should immediately restore any property protection systems that may have been damaged in the disaster, such as fire sprinklers and burglar alarms. These efforts will serve to limit subsequent insured losses to your business. Soon after the disaster, verify that your property protection systems are operational. If you lease space in a multitenant facility, you may need the help of your landlord or building management to complete this task. Your efforts may be complicated if your landlord is not on-site or cannot return to the facility immediately following the disaster. As part of your preparation efforts, request in advance an alternate contact number for your building management company in the event of an emergency. Or ask your building manager to supply you with direct contacts for service providers to the building, such as building security. If you have good relations with your neighboring tenants, you may elect to share this responsibility and distribute a contact list to divide and conquer. You could, for example, call the company that installed the smoke alarms and water sprinklers in your office building to report any malfunctions of that equipment. The tenant in the office adjacent to yours may contact the security company responsible for the building alarm system.

Working to restore common services provided as part of your office lease can be a sensitive issue. Your building management company likely wants to assume responsibility for this function, but if they cannot get their staff on-site in a timely manner, you need to demonstrate that you took steps to mitigate your property losses, irrespective of what the building management could or could not do in any particular situation. I recommend that you have a conversation with your building management staff before a disaster strikes. Ask them what they would like you to do in a situation in which they cannot be reached and building equipment necessary for common security is malfunctioning. Then, document the conversation with a brief follow-up memorandum. It is worth the hour or so invested in this effort to avoid costly misunderstandings.[1]

If it is impossible to immediately restore property protection systems following a disaster, post a watchperson. You may elect to hire a security guard to remain on the premises and alert the police of any suspicious activity. You may choose to alternate employee shifts to cover this duty. Be certain to document the additional effort and expense incurred in mitigating your losses, as this will be important to securing your insurance coverage. Such expenses are reimbursable by insurance companies, as they want to encourage loss mitigation efforts! Indeed, some insurance companies are raising the bar for loss mitigation requirements. Following Hurricane Katrina, insurance companies with major coastal exposures, particularly in California, issued statements with specific requirements for homeowners and small business owners to enhance the safety of their properties. Since California is typically a bellwether state for the rest of the United States, American small business owners need to take heed—and all others need to anticipate this trend.

Once you have restored service to any damaged property protection services, or put in place other means to compensate for the temporary loss of such services, your next step is to notify all the insurance companies whose policies may be implicated in your property loss. Prompt notification is essential to establishing your claim, although many states offer automatic extensions for notice when a federal disaster is declared. Your policy almost certainly specifies a time period following a disaster during which you must report any losses in order for you to claim policy benefits. Read your policy carefully and note any deadlines for reporting losses. Ascertain that at least one other person in your business is also familiar with the provisions of your insurance policy.

As you have read throughout this book, the key theme of contingency planning is developing redundant capacity to respond to a disaster. This includes redundant IT capacity (e.g., backup systems), redundant financial capacity (e.g., insurance), and redundant staff capacity. If you are incapacitated in a disaster, it is critical that you have a colleague or employee who can move the response process forward. It is more likely that you will not be incapacitated in a disaster; but that you will need all of the assistance and support you can get to react to the situation.

I have a friend who owns and manages a company that designs furniture specially developed for ergonomic considerations. On September 11, 2001, she was in Los Angeles, California, presenting her product line to a potential buyer. She remained stranded there for some days following the tragedy until the airports reopened. Meanwhile, her New York staff was unaware of the insurance arrangements she had in place for the business, which had sustained property damage. With no telephone service to Lower Manhattan, she was unable to advise them what to do. She attended to the matter immediately upon her return, but a prompt response could have accelerated the claims payment. You know how critical cash flow is to a small business. A delay of one to three weeks of an insurance claim settlement makes a difference. My friend has learned from the experience and has been more open about sharing such information with her staff. People genuinely want to be helpful in such situations; make it easy for them to help you by giving them the tools they need.

If you are in doubt as to whether an insurance carrier may be responsible for covering certain of your insured losses, err on the side of caution and notify them of the disaster. You should also consider whether to give notice to insurance companies whose policies have expired or to those who underwrite your excess coverage. If notifying an insurance carrier on an expired policy sounds like madness, let me clarify the point.

Insurance professionals distinguish between multiple time periods based on when loss events occur and when they are manifested. Consider an example that caused terrible dislocation to the insurance industry: coverage for asbestos-related risks.

Materials that we now consider toxic, such as asbestos and lead paint, were commonly used in constructing buildings decades ago. Workers may suffer respiratory symptoms and health problems as a consequence of their exposure to such substances, but it may take some time after the exposure before a medical diagnosis is made. The Lloyd's of London insurance market paid substantial claims to cover losses that resulted from the exposure to asbestos—which occurred when such policies were in force—even though in many cases, the consequences of the exposure were not apparent until years later, often after the expiry of the original insurance policies.

Let us move from this real world example to a hypothetical one. Let's say that you have an insurance policy covering losses incurred over the period of January 1, 2000 through midnight December 31, 2000. On January 1, 2001, your building is evacuated due to an exposure to a hazardous substance. Although your insurance policy expired at year-end, it may pay a benefit if it is determined that the hazardous exposure occurred prior to midnight on December 31, 2000. Perhaps the exposure occurred when the policy was in force, but the exposure was only noted several days later when a noxious odor was detected. It may be worthwhile to investigate expired policies to determine if they are implicated in your insured loss.

It may also be appropriate to notify the insurer that underwrites your excess coverage. If it appears that you will exhaust the underlying limits of your basic coverage and trigger excess cover, your excess lines underwriter should be notified. If in doubt, err on the side of caution and give notice. If it is subsequently determined that your losses are within the limits of your basic policy, no excess cover benefits will be paid, but at least you will not have precluded collecting on such a claim by failure to give timely notice of the loss.

Your next step is to prepare a preliminary report for your insurer outlining the type of loss, the date and time of the loss, the location of the loss, a contact person at your company (this is a task you may prefer to delegate when you are in disaster-operation mode), and the property implicated in the loss. Advise your insurer if the affected property is protected from further damage or if any facilities require temporary enclosures. Let your insurer also know if any utility lines have been damaged and are in need of repair.

In the event of a large-scale disaster, your insurance company will have a so-called CAT team in place to respond to it. "CAT" is insurance jargon for "CATastrophe" and "CAT teams" are assembled to deal with these extraordinary events. This means that to ensure a prompt response, your insurance company has likely mobilized a team in a location removed from the disaster. I have my insurance with a company that is headquartered in New Jersey, but the contact person assigned to my claim after September 11 was based in the company's Colorado office. He coordinated his efforts with a local colleague, when it was necessary to inspect my damaged property.

The advantage of this system is that your recovery process will not be delayed by reliance on a local insurance office that is recovering from the same disaster that struck your business. In my case, it meant that critical staff on-site in New York could be mobilized to inspect damages, while a remote team in Colorado (that was presumably not disrupted on September 11, 2001) could perform all of the necessary administrative tasks to process business claims.

I share this information with you because some of my neighbors delayed filing claims until telephone service was restored in Lower Manhattan, where their local insurance offices were based. Don't delay—your insurance carrier will put a CAT team in place to deal with the disaster and you can communicate with that team by e-mail and by fax. Visit the Web site of your insurance carrier to see if any announcements have been posted for policyholders affected by the disaster and follow the instructions contained therein.

Unless otherwise directed by instructions on your insurer's Web site, prepare and submit your preliminary report to initiate the claims process. But remember that it is not the final word. As you investigate the damage to your business caused by the disaster, you will likely revise the report. You should identify and separate the damaged from the undamaged property. Segregating the damaged property reduces the risk that further damage will be caused when, for example, an employee unwittingly begins to prepare your insurance report on a personal computer (PC) with a hard disk that had been corrupted in the disaster and software that was about to crash.

I recommend that you inspect your IT assets at least twice to make certain that you have not overlooked anything. I heard unpleasant grinding noises emanating from my PC when I returned to my office following the September 11 disaster. I suspect that I had not heard those noises earlier in the damage assessment process because of the background noise of construction work outside of my office building to restore other third-party services that had been disrupted. By reviewing each IT asset twice, I avoided the error of filing an incomplete claims report. When Stefan, my IT guru, heard the grinding noise, he recommended the replacement of one of the two mirrored hard disks I have in my PC before more serious problems could arise from the disk—another example of loss mitigation efforts!

Your next step is to begin the salvage operations. Assess whether production can be restored to the damaged facilities, and if so, make your best estimate as to when restoration is likely to be complete. Determine if your equipment can be repaired and if substitute parts and components are readily available. Investigate the possibility of recovering lost production time through overtime work, use of other suppliers, or processing of existing stock in inventory. The result of this process is a plan, developed with the input of your insurance company, to make the necessary repairs, secure access to alternate operating facilities, and to identify other loss mitigation efforts.

## SECURING INSURANCE FOR A PROPERTY LOSS

The first, critical step in securing insurance for your business property losses is to mitigate your losses, as we have discussed. Following that step, you should establish accounting procedures to track damage to property, plant, and equipment; damage to inventory; and costs incurred to mitigate those losses. Begin by establishing separate accounts to track all loss-related expenses. It is critical that you document all expenses paid to restore the business and get it up-and-running. If you purchased business interruption insurance, begin to document the revenues your business lost as a direct result of the disaster. Were customers unable to reach your business because civil authorities closed the premises? If you operate a business that relies on customer traffic, such as a retail store or a restaurant, every day that your facility is closed results in lost revenues and increased expenses. Because business interruption claims can be very large, it is possible that your insurance company will use the services of a third-party adjuster, in addition to its own internal adjuster. An external adjuster, typically a certified public accountant, is paid a fee by the insurance company to investigate and substantiate claims, so be certain to have accurate records.

To secure business interruption insurance, you must first determine the period of interruption. This is not necessarily a simple task. Consider our experience of the attack on the World Trade Center. Lower Manhattan was closed on September 11, but I was allowed to reenter my office on September 18.[2] However, not all services were available to support normal business operations at that time, so our interruption was only partially remedied. You may be able to operate on a limited basis for some time before full recovery is complete.

Make your best effort to assess lost production as reflected in marketing and sales records. Compare what your business would have produced had it not been interrupted to what it actually produced. The shortfall is the gross lost production. From the gross loss production figure, deduct any sales or production that your business was able to restore by using alternate offices, employing overtime workers, or other means. The difference is the net lost production to which you add the additional costs incurred in replenishing inventory and the expenses associated with loss mitigation. The result is the business interruption loss.

Other loss-related expenses relate to costs incurred to restore the business such as:

- Overtime wages paid to employees who work to restore the business

- Lease payments made for your alternate office facility when your primary office facility has been rendered unusable by the disaster

- Meals purchased for employees who worked overtime or off-site as a consequence of the disaster

- Watch protection expenses paid to security guards whose services were required as a consequence of the disaster

- Costs of purchasing property for temporary business use

It is not practical to produce an exhaustive list of such expenses, but you get the idea. Agree to a system for tracking these expenses; if in doubt as to whether an expense would be loss-related, agree on a means to "flag" it for review at a later time with your accountant. You may be able to deduct from your business taxable income loss-related expenses that were not reimbursed by insurance, so it pays to track these expenses with care.

For example, following the September 11 disaster, some small businesses in Lower Manhattan reimbursed their employees for the additional commuting expenses they incurred in coming to work. The train from New Jersey to the World Trade Center was not operational and several subway lines were closed. Clearly these expenses were related to the disaster! By the way, I recommend paying employees a reasonable per diem for additional commuting expenses, rather than invest time and effort in assessing the commuting pathway of each person. As the commuting expenses are trivial relative to other types of expenses, you should invest your time accordingly.

Be certain that each of your employees knows how to collect and record all loss-related documentation, including invoices, contracts, and timecards. The period immediately following a disaster is likely to be chaotic and you don't want to make extra work for yourself by having an inconsistent, or incomprehensible, tracking system. Expenses incurred in connection with professional services, such as expenses for the services of a certified public accountant or an attorney, are generally not covered by insurance policies.

Finally, you must prepare and submit your claim to the insurance company. The submission should include the date, location, and nature of your loss; the amount of loss claimed explicitly identified by category of loss; the lost revenues covered by business interruption insurance; and the expenses incurred to mitigate the losses. Attach supporting documentation for each claim of damage. If you need additional time to prepare, ask your insurer for a written extension of time to submit your claim.

Proper organization and documentation of your claim is vital. I received a call from my insurance adjuster's CAT team thanking me for the best-prepared claim she had received. She was not surprised when I told her that I had been a senior executive with a leading reinsurance company and so understood the procedures. During the course of our conversation, she related to me, on a no-names basis, the sloppy nature of many of the reports she received for policyholders. I received full payment within three days of filing my claim. I don't relate this anecdote to be self-serving, but to demonstrate how it is in your best interest to organize your materials and document your submission.

Think about the consequences of the disaster you have experienced. You know how disruptive it was to your business and to your personal life until some sense of normalcy was restored. Now imagine that the disaster was of a severe nature, such as a flood or earthquake. Many businesses in your area would be affected and your insurer would be dealing with many policyholders at a time. As you and your staff are working overtime to respond to the disaster, the insurance adjusters are doing the same. If you were an insurance adjuster, which would you handle first—the well-organized submission with supporting documentation or the incomplete submission that was prepared in haste?

You expedite the response process by making life easier for your insurance adjuster.

I organized my losses by type and attached written estimates of the cost of repair. The adjuster had only to review a bulleted checklist to ensure that my claims were covered under my policy, reviewed the supporting documentation, and contacted third-party service providers to ensure that replacement costs were accurate, and then organized an inspection of my premises. Once that task was complete, payment was made to cover my damages and the adjuster could resume the interpretation of many other disorganized submissions she received from other policyholders. Based on our conversation, I would say she appreciated the ease with which my claim could be processed. Cooperate with your insurance company's adjuster; it will make the response and recovery processes easier for both of you.

## IDENTIFYING IMPLICATED POLICIES

When your business sustains disaster-related losses, it is important to review all of the insurance policies that may provide coverage for the losses and liabilities to which your business is exposed. Remember you must give timely notice of your loss to the insurance carrier. Failure to do so could disqualify your claim from coverage. Therefore, you should invest time and effort to identify all insurance policies implicated in the disaster, rather than foreclose options for coverage by limiting the scope of your review. Begin with insurance policies that cover first-party property losses, or direct property damage, including collateral damage (such as from smoke, ash, or soot), and indirect property damage, including business interruption losses and loss-related expenses. Next, review the following:

- All-risk policies (remember these are the policies that cover risks to your business except for those that are explicitly excluded)

- Named peril policies, such as policies covering fire, flood, and other perils

- Business owner's policies—the package coverage I recommended

- Policies covering particular endorsements, such as boiler and machinery policies, interruption of electrical supply, and so forth

- Homeowner or renter policies, if you operate some part of your business out of your home and sought additional coverage for it

- Valuable papers and records policies

The next step in your review process is the evaluation of business interruption insurance, for businesses closed by property damage or government action. Such losses may be covered under an endorsement to your first-party property policy, or you may have a business interruption policy or a cancellation policy.

You should review possible workers' compensation claims to determine compensation for disability, including physical and psychological injuries to survivors of the disaster, and to family members of victims of the disaster for lost wages.[3] Review your workers' compensation insurance policy, your disability benefits policy, and your employment liability policies. Also consider life insurance policies and "key person" policies for your small business, in the event the disaster causes a loss of human life.

For injuries caused by the disaster to visitors to your premises, or for injuries to directors and officers not otherwise covered under workers' compensation, you should review the relevant health insurance policies, short- and long-term disability policies, and travel accident policies. You will also need to consider possible claims against directors and officers for any actions that they may have taken on behalf of the company that are said to have increased the losses to the company. In that context, review executive protection policies and your directors and officers (D&O) coverage.

Next, evaluate damages to any boats or water-borne vessels and review any marine insurance policies. For damage to automobiles, you should review business automobile policies, personal automobile policies, hired car policies, trucker's policies, motor carrier policies, and garage coverage.

You need to consider liability for third-party claims for any lawsuits brought against your business or any of your employees for harm or injury to property or persons arising from the disaster. Review your commercial general liability policies. If there is a possibility of pollution damage and cleanup claims, review your environmental impairment liability policies. If your business was involved in producing structures or equipment implicated in the disaster, you may be at risk for errors and omissions claims. Review your professional liability policies accordingly. If the disaster struck an overseas business facility, investigate your local coverage. Some governments require foreign businesses to purchase insurance coverage from local carriers.

Finally, review insurance policies that have expired, to ensure that no precedent events to the disaster occurred during a period of prior insurance coverage. Review your excess and umbrella policies, both commercial and personal policies. This "checklist" may seem excessive, but the effort to review the policies is well worth it. Your business has paid premiums for insurance coverage and you should seek to collect the claims to which you are entitled. I hope you reviewed your policies carefully when you purchased the coverage so that you are generally familiar with the provisions of the policies. Your insurance carrier will likely inspect your books and records. In the event your records were damaged in the disaster, make available your backup copies that you maintained off-site.

Finally, be aware that you may have to satisfy different deductibles for different insurance policies, or different components of the same business owner's policy. As you prepare your financial plan to recover from the disaster, include the costs of satisfying different deductible requirements.

## RECONSTRUCTING INSURANCE POLICIES

If your policy documents are not readily available, or were destroyed in the disaster, you may have to reconstruct the insurance policies for your business. Fortunately, this is not as difficult as it might seem. Insurance policies are generally "boilerplate" documents; that is, they are standard-form documents used throughout the industry. Even if you cannot obtain a copy of the exact insurance policy that you purchased, any commercial insurance broker can supply you with a standard-form policy and provide some guidance as to your likely insurance coverage. Begin with internal documents of your company, including the:

- Legal department

- Human resources department (particularly for insurance policies related to employment-practices liability, workers' compensation, life insurance, health insurance, and disability benefits)

- Accounting, finance, or purchasing departments

Of course, if your business has fewer than 20 employees, it is unlikely that you have organized functional departments as such. But you may have an employee who has records of insurance programs assigned to handle human resources matters. You may also retrieve secondary proof of coverage, such as electronic images of your insurance policy, from your electronic data stored off-site.

Once you have exhausted those possibilities, consult with external sources for copies of your insurance policy, such as your insurance brokers or insurance company. Remember that if you purchased surplus coverage for your business, you probably did so through a specialized surplus lines broker, so contact both your commercial insurance broker and your surplus lines broker. If these parties cannot produce copies of your insurance policy, request any other documents they may have relating to your coverage, such as copies of claims files. The Insurance Commissioner of your state may also provide assistance and/or counseling with respect to insurance problems and questions, including obtaining copies of policies, claims filing, and expediting settlements. For inquiries related to flood insurance, you should contact the National Flood Insurance Program.

Your last alternative is to seek secondary proof of coverage from external parties, such as:

- Additional named insureds under your policies

- Consultants

- Claims adjustors

- Outside legal counsel

- Outside accountants or auditors

- Agencies of federal, state, or local government

- Leasing companies with which you do business

- Financial institutions

- Any other party that may have required evidence of your insurance coverage

There are various means of reconstructing your insurance policy should it be destroyed in the disaster. The checklists provided here are not exhaustive. For example, following the disaster that occurred at Mount Saint Helens, a former colleague of mine could not retrieve her insurance policy. Still, she was able to obtain the policy from a local office of the Small Business Administration (SBA), as they had required her to have insurance in place as a condition of her business's participation in an SBA-sponsored program. I once worked with a biotechnology firm that sustained losses when Hurricane Gloria struck Connecticut over 20 years ago. The biotechnology company had received venture capital funding and, as a condition of that investment, had to maintain certain insurance coverage in force. As a consequence, the venture capital firm (which was based in California and therefore unaffected by the hurricane) was able to express-deliver original policy documents to the managers of the biotechnology company so that they could prepare their claims for property damages.

Two final examples: A friend whose office had sustained damage in the Northridge earthquake was able to obtain her policy from her landlord. The management of the commercial building where she leased a suite of offices required certain insurance coverage as a lease condition. Fortunately, the management company preserved these documents off-site, so they could be retrieved following the earthquake. I also have a French friend, a former fashion model with an MBA, who provides customized shopping tours of Paris and Milan to tourists. Her business records and insurance policies were destroyed in the floods that caused great damage in France not too long ago. She was lucky: The reinsurance company that covers her primary insurance carrier had requested copies of randomly selected insurance policies as part of a routine audit. Hers was among the sample and the reinsurance company was able to give her appropriate documentation to secure coverage of her losses.

Let's briefly summarize the recommendations of this section. Should your insurance policy be destroyed in a disaster, you may reconstruct that policy by consulting the following sources in the following order of preference:

- Internal sources for policies

- Internal sources for documentation relating to insurance coverage

- External sources of policies

- External sources for documentation related to insurance coverage

Of course, I hope that your contingency plan provided for secure, off-site storage of key company documents and records so that if your insurance policy is destroyed in a disaster, you will not lose time trying to contact external parties for assistance in policy reconstruction. However, if you have to learn the hard way the lesson on off-site backup of critical documents, I hope these suggestions for policy reconstruction accelerate your response to the disaster. Finally, the cost of procuring these documents may be covered under your insurance policy if you elected an endorsement for valuable papers.[4]

## ISSUES RELATING TO EMPLOYEE DISPLACEMENT

I sincerely hope you followed the advice given in Part One, Prepare, of this book and put in place contingency for valuable records. However, if you are reconstructing your insurance policy because your documents were destroyed in the disaster, then you likely have other records to reconstruct. I know of small businesses whose basic payroll records were destroyed on September 11, 2001. Laws vary from state to state, but generally, every employer must establish, maintain, and preserve weekly payroll records for a minimum period of six years, including the following information for each employee:

- Name, address, and Social Security number
- Number of hours worked daily and weekly, including the time of arrival and departure for employees working split shifts or overtime
- Amounts of gross wages, wage rates, and job classifications
- Deductions from gross wages
- Any allowances claimed as part of the minimum wage rate
- Monies paid in cash
- Student classifications and school statements
- Total wages and the value of any allowances for each payroll period for individuals working in executive, administrative, or professional roles

Generally, depending on their job functions, employees must be paid within 7 to 14 days of work performed. If your payroll records were destroyed in the disaster, make a reasonable effort to determine the hours that were worked and pay your employees as promptly as possible. Be advised that in certain states, failure to pay employees' wages exposes the business owner(s) to personal liability.

If your premises were rendered unusable as a consequence of the disaster, some of your employees may elect to work from home. If such employees are considered nonexempt under the wage-and-hour laws, the business must still record and maintain their work hours for payroll purposes and determine whether overtime compensation is payable. Nonexempt employees are also entitled to lunch breaks, even when they work from home. If your payroll records were destroyed in the disaster, we urge you to consult with experienced legal counsel to reconstruct your records in order to avert another disaster in the future.

## DISASTER RELIEF PROGRAMS

In this chapter, I present some basic information about disaster relief programs and some cautionary tales based on my experience. The Federal Emergency Management Agency (FEMA) is the agency of the U.S. federal government that may provide your business with low-interest disaster loans for businesses, working capital assistance for small businesses, and referrals to other agencies, programs, and services that assist in postdisaster recovery. FEMA assistance becomes available once the President signs a major disaster declaration. When the President has declared a geographic zone[5] a federal disaster area, certain types of federally funded assistance become available to the residents and businesses of that area.

Remember that not all disasters will qualify for FEMA assistance. The more common disasters that small businesses are likely to experience are discrete, localized disasters, such as a fire in the business facility or a disruption of the electrical power supply. While such events can have tragic consequences for the individuals who experience them, they are not of sufficient scale or scope to warrant the intervention of the federal government in the recovery effort. For the purposes of this section, I assume that your business has sustained a major disaster that was recognized as such by the U.S. federal government.

There are two approaches to the topic of disaster relief that I would like to take. The first concerns the needs of your extended small business family, as employees and residents in a disaster area; and the second concerns the needs of the small business itself, which is, of course, the focus of this book. The two are intimately related with one another: Your community has a stake in your business' recovery from the disaster and you have a stake in your employees' personal recovery from the disaster.

I had the experience of both residing in and owning a small business in a federal disaster area. As such, I was displaced for a period of time from both my home and my place of work and dealt with restoration efforts for both simultaneously. I became convinced of the necessity of household contingency planning on October 6, 2001 when I registered with FEMA. I learned that many of my neighbors were inadequately insured for the disaster. As you would expect, it was difficult to obtain accurate information about disaster relief programs on a timely basis. One of my neighbors, for example, was served with notice of foreclosure on her home when she missed mortgage payments for October and November of 2001, following her husband's death in the World Trade Center. Her mortgage bank was not aware (apparently neither was she) that the Federal National Mortgage Agency (Fannie Mae) had imposed a 90-day freeze on foreclosures, a waiver of delinquency fees, and reduced or waived interest charges on mortgages held by victims of the attacks. After visiting the FEMA Web site and reading the list of federal disasters throughout the United States over the past two years, I began to appreciate the need for information on contingency planning and disaster recovery for households.

So I want to remind you of the very personal needs of your employees, customers, and suppliers during a time of disaster. This, in turn, directly affects your recovery effort. It is hard to focus on business recovery efforts when you are worried about being turned out of your home; whether the bank has initiated a foreclosure; if you have lost a loved one; if a spouse has lost his or her job; or you are under otherwise severe economic or family pressure. I found it helpful to form a community of small business owners to share information concerning disaster relief programs to help individuals and businesses. Many hands make work light, as the saying goes, but it also conveys the sincere sense of caring and concern that we all feel. To the extent you have available resources, I would urge you to devote some time and effort to gathering information that may help your employees and their families recover from a disaster. Perhaps you could post notices on the company Intranet of appropriate relief programs for which employees may qualify. Don't forget to extend the same assistance to your local suppliers and customers. When you are recovering from a disaster, you will begin to appreciate (if you had not done so before), the extent to which we depend upon one another.

Now that we have acknowledged the need to attend to the very personal needs of your staff, let us turn our attention to your small business' recovery effort. If your business has been affected by a national disaster, the first step in working with disaster relief agencies is to register with FEMA. You may do so by calling their toll-free "800" number and completing an interview over the telephone. If you are a resident of a federal disaster area, you must also register yourself as an individual. There are different programs for families who live in disaster areas for which you may qualify. In this book, we cover only the programs relevant to small business. You may qualify for:

- Low-interest disaster loans for businesses and private not-for-profit organizations
- Working capital assistance for small businesses
- Disaster unemployment assistance
- Referrals to other agencies, programs and services

Once you register your business with FEMA, you will receive a disaster loan application from the SBA by mail. The SBA is the primary source of federal funds for long-term recovery assistance for disaster victims. For disaster damage to property owned by businesses and nonprofit organizations that is not fully covered by insurance, the basic form of U.S. federal government assistance is a low-interest disaster loan. Businesses may borrow from the SBA to fund repairs or replacement of real estate, machinery and equipment, inventory, and other assets that were not covered by insurance. The SBA's criteria has historically been that if 25 or more homes or businesses in a county have sustained uninsurable damage—which the SBA defines as 40% or more of the property value—loans to repair property loss will be made available. Over the past decade, the SBA has disbursed almost $1 billion annually in disaster loans.

If your business is a farm, business and farm loans are available if you have suffered damage to business property or economic injury. Low-interest loans are available through the SBA and the Farm Service Agency to repair or replace damaged property not covered by insurance, and to provide working capital. In addition, the U.S. Department of Agriculture's Extension Service provides information and materials to farmers to advise them on measures they can take to protect their farms against hazards associated with disasters. The Extension Service provides information on the cleanup of damaged property, sanitation precautions, insect control, food preparation in emergencies, recovery actions on damaged farms, and renovations of damaged equipment and property.

If your business has sustained losses that were not fully covered by insurance, the Internal Revenue Service (IRS) may afford you some relief. The IRS may allow casualty losses that your business suffered to be deducted on the income tax return if they were not covered by insurance. Your business may also file an amended return to receive an early tax refund. Your accountant can advise you accordingly.

If your business has sustained an economic injury, you may also apply for an Economic Injury Disaster Loan (EIDL). The purpose of this loan program is to provide funds to eligible *small businesses* to meet their ordinary and necessary operating expenses they could have met, but are unable to meet as a direct result of the disaster. These loans are intended to provide only the amount of working capital needed by a small business to pay its essential operating expenses and obligations until operations are fully restored. These loans will cover lost income, lost profits, or losses attributable to general economic conditions. The proceeds of these loans cannot be used to refinance long-term debt, but they can be used to make payments on short-term notes and accounts payable and installment payments on long-term notes, to the extent your business could have made such payments had the disaster not occurred.

Federal law requires the SBA to determine whether EIDL applicants can obtain credit to finance their own recovery from the disaster from nongovernment sources without creating undue hardship. The SBA has determined that over 90% of disaster loan applicants do not have sufficient financial resources to recover from disasters without the assistance of the Federal government. However, because taxpayers subsidize EIDL loans (the maximum interest rate assessed by EIDL loans is 4%), applicants with the financial means to fund their own recovery are not eligible for the program. EIDL loans are extended on the following terms:

- **Credit Requirements.** The SBA must be persuaded that your business can repay the loan.

- **Collateral Requirements.** Loans in excess of $5,000 require the pledging of collateral to the extent that it is available, as well as personal guarantees by the principals of the business.

- **Interest Rate.** The interest rate is recalculated each quarter with a maximum of 4%.

- **Loan Term.** SBA will set the term in accordance with the borrower's ability to repay, to a maximum term of 30 years.

- **Limit.** The amount of each loan is limited by the actual economic injury, as determined by the SBA, that is not compensated by insurance and is in excess of the resources the business and its owners can provide, and is not otherwise open to financing by private sources of credit.

- **Insurance Requirements.** SBA requires borrowers to obtain and maintain insurance on the business property as well as insurance on the property collateralizing the loan.

The SBA may provide staff to assist you in preparing your loan application. It is not necessary to demonstrate that you have been declined for private bank loans before applying to the SBA program; the SBA will apply its own criteria to determine if your business could obtain funding elsewhere. The SBA disaster loan program is administered through regional offices; consult www.sba.gov for current contact information.

In determining the amount of an EIDL loan, the SBA will prepare a pro forma analysis of your business income statement and balance sheet. That is, they will make a snapshot of the expenses that your business could have met and the working capital position that your business could have maintained had the disaster not occurred—in other words, your business financial statements pro forma for the disaster. They will also consider the total amount of your existing debt obligations; the operating expenses that mature during the period affected by the disaster and the sum you need to maintain a reasonable working capital position during that period.

In addition to the Economic Physical Disaster Loans for small businesses and the Economic Injury Disaster Loans for small businesses, the SBA offers two other loan programs that may be relevant to your needs. The SBA offers disaster assistance loans for homes and personal property; these are loans to homeowners or to renters to repair or replace disaster damages to uninsured real estate or personal property they own. Renters are eligible to borrow funds to cover personal property losses only. If the SBA declines to extend such a loan to you, it will refer you to the Individual and Family Grant program (administered by state governments) to be considered for a grant of up to $14,000 to assist you with disaster-related expenses. This program may be of interest to you or to your employees, so make them aware of it. I hope you are not in need of loans to cover physical damages to either your business or personal property. At pre-disaster market rates, you could have obtained coverage for $70,000 of property for under $400 in New York City. This is a far better arrangement than obtaining loans—even for those with interest rates capped at 4%.

The final SBA loan program to consider is the Military Reservist Economic Injury Disaster Loan Program, which extends loans to eligible small businesses to meet ordinary and necessary operating expenses that it could have met, but cannot meet, because an essential employee was called to active duty as a military reservist.

If you have liquid financial assets that could otherwise finance some of these needs, you may obtain some relief once the government declares a disaster. Banks that are members of the Federal Deposit Insurance Corporation, the Federal Reserve System, or the Federal Home Loan Bank Board may permit early withdrawal of time deposits, without penalty. Ask your financial institution if it has obtained the necessary waiver from their regulatory agency. Be sure to ask, because often the bank tellers are not aware of this provision. I stopped a friend, whose business was based in California and was affected by the Northridge earthquake, from incurring a substantial penalty for early withdrawal of a certificate of deposit by advising her of this disaster-related program. She wrote a letter of inquiry to the manager of her bank's local branch and the early withdrawal penalty was waived. Beware that often, information is not widely disseminated throughout large organizations and this will be a source of frustration to you as you implement your recovery efforts.

I can tell you from experience that government employees, bank employees, and relief workers often give out incorrect information to applicants because they are not aware of the program requirements or amendments. If your need of access to funds is so urgent that you are prepared to incur penalties for early withdrawal for time deposits, write a letter to your bank explaining your circumstances and how your business was affected by the disaster. Follow up when you are further along in restoring your business and have time available. You may be able to obtain reimbursement of the penalties you incurred if the bank staff subsequently learn that penalties are often waived in the case of disaster.

Should you require assistance in preparing an application for an SBA loan, there are a number of resources that may be available to you, including the SBA itself. You should also consider your local business school or state university; many business school campuses have small business clinics to provide free or low-cost assistance to business owners while giving their students valuable experience. The students generally work under the supervision of a faculty member, many of whom are experienced business people. This can be a real source of value to your business. Check with local professional organizations. Following disasters in New York and Georgia, local societies of Certified Public Accountants offered small business owners assistance with preparing SBA loan applications and with applying for tax filing extensions. Free or reduced cost legal services may be available to your small business following a disaster from the members of your State Bar Association.

I hope that your insurance program covered the property damage to your business and provided a reasonable settlement to your business interruption claim. If that is the case, you may not need an SBA loan. If not, read the next chapters with care. My advice in these matters is to plan for events that you can reasonably anticipate, such as securing adequate insurance coverage. Should you be approved for an SBA loan, congratulations, but I advise small business owners not to rely on the availability of such funding for contingency purposes for the following reasons:

- **Size of Business.** The SBA defines small businesses in its regulations and has established a size standard for each industry, based on either the number of employees or the average annual revenues of the business. Let me share with you two examples that were reported in our local press. A Lower Manhattan restaurant, American Park, was closed following the September 11 disaster. Employees assisted the business owner in cleaning the damaged property and the business applied for a loan. The SBA rejected the application because the restaurant company's revenues exceeded the cap established for New York City. The restaurant company was turned down for several bank loans, for reasons such as failing to meet the lending criteria or bank requirements that 80% of the shareholders of the business would be required to personally guarantee the loan. Another of my favorite Lower Manhattan establishments, the Century 21 department store, was closed for five and one-half months following the attack on the World Trade Center that shattered the store's windows, destroyed glass merchandise cases, and activated the sprinkler system that caused the lower level to flood. The chief operating officer of the company was quoted in the press as stating that the company was denied an SBA loan as it had more than 50 employees. The store's refurbishment cost the company approximately $10 million.[6] Because of the company's size, it was in the middle between funds available for large corporations and grants for the smallest businesses. I call this the "Goldilocks" phenomenon: Some businesses were too small to qualify for assistance, some were too big, and a relative few were just right.

- **Creditworthiness.** Because the assistance is in the form of a loan, SBA requires reasonable assurance that the loan can and will be repaid. Many small business owners did not qualify for a loan, or were reluctant to assume additional debt, as they were already experiencing a general economic downturn.

- **Causal Relationship.** To qualify for an SBA loan, the economic losses to the business must be directly tied to the disaster. Less tangible factors affecting your business, such as a reluctance of your customers to visit the disaster area (and thereby patronize your business) are not always clearly linked to the disaster by the SBA's criteria.

- **Personal Guarantees.** One attorney wrote to the Editor of *Crain's New York Business* that his small law firm had been approved for an SBA loan on the condition that he pledge his home, his primary residence, as collateral. Given the uncertainty about when Lower Manhattan would recover from the disaster, many small businesses were reluctant to put themselves at greater risk. Indeed, we incorporate our businesses, in part, to give some measure of protection to our personal assets. Since there is likely to be uncertainty as to when roads will be repaired or traffic routes reopened or public transportation access resumed following a disaster, your business recovery is at risk for events beyond your control. As such, we would be reluctant to put our homes at risk to secure loans. Consider if you have other assets available to offer as collateral, but be advised that the SBA generally prefers real estate collateral.

Don't expect that an SBA loan will be available to you to cover your disaster-related expenses or that it is necessarily your best option to pledge your home as collateral for the loan. A carefully crafted insurance program is the cornerstone of your contingency plan and with that in place, you will be less dependent on other types of assistance. The aforementioned Century 21 department store relied largely on its own financial reserves as well as insurance to fund its restoration efforts, with the goal of preserving as many jobs as possible. Floor managers of the downtown store were transferred to Brooklyn and Long Island, along with one-third of the sales clerks and cashiers. The remaining employees were laid off and subsequently called back when the store reopened for business. This brings us to the next element of disaster relief: disaster unemployment assistance.

The U.S. Department of Labor provides benefits and services to those who lost earned income or became unemployed due to the disaster, either through unemployment insurance or disaster unemployment assistance. Self-employed persons, sole proprietors, small business owners, and others who would not otherwise qualify for unemployment insurance may obtain disaster unemployment assistance. This program is also helpful to those who recently entered or reentered the workforce, and therefore have not accumulated sufficient credits to qualify for traditional unemployment benefits when disaster strikes. The procedure is to apply for traditional unemployment insurance, and when such benefits are denied, appeal for disaster unemployment assistance. You will have to be persistent because unless your state's department of labor has experience in working with federal programs to recover from disaster, their staff may not be familiar with the program. I can tell you of many, many New York City residents who were turned away by workers at the State's Department of Labor because they did not qualify for unemployment benefits. It took time for the details of the disaster unemployment assistance program to be disseminated throughout the Department of Labor in Albany, New York. Should you be in the unhappy position of having to lay off employees following a disaster, advise them of the disaster unemployment assistance program. Some of your employees, such as the recent hires, may not qualify for traditional unemployment benefits. Try to ease the pain by providing information regarding other types of disaster-related programs for which they might qualify, as we had discussed earlier in this chapter.

The coordination and assignment of roles and responsibilities to various government agencies may confound your recovery efforts. I had the experience of helping a poultry farmer in the Gulf Coast who had sought counseling from the SBA. The SBA would not help him because it does not extend agricultural loans. For the purposes of one government loan program, the poultry farm was considered a small business, but for the purpose of another government program, it was not. When confronted with this case, the SBA punted this matter to the U.S. Department of Agriculture.

I conclude this section by discussing assistance offered by disaster relief agencies. The leading disaster relief organization, the American Red Cross, provides assistance to individuals and not to businesses. However, if you are self-employed or if your business is a sole proprietorship, you may qualify for individual assistance. For other types of small businesses, such as limited liability companies or subchapter S corporations, it is worthwhile to consider the resources of the Red Cross in providing free or low-cost counseling services to deal with the psychological consequences of the disaster. The Red Cross is very experienced in dealing with emotional reactions to disasters, ranging from relatively minor anxiety all the way to post-traumatic stress disorder. I would urge all small business owners to visit a Red Cross counselor immediately following the disaster. You will be feeling the stress of recovering from the disaster and the need to take care of your employees. It can be extremely helpful just to talk to someone who is not completely burned out by the challenges you are now facing. It is comforting to know that you are not alone and that your reactions to the disaster are common. Finally, the advice of an experienced counselor can help you recognize symptoms of difficulty among your own employees and encourage them to seek appropriate help.

The challenge of writing this section of the book is that disaster relief is not uniform and different services may be made available in different cases. The victims of the bombing in Oklahoma City, for example, did not have access to the same types of resources that were made available following the attacks on the World Trade Center and the Pentagon. Even if you do ultimately secure assistance, such as an SBA loan, the process of applying for assistance consumes time. Your business will need funds until the assistance is disbursed. Remember that both public and private disaster relief programs require the small business owner to produce many records, such as tax returns, as part of the application. Your backups are critical to your ability to secure aid in a timely manner.

Don't be one of the small business owners who learn this lesson the hard way. I had the privilege of facilitating three-hour workshops on small business disaster preparedness in September 2006 at the annual conference of the Association of Small Business Development Centers (SBDC) in Houston. One of the highlights of the conference was the reunion of the SBDC counselors who volunteered to help their peers in the Gulf Coast assist small businesses in recovering from Hurricane Katrina. I found it excruciatingly painful to relive the same frustrations and difficulties involved in disaster preparedness and response, most of which can be mitigated. As the counselors were sharing their experiences, one of the common themes was that with few exceptions, small businesses had not backed up their critical data, including their tax records. In order to produce some documentation for SBA disaster loans, Gulf Coast small businesses faxed requests for income transcripts to the IRS. Of course, with thousands of small businesses making their requests at the same time, the response was not immediate, and delays are costly. But there are even worse outcomes.

Let me share with you the experience of Ariel Goodman, whose small business was based in the World Trade Center. Ariel also lived in an apartment building directly facing the World Trade Center. Following the terrorist attacks, the Department of Health condemned her apartment building. What was doubly unfortunate was that her business records were backed up at her home and her personal records were backed up at her office. In the space of a few minutes, she lost both simultaneously. Obtaining backup tax records from her accountant was not an option, as her accountant's office was also located at the World Trade Center and he had not thought to back up records off-site. That left her with the option of contacting the IRS for a transcript. The IRS had a snafu of its own and was unable to provide the transcript, although it did furnish her with a statement to the effect that she was current on all of her business tax filings. That, however, was not sufficient documentation for most private or public disaster relief programs. Ariel, by the way, founded From the Ground Up, the nonprofit association of Lower Manhattan small businesses affected by 9/11.

It bears repeating again and again: Don't count on big government or big business to come to the rescue of your small business. They won't: They will make self-serving statements about their disaster aid programs and how they are helping mom and pop shops, but you will be much better off putting your own preparedness plan in place than becoming a "victim" or a body on the dais when your local politician wants to make a speech about all that he or she is doing to serve the constituents after a disaster. Government relief programs are not designed to help individuals, families, or small businesses: They exist to redistribute wealth to more powerful interests. I was particularly so appalled by an SBA official's letter to the editor of one small business magazine that I had to respond. Do you remember how many airlines received bailouts from the federal government in the aftermath of 9/11? Nearly all of them were unprofitable before the disaster. So I wrote my response, which was published by *Inc.* magazine in its February 2003 issue:

> In his letter to the editor (Mail, December), Michael Pappas affirms the Small Business Administration's requirement that if borrowers have personal collateral, they must pledge it, including their own homes, to qualify for assistance from the SBA. His point about the need to protect taxpayers' interests is well taken. Does this mean that airline executives who are seeking massive taxpayer bailouts to cover their past poor management decisions will be required to put their homes up for collateral to secure government guaranteed loans? Or is it only the little guy whose livelihood was destroyed by circumstances beyond his control who must risk homelessness to secure assistance from the federal government?

Craft a simple disaster preparedness plan and you can avoid the bureaucrats altogether.

## SOMETIMES "AID" CAN BE HARMFUL

I participated in many disaster relief programs (although not the SBA loan program) and I will tell you that I would never do so again. Nevertheless, the experience was instructive because I can pass on lessons learned to you.

**Lesson 1: Your time is your most precious asset and it is better spent on growing revenues and pursuing business opportunities than trying to qualify for many aid programs.** These programs have onerous documentation requirements, each one is different, and they generally yield a poor return on the time invested. There is always a psychological need to feel like you won something for nothing, so you may feel that you are leaving a benefit on the table if you do not apply for the aid. After all, you paid your taxes and you want to get some of your money back. But it can hurt more than help your business.

I had applied for the Lower Manhattan Small Business Recovery Grant. Because my business was based in "Zone 1" (very close to the World Trade

Center), I qualified for the second largest grant award, which was $2,500. Only businesses based in the World Trade Center, designated "Zone 0", qualified for more. Businesses further removed from the World Trade Center were designated Zones 2, 3, and 4 and qualified for smaller awards. I did not rely on the assistance of an accountant or a lawyer to complete the grant application, which expense would have reduced the proceeds of the grant. Even so, the grant, which is taxable, paid less than minimum wage for the time required to complete the applications. Obviously, that was a losing proposition, but I did not know that at the outset. I had prepared my application in good faith and the state agency that administered the program changed the requirements over time, demanding more and more documentation. Since I had already done the work to prepare and submit the application, I was aware of the sunk cost of my time, so I followed the process through to completion. But with hindsight, my time would have been better invested in revenue-generating activities.

**Lesson 2: Government aid programs benefit the more affluent at the expense of the poor and justify the existence of large bureaucracies.** We are all familiar with the example of the subsidies provided in the form of government flood insurance to wealthy homeowners with coastal properties. Let me share with you one of many less well-known examples. In the aftermath of 9/11, the Individual and Family Grant Program (a program of the federal and state governments, administered by FEMA for the federal government) provided for free HEPA air filters for residents of Lower Manhattan. The purpose of this benefit was to address the health concerns arising from the poor air quality. In order to avail yourself of this benefit, you had to purchase a HEPA air filter, complete a one- or two-page form and submit it with your sales receipt. You would be reimbursed for the purchase within 90 days. It sounds simple and fair, doesn't it? Well, experience revealed that it was neither simple nor fair.

Lower Manhattan comprises very different socioeconomic groups in a very small physical area. In Chinatown, for example, which was part of the land mass declared a federal disaster area on 9/11, there are many immigrants living below the poverty line. A ten-minute walk can get you to Tribeca, home to multi-million dollar lofts owned by Wall Street investment bankers. Tribeca was also part of the federal disaster area. Residents of Chinatown protested that they live paycheck to paycheck and don't typically have the hundred or so dollars in available funds to purchase a HEPA air filter and await reimbursement for several months. For the more affluent residents of Tribeca, the air filter was a freebie. But there was a hidden cost to this benefit. About six months to one year after receiving reimbursement for purchased air filters, the beneficiaries received letters from FEMA stating that inspectors would visit their homes to inspect the air filters to ensure that they had really purchased them. Now this is absurd: The presence of an air filter in your home does not prove that you purchased it with the FEMA-reimbursed funds. You could simply run out and buy an air filter the day before the FEMA inspector comes. Nor does the absence of an air filter prove that you misused the funds: You could have legitimately purchased the air filter, submitted the receipt for reimbursement, and then discarded the filter six months later if it was not working or you determined it was no longer necessary. I stayed with my neighbor during the six-hour window that she was to be home for the inspection.

Guess how many FEMA inspectors it takes to look at a HEPA air filter? Three: one to fill out a form, one to speak with us and one to admire the view from the apartment. They never looked at the filter. The value of six hours' labor of a small business owner exceeded the value of the "free" air filter, so take that into consideration when evaluating government assistance programs. I should also add that the small business community really stepped up to help one another. When a distributor of air filters in upstate New York read that the poorer residents of Lower Manhattan could not afford to purchase the filters and wait for reimbursement, he and his son drove down in two trucks to distribute free air filters. In advance of their arrival, they had faxed flyers to local small businesses announcing where and when they would park their trucks. Small business owners photocopied the flyers and made them available in the lobbies of downtown apartment buildings. All you had to do was to meet the truck, show a New York State driver's license indicating a residential address in Lower Manhattan, and receive a free air filter. No paperwork and no receipts, and people were on the honor system not to take more than one unit per household. I watched their distribution one morning and was impressed by its efficiency. City officials thwarted that act of generosity within one week, as the distributor did not have a permit from the City to give out free HEPA air filters or to park his trucks!

**Lesson 3: Government aid programs motivate counterproductive conflict on the division of the spoils.** Members of From the Ground Up, wearing T-shirts identifying the group, were accosted by small business owners in Florida. The Floridians expressed anger that New York had received generous disaster aid post-9/11 and the residents of Florida had not fared as well following the 2004 hurricane season. That is certainly not true, but it is probably better for New York politicians to pretend that their constituents were well-served, than to have us compare notes nationally and find out that, by and large, small business disaster relief programs do not necessarily benefit small businesses.

This is a topic that I have written about at length for our Web site (see www.preparedsmallbusiness.com), because as disaster relief programs are under Congressional review, the risk is that the information in this book will date too quickly if I try to present it here. But the bottom line is: Don't count on the government to help you. You will be disappointed.

## WORKING TOGETHER

I would like to close this section with a piece of advice: Work with other small business owners to resolve issues of mutual concern. There is strength in numbers and you may be able to provide information and advice to your peers in the small business community and they will almost certainly do so for you. You will be surprised to learn how much information is conveyed, following a disaster, by word of mouth, even in our mass media age. There is a great deal of confusion following a disaster. Program requirements change and employees of relief agencies often don't have the latest information, the news media can occasionally get the details of disaster relief programs wrong, and you will be surprised how much you learn by sharing with your peers in the small business community. Consider the value of the small business community in addressing the next element of your reaction plan: communicating with your stakeholders following a disaster.

## COMMUNICATING WITH STAKEHOLDERS

Following a disaster, you will need to communicate your recovery efforts to a number of stakeholders, including employees, their families, suppliers, customers, and other constituencies, such as your landlord, the tax authorities, your insurance company, your third-party service providers, and many others. People will often assume the worst, so any information you can convey regarding your contingency planning will offer some reassurance. Indeed, to the extent your contingency planning efforts can assist others in your community, you may generate some additional goodwill for your business. I remember that after we were evacuated from Battery Park City to New Jersey on September 11, the police boat brought us to Exchange Place. Small business owners who were tenants of nearby facilities had placed telephones in their lobbies so that people could call their loved ones anywhere in the country and let them know that they were safe. Since we had lost our telephone service in Lower Manhattan earlier that morning, and our families had almost certainly seen the disaster on television, their generosity was greatly appreciated. I would certainly be more likely to patronize these businesses for their support of the community.

In the recovery period that followed, many small businesses posted on the Internet details of their available space to assist other small businesses that had been displaced. A spare room here or an extra suite of vacant offices there, made all the difference in the world to businesspeople struggling to get back on their feet. Other businesses donated surplus equipment, such as computers and printers, to assist the businesses whose property had been destroyed. A local company made available wireless Blackberry units to small businesses in Lower Manhattan to assist them until telephone service could be restored on a permanent basis. The company offered three months of free wireless service, which was a great help to small businesses who were working remotely and perhaps communicating with colleagues who were temporarily working from home. To the extent that your business can assist in the recovery effort, you should do so.

You will need to communicate with other stakeholders concerning your recovery efforts. For some, you should rely on expert legal advice as you may be surprised to learn of some of the risks to which your business is exposed following a major disaster. We were surprised, for example, to learn that business leases do not automatically terminate when the premises are destroyed. We were also surprised to learn of certain contractual obligations that survive a disaster. Of course, I am not an attorney, but I consult one where appropriate and would advise you to do the same. Legal issues frequently complicate recovery efforts: I have a friend whose husband died in a disaster that struck Georgia some time ago. The husband had operated his business as a sole proprietorship, which meant that his personal assets were available to satisfy his business debts. The surviving spouse did not fully appreciate the consequences of his elected form of business organization, but fortunately she consulted with legal counsel. She successfully petitioned the court to continue her husband's business on behalf of his estate.

There are certain communications that should be conducted through legal counsel, such as certain types of disputes with your insurance company, tax issues, and other contractual matters. It will facilitate your recovery from the disaster if your legal counsel is briefed on the state of your business as part of your contingency planning. Indeed, your counsel will provide some key input on the development of the contingency plan. If you have to assemble documents and obtain new counsel after a disaster when you are responding to time-sensitive matters, you will delay the recovery process. Nevertheless, I would prefer that you act with caution and appropriate legal advice to deal with matters after the disaster than make poor decisions in haste because you were ill-advised or not advised at all.

Communicate with employees and keep them up to date as to the status of the business is critical, both to ensure their effective cooperation and to alleviate their anxiety about the future. You may post information on the intranet on a daily basis to give everyone a common place to "meet" if you are operating from multiple remote locations.

Finally, you must communicate with your customers. Let them know when you can deliver products and services that your business has committed to and keep them apprised of your efforts. You may lose customers immediately following the disaster before your business is operational. This does not reflect any lack of customer loyalty; it is simply that they must conduct their business with or without you. Communicating that you have reopened for business is important and you may need to offer some incentives to bring your customers back. In Lower Manhattan, restaurants that were temporarily closed contacted the customers on their mailing lists and announced that they were open for business. Some offered promotions, such as free desserts with dinner. Others offered their customers helpful information, such as which subway routes continued to service the neighborhood.

Hairdressers who had formerly been employed in the World Financial Center (adjacent to the World Trade Center) passed out flyers on the street to advise local residents of their new places of employment. Service businesses contacted customers directly or posted notices on their company Web sites. You will have to be imaginative because your insurance policy will not cover the costs of advertising your return to business following a period of interruption. In my opinion, the most effective way to communicate with the community and with your customers is with other businesses. Customers may be reluctant to return to a disaster site due to the uncertainty of the conditions there. Are there new routes available to reach your business? Is parking available? Is it safe to breathe the air in the affected area? These concerns are not unique to your business; your neighbors have the same issues. If you work together to communicate the recovery of your area, you can leverage limited resources to achieve a common goal. I have three specific suggestions.

First, some media outlets may offer discounted advertising rates to businesses located in areas that are recovering from disaster (an excellent example of building goodwill). You may take out inexpensive advertisements in publications your customers are likely to read and announce the reopening of your business. Perhaps you can make it an event, with beverages and refreshments, and invite your local political and community leaders. You might also consider cooperative advertising. If your business is located in a major retail center, for example, you could defray advertising costs by taking out a large advertisement listing all the businesses that have recently reopened.

Second, consider contacting the media and suggesting a story about how your business experienced disaster. The media are always looking for a story and you could write a "pitch," a proposal for coverage that would appeal to a specific interest. Perhaps you learned lessons in disaster recovery that you would like to share with others in your community. Perhaps your business has a particularly compelling human interest story that puts a face to a disaster. Maybe you would like to publicly thank all those who contributed to your efforts to recover, such as the firefighters, the employees of the electric company, or the postal delivery person who went out of his way for your business. A media story is free advertising and can announce that you are back in business.

Finally, work with other small businesses to promote your recovery efforts. Your combined resources can achieve much more than any single business could do independently. For example, Wall Street Rising, an organization formed to restore the vitality of Lower Manhattan and that existed prior to September 11, 2001, launched a Web site and distributed a "Do It Downtown!" discount card that offered discounts to local businesses to encourage people to come back to Lower Manhattan. You may consider a similar effort for your community or you may work with your local chamber of commerce to communicate your ongoing commitment to recover from the disaster. In addition to leveraging limited resources, efforts such as these build morale. It is a sad experience to return to your place of work and see the physical damage, to think of the loved ones who have been affected by the disaster, and to remember what was. Working with others in your community will build commitment and support, and you will need both.

## NOTES

1. Misunderstandings arising between a small business owner and his or her landlord can confound disaster recovery efforts. I would like to help you avoid two common sources of misunderstanding. The first concerns policy endorsements for Boiler & Machinery Insurance that covers damage arising from your building's boiler and/or electrical apparatus. Many small businesses forego such coverage because they mistakenly believe it is included in their standard form coverage (it isn't) or that their building management has appropriate insurance in place. The building very likely has such insurance in place, but unless you are a named insured on their policy, it will be of little benefit to you. Since the incremental cost of this endorsement to your property insurance is modest, I urge you to obtain it. The second source of misunderstanding concerns rent adjustments for periods of business interruption. I will cover this in greater detail in the next chapter. Be advised, however, that you cannot rely on your landlord to insure property risks that will disrupt your business.

2. This is only because my office is located on Wall Street and there was enormous symbolic importance attached to reopening Wall Street and the New York Stock Exchange. Had my business office been located even just one block away from its location, access to the office would have been further delayed.

3. You may also obtain assistance from the Social Security Administration to expedite delivery of checks delayed by the disaster and for assistance in applying for Social Security disability benefits.

4. You may have to produce key documents, such as property titles and deeds. If they are destroyed in a disaster, valuable papers and records insurance will cover the costs of replacing those documents crucial to your business.

5. Once a disaster is declared, FEMA will identify which counties qualify for public assistance. It will then extend assistance to the affected state and local governments for the repair or replacement of public facilities damaged by the disaster.

6. The *New York Post*, February 28, 2002.

# PART THREE

# RECOVER

Once the immediate effects of a disaster have passed, it is time to recover. You have taken corrective action as a direct response when you were directly hit by the disaster. Most likely, your disaster was a "minor" event, and you did everything possible to mitigate your losses. However, if it was a major disaster, you will need time to look forward and recover from the event. Maybe you have to reconstruct some data or maybe rebuild the whole office. Whatever the case, you have to keep your business interruption as brief as possible and resume normal operations and productivity as quickly as possible.

While you are working hard at rebuilding your business, you will face some unexpected challenges. Your business may suffer some attrition of customers and employees. Disputes with suppliers or customers that arise from the disruption of normal operations may result in litigation. This will exacerbate your stress and further delay your recovery. I have seen many situations in which the disaster recovery effort was delayed; in particular, the process of data recovery was stopped because employees were needed for critical delivery obligations. It is time consuming to restore data and this causes additional aggravation and frustration for the employees and clients. If I have not already convinced you, this is yet another reason why you simply cannot afford lengthy data recovery operations, particularly if you own or operate a small business.

Confounding recovery efforts are the emotional and psychological consequences of a major disaster. These changes in mental status can range from frustration, to feelings of being overwhelmed, to major disorders like post-traumatic stress disorder or depression. These feelings can be particularly acute if you have lost friends or colleagues. Such conditions are difficult to diagnose, and you should turn to medical professionals to counsel your employees.

In addition to these direct effects, you will also face issues with third parties. For example, your bank might refuse to extend your credit line because it doubts your ability to recover and resume profitability. This comes at a time when you are most urgently in need of credit. Your valued clients may cancel contracts—they simply cannot wait until you have reestablished your business operations, and may move on to another supplier. Alternatively, your clients may also be in the immediate disaster area, and the financial costs of their recovery efforts preclude purchasing products and services from your business. You may have some disagreements with your insurance carrier regarding claims settlement.

You must become comfortable with ambiguity, because you will face new challenges. Your attention should remain on rebuilding your business and swiftly recovering from the situation. You may see the disaster as an opportunity to start anew, to leave behind obsolete procedures and processes, to import some new ideas, to have a stronger sense of teamwork within your company and to appreciate what is really important in your life.

At this time, you need to establish clear priorities on how to restore your business after a major disaster. Priorities may shift and people will be reassigned tasks, but in general, I suggest that you follow this scheme:

- **Provide Security.** In any unforeseen event, but especially in the context of a disaster, business security is often compromised. This includes physical security due to diverted attention of security personnel, as well as data security. Backup systems in a recovery operation are vulnerable to security breaches when the main focus is on reestablishing operations. The disaster recovery process should include only essential staff. Remind your staff that you are more vulnerable to possible security breaches during this period. Simple tasks, such as retrieving data from the backup system, could open short-time data security holes that an experienced user could exploit to obtain confidential data of the company. Protect your valuable IT equipment following a major disaster. Often, such equipment is removed from the premises as it appears to be damaged, but even so, a trusted systems expert should inspect all IT equipment to ensure that it really is beyond repair and that all sensitive data are thoroughly deleted.

- **Office Space.** You need space to accommodate your employees and you may also not be able to return to your former worksite. Let me share with you a personal example. A friend set up his small business in what he thought was a secure office building. A water line broke and released water into the desktop computers. As a consequence, those computers were damaged beyond repair. Fortunately, the damage was soon brought under control; systems were replaced and data were restored. However, two weeks after the water leakage, mold developed and the office required four weeks of intensive renovation. It was not safe for the workers to enter the office during this time, as hazardous chemicals were used to remove the mold.

This is a true story. What made this gentleman's situation even more wretched is that he had no insurance.

- **IT Infrastructure.** Determine if third-party services require repair. You may have to reorder certain services since long lead times often precede new installations following a disaster. The next priority is the reestablishment of communication services, phone, fax, and e-mail, followed by retrieving essential data, such as client contact lists. It is important to prioritize this work and to protect the system staff from impatient users who will ask them to set up their desktop workstations first. You should know that it will be fairly difficult to estimate repair times in advance. For the IT infrastructure, it will very much depend on how much time had been available to perform a clean shut-down of all systems and which parts might have been damaged due to power failure or physical destruction. For services that rely on third parties, such as your phone and Internet services, many other businesses were likely also affected. Although your phone company will do whatever it can to restore your service, it may be hard to estimate when that will happen. Sometimes, service providers protect themselves by erring on the side of caution—don't panic! When I first returned to my Wall Street office after the September 11 attack on the World Trade Center, a representative of my telephone company advised me that it would take at least five months for office telephone service to be restored. Service was restored in less than two weeks. Focus on the items that are within your sphere of control and you will not only be more productive, but you will also reduce your stress level.

- **Business Administration.** During the ongoing recovery process, a core group of key employees will have to cover all departments, assume full operational capability, and make decisions on the most critical matters. They must ensure that all outstanding obligations are satisfied in an appropriate manner, which will also set priorities for establishing further vital business functions. In addition, you will need an experienced person to oversee Human Resources (HR) and other administrative functions of your business. That person will provide services such as recovering contracts for evaluation, filing insurance claims, or providing information to employees or to the families of employees.

- **Marketing and Sales.** The next priority is for the marketing and sales groups to establish an emergency public relations program. They will immediately contact clients informing them that the company did have a disaster recovery plan and was prepared to handle the disaster. They will also announce the recovery time schedule, and discuss implications for contracts with third parties. They will also handle requests from the media for information or interviews. Depending on the nature of your business, you may find a way to recoup lost revenues and generate some goodwill by assisting other businesses in your community with their recovery efforts.

- *Accounting and Payroll.* Your controller, treasurer, or chief financial officer is a key part of the recovery process. Keep in mind that your employees must be paid in a timely manner, especially during the disaster recovery period. Your accounting team also needs to make sure that the company fulfills its financial obligations, provides a schedule of necessary bill payments, and estimates the approximate recovery costs for which you may need additional credit.

At this point you should have established a solid foundation on which to rebuild your business. Make time to reflect on what has happened and what you have learned from it. Your contingency planning and disaster recovery effort must adapt to changing conditions and new technology. Evaluate your staff's performance and handling of the crisis. Is additional training required? Assess your experience with third-party providers. Did they handle the crisis as well as you did? Perhaps there are measures that can be taken to reduce the risk of reoccurrence of this particular disaster. You might have found that you need different equipment, faster backup times, better organization, and so forth. You can learn many lessons from such extreme circumstances.

# 12

# IT Strategy

Disaster recovery begins when the actions to minimize IT damage become a structured effort. Guide your employees through this process, and then scope out the remaining work and the responsibilities of your employees to complete the recovery effort.

If you prepared carefully, most of the "daily" disasters, like human error, equipment, and third-party failures, will be satisfactorily addressed during your immediate reaction to the event. The recovery portion then focuses on fixing some loose ends, documenting and analyzing the impact of the disaster, and determining how it can be avoided in the future. Over time, you will learn how to handle these small crises more efficiently. Update your procedures often in order to be consistent with the current best practices in disaster recovery.

When you are undergoing a major disaster, your recovery time can jump from minutes to days to months. You may have to rebuild your whole company from the bottom up. The recovery effort then becomes a full-fledged project that requires organization, planning, and project management around the prerequisite that you maintain core business operations for which you need particular IT support. It is critical to get all systems running in normal operation mode in the shortest amount of time possible. You won't be able to devote your resources to system upgrades or enhancements. Your goal is to establish some normalcy to your business operations as soon as possible. You have to take careful and small steps to first assure a minimal operational environment, and then proceed toward full recovery. Begin by assessing what is immediately required to continue operations, even if not all IT systems can be ready, and determine how to continue rebuilding your IT equipment. Make an inventory of what is needed, and if you require certain parts, purchase them right away.

If your network infrastructure has been affected, it must be rebuilt, even if it is only one network segment. Because this is so critical, network replacement equipment should always be in your spare parts inventory, which could be at the same location as your disaster recovery site. The next priority is access to data, either recovered or from your backup system. Depending on your sensitivity to downtime, this data must be available within minutes to hours and provided for access at one location. After that, the network is reestablished.

The next priority is to reinstall your desktop computers from disk images that you saved as part of your Stage II plan. If some functions do not perform properly, don't invest time at this critical point to resolve errors. In a crunch, use the simplest setup possible. This will at least ensure that users can again access to and share their files.

You need to determine which third-party services continue to function. If some or all of them are down, prepare a plan of the "hierarchy of needs," the services you need back, ranked in order of urgency. Contact your providers' technical support departments, or better yet, your direct support contact, to alert them to your circumstances. They can help you much better if they understand the constraints under which you are working. You could also establish temporary service by backup methods, such as a dial-up solution, or you could try to connect to the Internet and make access available throughout the network.

If there was an incident with hazardous materials, you may need to take specific precautions and to rely on a team of specialists to clean your office. Fire, natural disasters, and terrorist attacks may destroy a good part of your IT equipment. Even if you have the funds to replace damaged equipment, you will likely not be the only business in need of replenishments. It will be difficult to obtain new equipment quickly. Expect to encounter shortages of replacement parts and production or delivery delays.

Your recovery effort will be greatly facilitated by thorough preparation and training for this contingency. Basic checklists of anticipated needs can save you time in determining recovery and testing steps to take. It is much easier to develop a plan and prepare checklists of "to-do" items in a period of calm, before a disaster strikes. As the business evolves, so do the checklists. They should reflect changes to keep them up to date. Always keep this information accessible in hard copy within the company and also off-site so that someone else could act in your absence, if necessary.

Once you have successfully managed to work through a disaster situation, remember to document all the actions taken and changes made to improve your disaster recovery capability in the future. Do not forget to express your appreciation to your staff and your vendors for the support they have provided!

## HUMAN ERRORS

Human errors are to be expected, but when they are excessive, it is time to scrutinize your business procedures. This can be a contentious process. Usually, several people contribute to the retrieval of an important lost file. This can lead to a heated situation. IT people are notorious for complaining about "stupid" users and the extra work caused by such incidents, while the user feels embarrassed and intimidated.

Observe how much more pleasant the situation becomes when a backup system is available from which files can be retrieved individually by the user without intervention from anyone else. Additional work is required to install the backup system and to configure it for your specific needs, but in the end it is time saving for everyone. We have seen that everyone appreciates the value of simple tools, like the backup file synchronization.

How can we minimize human errors in the future? You cannot eliminate human errors, but you can take measures to reduce them. Do users receive adequate training? Do they bring the right skill sets to the job? We often see users writing collaborative documents, but are unaware of, or sometimes even unwilling to use, version control tools. Often, sending documents via e-mail creates a proxy for version control. At least this way, the documents are time-stamped. But this is an inefficient and vague control mechanism. The burden is always passed to the recipient to reconstruct the document to reflect all editorial changes. In such a scenario, conflicting versions of the document appear.

## EQUIPMENT FAILURES

Your recovery path from equipment failure will be determined by whether you suffered a loss of data. Data loss usually occurs when a hard disk malfunctions, but can occasionally be the result of a software glitch, a power failure, or a system crash. The disk most likely shows some signs of malfunction and remains in physical working order. Even so, it makes sense to replace the faulty disk and restore the data from the backup, so that the user can continue to work. Then determine if the disk can be salvaged by reformatting it. Nevertheless, given the continued decline in disk prices, it would likely make sense to discard the disk.

If your machine does not boot up promptly, but otherwise appears to be in working order, it does not necessarily mean that you have to reinstall everything. Disk recovery tools are often very effective in repairing and installing new boot information. You need to rely on your data backups, however, because if your disk crashed, and your data are not available on a backup, you need to pass the disk on to a data recovery professional. These services can be quite costly. Typically, a fee in the range of $100 is assessed simply to accept the disk for a preliminary diagnosis. After that, the cost of recovering your data can easily run into thousands of dollars. Are your data worth that sum? Probably, so you may pay, but you will have learned the hard way that maintaining proper data backups is much less expensive and the turn-around time during recovery is much shorter.

Other personal computer (PC) components that are likely to fail are the fans, the power supply, and the main board. If these parts fail, it saves time to simply replace the whole unit. Have a PC technician look at the old unit. If it can be repaired, fine, but very often it is simply not worth it.

There is a whole category of equipment failures that aren't really equipment failures. These are cases where a cable is loose or broken; the environmental conditions are unsatisfactory; and so forth. These cases are actually difficult to identify because often, as in the case of a loose cable, the connection is intermittently disrupted and then fails completely. Do not be afraid of the perceived complexity of the systems. Most often, malfunctions have simple causes. It is therefore a good idea to check first all connectors and to have replacement cables available.

Once equipment is rebuilt, thorough testing should be performed before it is connected again to the network. Special disaster recovery configurations, such as a specific preinstalled hardware profile, would allow even a limited machine to boot and to connect to the most important services.

Ask yourself what you have learned from your system crash. How likely is it that it would happen again and what would be the consequence? Would it be advisable to establish a more solid hardware base, such as the use of mirrored disk systems in the affected workstation? Did you have all the spare parts, or some systems, to immediately replace the broken equipment and to begin data restoration efforts as previously described? Why did this equipment failure occur? What was the impact? Would it be cost-effective to establish preventative measures, such as a mirrored disk system, or more frequent backups?

Some vendors will try to convince you that they have convenient solutions to the problem of equipment failure. There is a very strong correlation between *perceived* convenience and costs when it comes to contingency. I underscore the word *perceived* because real disasters often reveal the complexity of solutions that had initially been purchased because of their "convenience." Salespeople often have difficulty assessing the level of contingency your business needs and, as a consequence, often offer high-level contingency solutions with a commensurate high price. I suggest, however, that you first estimate the level of contingency you need and benchmark all choices against that requirement so that you can have an informed conversation with your IT staff and with sales vendors. Contingency will only be as good as its weakest link, so a flawless backup unit will not protect your business against a human error.

Equipment failures are best handled through organized plans for equipment replacement. Equipment failure through hardware malfunction is most likely a localized problem, unless, of course, it is a network component for which either an alternative network route should be implemented or a spare part must be readily available. When a serious disaster strikes, it will be difficult to immediately procure equipment parts. Manage your in-house stock accordingly. Make certain that you purchase business products for professional use and avoid products developed for home or consumer use.

In the event of equipment failure, you should first isolate this system from the network as it could be a symptom of a virus attack. You want to stop a potential virus threat from propagating throughout your network. Furthermore, it is much easier to locate and identify the error if you can be certain that no external parties interfere with your system.

## THIRD-PARTY FAILURES

Many companies rely on Internet connections, especially for e-mails. It has become a standard tool for unofficial communication. How much you depend on the Internet will become clear once the service fails. You have to resume services as soon as possible. If you followed the advice in Part One, Prepare, of this book, you probably will not have to do much at this point. Your secondary Internet connection has automatically taken over or you need to manually patch a network cord. And you always have the backup of using one or several dial-up lines to establish an Internet connection. But note that these dial-up connections should not be made from individual PCs for security reasons. They should be done through a specified dial-up location, preferably a dial-up and router combination.

Most often, however, the issues do not present themselves in a clear fashion. Users may complain about a "slow" Internet connection although your company has signed on to a DSL or cable high-speed Internet service. E-mail transmissions are erratic, connections occasionally time out, and Web browsing appears sluggish. It can be difficult to assess if these conditions are the result of a local technical problem or a problem with third-party providers. These conditions may occur every day, usually at peak traffic hours. Your Internet provider may tell you that everything is fine with their networks and their service. If you read Part I: Prepare carefully, you know that there are two issues you need to investigate, the actual bandwidth you are using and the average latency time you receive from your most contacted external hosts. In many cases, you will find that this sluggishness is caused simply because your traffic passes through so many different network routers. With all network routers busy, even a small data packet will travel at one-tenth its usual speed. You will also find that the available bandwidth to one individual during peak hours shrinks because too many people share the connection from Cable to the Internet. In either case, a call to customer support at your Internet service provider (ISP) will not help.

You will need to call your high-level contact at the service provider, explain the situation, and ask that your traffic be routed in a different manner, perhaps directly to the Internet backbone providers. You will have a tough time convincing them as they don't want to prioritize one client over another, but if you are successful, you will be amazed at the results. If you are not able to convince them, consider your options carefully. It might be time to upgrade your connection, from DSL or Cable access to a true data line, such as a T1 line. It might help to simply change the provider. You need true quality of service from your ISP to properly conduct your business. Your ISP owes you a full explanation for the poor service. If you are dissatisfied with their response, change to another provider.

After a power failure, carefully restart the system by first bringing all network components live, then the servers, and finally, all the user workstations. You need to run system and disk check software on each workstation that was not cleanly shut down when the power failure occurred. You may have serious data corruption issues on some hard disks. Some PCs may not boot up. It is probably more efficient to replace the PC with another unit from your stock while using recovery tools to bring the damaged PC back to life.

A power failure will also affect your phone system. Telephones directly connected to analog lines, however, will continue to work because the power is provided to them through the wire directly by the phone company. So it is just a matter of restarting your phone system to see if it recovers automatically—it usually does. If not, call your phone technician right away.

Assess how your company responded to the power outage. This response gives you valuable feedback about your preparedness for the most severe disasters. Did you have all essential machines on UPS units? Were they monitored by the machines that connect to them, and did the equipment sense the power loss and cleanly shut down all the systems? You will probably find that you never again want to go through the agonizing and nerve-wracking experience of a corrupted disk structure and will invest in UPS units, even though you may never again need them.

## ENVIRONMENTAL HAZARDS

Environmental hazards of sufficient severity to interrupt business operations are relatively rare. You do not anticipate such an event unless you are in an area with a known exposure. The first step in recovery is to ensure that the hazardous condition no longer exists. Minor hazards, such as noxious odors, may pass within hours. More severe cases of contamination by chemicals, biological agents, or radioactive agents will require a more extensive, professional restoration effort. In some cases, it might not be possible to decontaminate your premises and equipment. In the worst-case scenario, the site may be scheduled for demolition.

Most likely, you can continue your remote operation—Stage I, so it is still possible to run a full backup of all systems. If the situation is quickly brought under control, people can reenter the building within a couple of hours. But if the situation persists, you need to continue your company's operations from your alternate site and build-up a small infrastructure that can support the critical business functions.

Work closely with your third-party vendors because you will need some temporary services from them at your alternate site. But remember to use a vendor that can guarantee you that it can provide the service to you and will not be affected by the disaster. You should also ask for special rates for disaster recovery site installation.

If you can indeed return to your premises, you may encounter other residual problems, such as corrosion on equipment parts, damage from the cleaning effort, and so forth. Work with your insurance carrier to reach an agreeable settlement that will replace the damaged assets.

## FIRES AND OTHER DISASTERS

When a fire strikes, there is a risk that your office will be destroyed or it may suffer some damage. You will have to move operations to an alternate site until your office can be restored or rebuilt.[1] Your first priority is to build up the recovery site so that the critical staff can convene there and resume work. You should have on hand spare equipment and additional components like network devices and cable. You need to work with the team that will assume responsibility for core operations in the recovery period to ensure that their needs are met. I hope your preparation included conducting emergency drills and assessing the needs of the staff operating from the alternate worksite, so you have anticipated much of what you will need.

The transfer of the operation to the disaster recovery site will be smoother if you were able to perform a clean shutdown of all equipment in your primary worksite or, if you were very lucky, there was enough time to run a full backup of all machines and copy data over to your off-site server.

When building your small remote operation—Stage II, your security scheme will change significantly. The core team needs unencumbered access to information because they will perform additional roles.[2] Expect these adjustments on the operational side will take a significant amount of time. Advise your staff on the new access rules and remind them of their responsibility to safeguard confidential company information.

When recovering from a severe disaster such as a fire, the ideal situation for a small business is to be hosted by a larger company that can provide temporary accommodation until a new office site can be established. It is not only because many services are available that you would not buy for your alternate site, but it is also reassuring to your employees to feel welcomed and to work in a secure environment. Returning to your old worksite will bring back memories of the disaster. It is important to maintain an *esprit de corps* to deal with these emotions.

## TERRORISM AND SABOTAGE

The recovery from an act of terrorism or sabotage has more to do with dealing with psychological trauma than with repairing the attendant physical damage that may be similar to that caused by a natural disaster, such as a fire. The questions about motives or the outrage about such inhumane conduct will persist in the months to follow and will likely be a part of the community's grieving experience. There is nothing that you, as a small business owner, can do to prevent it. You can increase security measures at your facilities and try to keep a low profile.

You must organize a detailed investigation to detect any subtle damages to your business. The most common form of sabotage consists of virus attacks on your IT infrastructure, but the damage can be mitigated by good backup procedures and rigorous use of firewalls and virus detection software. The greatest degree of financial harm inflicted upon your business will result from three efforts: (1) trade secret theft, (2) accounting record manipulation, and (3) employee misuse of IT resources. The damage can be subtle and it may take some time before its effects become apparent. Mischievous transactions may include the placement of a Trojan horse or some other method to penetrate your business' computer network to obtain access to restricted information. If you suspect that your business may have been a victim of such acts, consult an IT professional. Consider reporting such incidents (in the United States) to the Federal Bureau of Investigation (FBI). These acts occur more often than we think, but companies rarely report them out of embarrassment. The FBI may be able to assist businesses in a discreet manner.

## NOTES

1. When recovering from a disaster such as a fire, there are companies that specialize in providing property restoration services. It is important that you do not attempt the cleanup yourself or with the use of untrained personnel. In a well-intentioned attempt to remove soot and ash, you may cause the particles to become airborne and so possibly cause more respiratory problems for those who work in the area. This is a job that you must leave to professionals. Your insurance carrier can recommend a qualified restoration service in your area.

2. As you recover from a major disaster, you will likely not have a full complement of staff. Some of your employees may be unable to return to work immediately following the disaster. Remember to anticipate that some of your employees may be military reservists who will be called to active duty in certain types of disasters. Other employees may be forced to work from home if their commute to the alternate location is impaired or if they have to attend to family needs.

# 13

# Financial Liquidity

In the recovery process, you will address issues that were unresolved during the initial reaction to the disaster. You may have to resolve disputes with your insurance company regarding damaged property or other business losses. You may face the risk of increased insurance premiums as a result of the disaster. In this chapter, we consider how to work through those processes. The recovery process, however, is not just about unfinished business from the initial reaction to the disaster. Recovery is a forward-looking process. You will reflect on how your small business reacted to the disaster, what you learned from that reaction and what you will do differently in the future. You will almost certainly learn lessons that you can apply to your current and future business processes.

Now that the initial reaction to the disaster has passed, you are likely experiencing a range of different emotions. Those reactions were probably suppressed when you were busy trying to rebuild your business and resume operations. The frenetic activity occupied your mind and left you with little time to think about your losses. Now that you have some time alone with your thoughts to reflect on the experience, you may experience some disquieting moments. By now, your friends and family who were unaffected by the disaster have moved on. The disaster is no longer a news item. You are only just beginning to deal with the feelings provoked by the disaster. I will give you some advice on how to cope.

## RESOLVING INSURANCE DISPUTES

From time to time, disputes arise concerning proper settlement of insurance claims. I hope that you do not have this experience, but if you do, you are not alone. Major disasters are invariably followed by stories in the media about the challenges of collecting on insurance claims, such as denied claims, delayed claims payments, and payments made for significantly less than the policyholders had expected.

I cannot anticipate every circumstance that may give rise to a dispute with your insurance company, but I can advise you on steps to take to mitigate your risk of such disputes and/or expedite their resolution. If you cannot resolve the dispute to your satisfaction, you have the option of retaining legal counsel and bringing suit against your insurance company. This is an option you want to reserve until you have exhausted all other means of resolving the matter. Managing a small business is completely engaging in the best of circumstances; your resources will be even more limited following a disaster. It is not in your interest to become enmeshed in litigation. Unfortunately, insurance companies often appreciate the reluctance of small businesses to engage in costly, time-consuming litigation, and so may be less motivated to respond to threats of lawsuits.

Ironically, liability claims are, in my experience, less likely to be denied by insurance companies. If any aspect of the disaster gives rise to liability claims against your company, for example, a claim against the directors and officers of your company for their alleged failure to properly implement contingency plans for the business, you must give immediate notice to your insurance company. Further, you must work with your insurance company to mitigate your insured losses, exactly as we discussed in the previous chapter. If you have liability insurance, and, even better, an umbrella cover, your insurance company will almost certainly want to select the legal counsel who will represent your small business. Your insurance policy likely contains a provision for the selection of counsel.

You can appreciate their preference; as a large, well-capitalized corporation, the insurance company routinely deals with litigation and, as a consequence, has established relationships with many law firms experienced in defending such suits. Due to the volume of business generated for the legal profession by the insurance industry, insurance companies have typically negotiated fees with certain law firms at preferred rates. The insurance company would prefer to select experienced counsel with whom they have an ongoing relationship than to rely on an inexperienced entrepreneur to select his or her own counsel and hope that a wise choice was made. At the same time, it expedites claims settlement if the insurance company can work with legal counsel who is familiar with the corporate policies of the client, so the insurer need not explain, over and over again, to a succession of law firms their approach in resolving claims and their corporate policies. Finally, the insurance company almost certainly benefits from a preferred fee structure, given the volume of business it may do with any single law firm. In this case, the insurance company's size works in your favor.

In liability claims, you and your insurance company are partners in mitigating losses. As a consequence, it is critical that you document your loss mitigation efforts; they are crucial to your defense. Your insurance company will rely on the advice of counsel to determine whether the plaintiff, the party who seeks to bring a liability claim against your small business, has a valid legal claim. Based on the findings of their own investigation, they will determine how to resolve the case. I don't wish to trivialize such claims; they can be emotionally draining for the defendant and, in the context of your disaster recovery efforts, counterproductive. I simply mean that in my experience, you are less likely to have a dispute with your insurance company regarding whether a liability claim is covered by your policy. You are also unlikely to have a dispute with your insurer about the valuation of the claim, since your business will not be the direct beneficiary of any such payment. If there is a dispute, it will be between your insurance company and the plaintiff. The best advice we can give you with respect to liability claims is to give timely notice to your insurance company, document your loss mitigation efforts, and cooperate with your insurance company in resolving the claim.

Next, let us consider claims concerning property insurance. The three suggestions from Part One: Prepare—regarding documentation, furnishing notice, and completing valuation—should minimize the risk of disputes with your insurer. Documentation refers to proper maintenance of records of the assets of your business. If you have, for instance, receipts and invoices showing the sums paid for your business assets and descriptions of those assets—thereby allowing both you and the insurance company to agree on replacement costs—it should be relatively straightforward to agree to a claims settlement. The difficulties reported by some insurance companies adjusting claims for small businesses concerned documentation of the damaged business assets. The records of many businesses based in disaster-affected areas and in adjacent properties were destroyed. It may not be possible to reconstruct an inventory of property, plant and equipment, such as by means of procuring statements from the business' credit card company.

If you follow the program I have outlined for you, you will minimize the risk of such disputes. Maintain careful records of your business assets, including receipts, invoices, cancelled checks, photographs, serial numbers, and so forth. *Keep a duplicate (or even triplicate) copy of these records off-site!* Imagine that your office building were destroyed in a catastrophe and with it, all of your business records. Your business may never recover. I keep electronic records, with digitized photographs of certain assets and such records facilitate my business procurement processes, irrespective of contingency planning for disasters. I urge you to do the same.

The next step is giving notice to your insurance company of possible claims. Don't risk a possible denial of a valid claim for failure to give timely notice of the disaster and remember to review all policies implicated in the disaster, including policies that have expired and umbrella or excess coverages. It is better to invest time in determining that a certain policy does not indemnify a particular loss than it is to forfeit the indemnification for lack of a prompt response. In giving notice of a loss, if you fail to properly identify the peril for the insured coverage, your claim may be denied and a dispute may ensue. A real-world example will illustrate this point.

A sole proprietor who worked from her home near a disaster site (a fire) sustained a systems crash. She concluded that the crash was most likely due to the loss of electrical power, a result of the disaster, and so notified her insurer. As her policy did not include an endorsement for interruption of power supply, that portion of her claim was denied. In fact, the damage to her computer was the result of soot and ash clogging the fan of her computer, a peril that is covered by her policy. The denial of coverage and dispute that followed could have been avoided by proper diagnosis of the problem, or a description of the problem without a diagnosis. Had the insurance company sent an adjuster to inspect the damaged computer, he or she would have seen the soot and ash in the machine and likely authorized the claim. Her hasty diagnosis resulted in a denial and then a delay of her claims payment. When submitting an insurance claim, remember the words of Sergeant Joe Friday, "Just the facts, Ma'am." Don't foreclose a valid claim by a hasty self-diagnosis.

I recommend that you have an IT expert examine your computer and related hardware assets following a disaster. Since damage to these assets can be subtle, inspection is best left to an expert. Since we are considering an example of a sole proprietor with an insurance-related dispute, I will take the opportunity to remind sole proprietors of their need to secure insurance coverage for their business-related assets and thereby avert disputes.

In the United States alone, more than eleven million people are self-employed. Many work out of their homes. The rise of outsourcing and attempts to reduce labor costs will likely increase this number. If you work from home, if you are self-employed, or if your business is organized as a sole proprietorship, be certain that you have adequate insurance. Earlier in this book, I suggested that you consider securing insurance coverage from partner companies to associations serving the small business community. Some of these affiliated companies offer insurance policies specifically designed for self-employed individuals and those who work from home. You can obtain a basic insurance policy designed for the needs of home-based workers for as little as several hundred dollars annually. Investigate whether such coverage is appropriate for you. If you file a claim related to your home business with your homeowner's or tenants insurance company—which generally do not cover home-based business activities—you may find yourself embroiled in a dispute with your insurer.

Finally, many property-related disputes with insurance companies concern the valuation of the damaged or destroyed property. Mitigate such risks by insisting that your policy cover the replacement cost of damaged assets, and keep records of your business assets. This is particularly important with respect to IT-related assets. Manufacturers of computers and other related hardware frequently introduce new models of equipment and discontinue older models. To determine a fair replacement value of IT assets requires a detailed list of performance specifications. If the insurance company has documentation that, for example, the ten computers destroyed in your building fire each had Pentium III chips, 256 megabytes of RAM, 20 gigabytes hard disks, 15 inch flat screen monitors, and a color laser printer over an Ethernet network, such information will expedite your claims settlement. However, if the records you produce show that in 2000, your business paid $25,000 for these ten computers including the printers, agreeing to a fair replacement value for those computers can be a contentious process.

If you properly document the value of your assets, give prompt notice to your insurer and agree to a replacement cost valuation method. This will minimize the risk of disputes with your insurance company for a fair claims settlement. What if you follow all of these precautions and a dispute arises anyway? You will need to pursue two courses of action simultaneously. First, explore alternate means of generating cash to finance the replacement of the damaged assets that are absolutely essential to the recovery of your business. This is critical since you cannot anticipate with any degree of certainty when your claim will be resolved, and you need the funds to replace business assets to get your business up and running as soon as possible. Don't delay your recovery efforts pending resolution of all insurance claims. This book does not cover topics of capital raising, but as a small business owner, you are familiar with various means of bootstrapping. Did you finance your purchases with credit cards? Contact your credit card providers and try to negotiate a lower interest rate or raise your credit limit. You will be surprised how many credit card holders are able to reduce their interest charges by several percentage points with relatively little effort. The credit card company wants you to pay them interest charges, not to go out of business. Explain to the credit card issuer your disaster recovery efforts.

Are there receivables that you can factor? Are you able to lease or temporarily rent your necessary equipment? Do you have access to a line of credit? Does your business have cash reserves that you could draw down, pending resolution of your insurance claim? Are you operating your business from your alternate location? If so, do you have surplus space that you could sublease to another business displaced by the disaster? Remember that even as you are resolving your property insurance claim, you are demonstrating to your insurance company that you are taking steps to mitigate your business interruption losses.

If your business is a copy shop, for example, and you and your insurance company cannot agree on a replacement cost for the damaged photocopy machines, work with your insurance company to develop a plan for resuming business operations. Presumably, you cannot reopen your doors for business without replacement photocopy machines. If you have a business interruption cover in place, gently remind your insurance company that reducing the amount of your property damages may increase your business interruption damages.

Ask your insurance company to advance you funds for the undisputed portion of your claim, provided, of course, that you do not have to waive your rights to pursue other elements of your claim. If your business is a copy shop, and you and your insurance company can agree to a fair replacement cost of the black and white photocopy machines, for example, ask that that sum be paid to you while you continue to work to resolve your dispute about the valuation of the color photocopy machines. As you seek the funds to replace the assets damaged in the disaster, you must simultaneously work toward resolving the disputed portions of your insurance claim.

I recommend that you propose arbitration to your insurance company. Reinsurance contracts—contracts between primary insurance companies and reinsurance providers who assume certain insurance liabilities—typically contain so-called arbitration clauses. Such clauses specify that disputed claims are to be resolved by arbitration and they identify the venue and forum for such arbitration. Arbitration provides a means for resolving disputed insurance claims without recourse to litigation. Commercial insurance policies typically don't provide for arbitration but ask for it anyway. An impartial party can often resolve the dispute promptly, provided, of course, it is agreed in advance that the arbitration is binding on both parties. The office of your state insurance commissioner will be able to refer you to parties who can arbitrate your dispute.

If arbitration is an unacceptable option to the insurance company, and you are forced to litigate your claim, first contact your insurance commissioner to file a complaint. You may learn that your business is not the only one with difficulties resolving insurance claims with a particular insurer and your complaint may prompt an investigation by the commissioner. You may also be able to access low-cost or *pro bono* legal representation in the case of a major disaster. Contact your local bar association and explain your circumstances. Following any major disaster, a number of small business owners will face bankruptcy and can often secure *pro bono* legal counsel to litigate their insurance claims. The likely remaining source of disputes with your insurance company concerns business interruption claims and they tend to be the most contentious.

## SECURING BUSINESS INTERRUPTION INSURANCE

In Part Two: Respond, we considered the steps you need to take to secure insurance coverage following a disaster. You begin by reviewing all the insurance policies that may be implicated in the property loss and taking steps to reconstruct policies that may have been destroyed in the disaster if you failed to keep backup copies of the policies off-site. I advised you to give prompt notice of the disaster to your insurance company and to work with your insurer to mitigate the losses. You must be careful to document the losses and expenses incurred in mitigating those losses, as such expenses may be reimbursable. The insurance company's input into your loss mitigation efforts reduces the risk that they will subsequently characterize such efforts as inadequate or deny reimbursement of your loss mitigation expenses. You then prepare and submit your claim.

Let's assume that you have followed these steps properly and a dispute arises with the insurance company regarding your business interruption claim. I advise the same course of action as recommended for resolving disputes over property claims: Request an advance of the undisputed portion of the claim, continue to work towards rebuilding your business, propose that your insurance company agree to arbitration to resolve the dispute, and, if necessary, write a letter of complaint to your state's insurance commissioner and litigate your claim. If you have followed these recommendations for documenting losses and loss mitigation efforts, you will be in a strong position to present your claim to the arbitrator (or judge and jury) and to do so immediately. If you believe litigation is inevitable, redouble your efforts to secure payment for the portions of your claim that are not in dispute. Those funds may be necessary to cover your legal costs, and advance payment of those claims will preempt the insurance company from withholding them pending resolution of all of the claims.

Reinsurance contracts typically require arbitration to resolve disputed claims and specify which laws apply for the interpretation of the contract. Since insurance laws vary from state to state and from country to country, and since the insurance company and its reinsurer are very likely domiciled in different states or different countries, it is important that the parties agree in advance which laws apply to the contract. Very often, reinsurance contracts are written "to be construed in accordance with the laws of the United Kingdom," even when neither the insurance company nor the reinsurer is domiciled in the United Kingdom. This is because, owing to the development of the insurance market from its beginnings in a London coffee shop to the role that the Lloyds Insurance Market plays in the world today, the United Kingdom has a very well developed body of case law with respect to insurance. An arbitrator would have many precedents to guide him or her in resolving the dispute.

Insurance contracts are not written in the same manner. They rarely require arbitration to resolve disputes and often fail to specify how disputes would be resolved, leaving the policyholder with only one apparent option: litigation. Insurance contracts often do not identify in which forum litigation should take place. In such a case, you should select the most appropriate forum in which to litigate your claim. Your legal counsel can advise you of the best choice. In the United States, New York is considered a leading state with respect to insurance regulation and its policies and practices are often adopted by the other states. While your commercial insurance policy may not specify the forum for litigation, it will almost certainly specify a timeframe within which such litigation must commence. Typically, insurance policies specify that the policyholder has a certain period of time following the date he gave notice to his insurance company of the loss (or from the date the insurance company notified him of its denial of all or part of his claim) to bring a lawsuit against the insurance company to collect the claims that are in dispute. Understandably, insurance companies don't want to be served with lawsuits from insurance policies that expired decades ago. The typical period to expiration of the right to bring suit is three years; read your policy carefully.

The rules of construction of insurance policies favor the policyholder. That is, if there is any ambiguity in the wording of your insurance policy, it must be construed in favor of the policyholder. The reason is as we discussed in Part II: Respond—insurance policies are standard documents issued by insurance companies. The policyholder has little or no input into the drafting of the insurance contract; it is typically a "boilerplate" document. However, disputes with insurance companies regarding business interruption claims are less likely the result of contract wording and more likely the result of identification of the "triggering" event (i.e., the disaster that disrupted the business operations).

Because business interruption insurance is typically an endorsement to property coverage, it does not cover losses of business income that occurred independently of an insured property loss. For the business interruption insurance to apply, an event that triggers coverage occurs, causing damage to the insured property of the policyholder that interrupts the operations of the business, thereby causing a loss of income. For our purposes, we assume that the triggering event is a major disaster. One issue likely to give rise to disputed insurance claims is for business interruption cover following a disaster in which the policyholder did not sustain damage to his or her property.

Imagine, for example, that you own and operate a travel agency in a disaster zone and that your premises were sufficiently removed from the epicenter that they did not suffer any physical damage. Nevertheless, the civil authorities closed your business premises as a direct consequence of the disaster. Employees and customers were denied access to your premises. Do you have a valid business interruption claim?

The answer is maybe. Business may be interrupted by action of civil authority and your insurance policy may have a specific provision covering claims arising from such action. In that case, the answer remains "maybe." The insurance company may take the position that the provision does not apply unless the triggering event, property damage caused by a peril covered in the policy, occurs. The insurance company may or may not persuade a court of its interpretation. Businesses that lost revenue when they were closed in compliance with curfews following the assassination of Dr. Martin Luther King won their claims for business interruption insurance, despite the fact that their businesses did not suffer any damage to physical property. However, other courts have denied policyholders claims under similar circumstances when civil authorities imposed curfews.

Consider another well-known legal case concerning business interruption insurance. A movie theatre chain closed its movie theaters in compliance with curfews imposed by civil authorities following the Rodney King verdict. The insurance company denied the business interruption claim and the court ruled in favor of the insurance company on the ground that the theaters did not sustain physical damage as a consequence of the riots following the verdict. The court was not persuaded by the fact that the curfew prevented customers from going outside and patronizing the theaters.

The lesson learned here is that in the case of business closings due to the action of civil authorities, it is not clear that business interruption claims will be recognized as valid by insurance companies, or that policyholders whose claims have been denied will prevail in legal proceedings. The hypothetical travel agency in the disaster zone may have a stronger claim if it lost electricity and telephone service as a consequence of the disaster, thereby identifying a "triggering" event. As each case has unique circumstances, should your claim for business interruption following the actions of civil authorities be denied, seek legal advice as to how to proceed.

Let's consider another common source of disputes regarding claims for business interruption insurance: disputes concerning physical damage to IT assets, such as computers and related hardware. I remember well how reinsurance companies took note of cases in which insurance companies denied policyholders' business interruption claims when electrical outages (or power surges) destroyed data stored on computers. The insurance companies denied such claims on the ground that the computer systems were not physically damaged. The businesses argued that the data on the computers were destroyed and that they were the property of the company. In some cases, the insurance companies prevailed, arguing that data stored in electronic format were not tangible physical assets of the business. In other cases, the businesses succeeded in persuading the arbiter of the dispute that the data were intangible assets and were no less valuable to the company than other physical assets. You can appreciate how complicated these disputes can become.

Even property damage itself may not be deemed adequate to substantiate a business interruption claim. Following major floods in Europe, a small business operating near a theme park sought business interruption protection. The flood caused some damage and mold in the park, which closed for repairs and safety checks to the amusement rides. When the park reopened for business, visitors were fewer in number and revenues had declined. The insurer denied the claim on the ground that most of the park was accessible to the public. The small business owned and operated a restaurant and a take-out food-service facility adjacent to the park and derived all of its revenues from diners visiting the park. The fact that the restaurant's business was supported by the theme park and, in the absence of visitors to the park, there were no diners to patronize the restaurant, was viewed as immaterial by the arbiter. Perhaps if the restaurant owner had negotiated an endorsement to his policy to connect the protection afforded by his insurance to events occurring at the adjacent park, he may have succeeded in establishing a valid business interruption claim.

Successfully securing a business interruption claim requires satisfying the precise requirements for property damage and attendant income losses, and persuading an insurance adjuster, arbitrator, or court of those facts. Unfortunately, the interpretation of "triggers" of business interruption insurance and the quantification of damages can vary considerably from case to case. It may be of small consolation to small business owners, but large corporations face the same problems with business interruption cover. I remember two negotiations to structure a business interruption insurance program for two separate companies, one a computer chip manufacturer and the other a pharmaceutical company. Both negotiations were unsuccessful.

The situation faced by the chip manufacturer was unique: The company was a specialized niche producer of chips whose lifecycle was short. Should the manufacturing facility be destroyed by fire or earthquake, the chips it had manufactured would be obsolete by the time the facility could be rebuilt. The company managed its operations by successfully retrofitting its existing facility for each new element in the manufacturing process mandated by a new generation chip design. The insurance company and the chip manufacturer were unable to agree to policy terms with respect to how to calculate an appropriate benefit if a disaster destroyed an existing facility that could therefore not be quickly upgraded to manufacture the next generation product. In case you are wondering how the company devised its contingency plan, the answer is that they built in redundancy. The company expanded production capacity at each of its five plants worldwide, each of which was located in different geographic areas. Should a major disaster destroy one plant, each of the remaining four plants would increase its production quotas by 25% to compensate for the lost production of the fifth plant. The company insured its property risk, so it would recover some funds if any of its facilities were destroyed, but it retained its business interruption risk.

The pharmaceutical company case is interesting, in that it is analogous to the small business operating a restaurant adjacent to the theme park as we discussed earlier. The company manufactures drugs to treat relatively minor medical conditions. The company's senior management was worried about product tampering; that is, not tampering with their products in the manufacturing process, but tampering with the competitors' products. The company was confident of the security of its own facilities and the protections it had put in place, but it was less confident of the security practices of its competitors. Management feared that should one of its competitors be affected by product tampering, consumers would be reluctant to use this particular class of drugs, including the drugs produced by this specific pharmaceutical company. The company did not succeed in obtaining a business interruption policy for this particular peril because it could not agree with its insurer as to what constituted an event trigger or an appropriate recovery.

In the Gulf Coast, small businesses are right now involved in disputes concerning their business interruption cover. Contentious issues include determining the period of coverage: Presumably all parties can agree that the losses began when the hurricane made landfall, but when did they end? What exactly was the period of interruption? When were neighborhoods reopened to pedestrian traffic? When were roads and commonly used traffic routes reopened? When did sales volumes return to their predisaster levels? As you can see, these disputes are not easy to resolve. The best advice that I can give you is to follow the recommended procedures for documenting losses, mitigating losses, and giving notice. In my opinion, even the most experienced legal counsel cannot predict the outcome of a business interruption insurance dispute. But if you take all the steps I recommend to secure your coverage, you will have maximized your prospects for a recovery under the provisions of your policy.

## NEGOTIATING CONTINUING COVERAGE

Insurance is a cyclical business characterized by a hierarchy of capital strength and hence, appetite for risk. The insured party has the lowest appetite for risk and the smallest capital base. Your business is an insured party or a policyholder. Your business has a relatively small base of capital and commensurate appetite for risk. If, for example, your factory is damaged in a fire, you want an insurance company, with its capital resources and greater appetite for risk, to cover your damages—less a relatively modest deductible. You pay a premium to your insurance company for indemnification against specified risks. Should a loss occur, the insurance company will pay the claims.

The insurance company, of course, collects premiums from many policyholders diversified across many perils, many periods of time, and many geographic regions. Thus, the insurance company has a greater appetite for risk. The insurance company, in turn, cedes certain of its risks to the reinsurance market, for which it pays a premium and it retains other risks. The reinsurance market, in turns, cedes certain of its risks to the retrocession market. The retrocession market consists of relatively few, large-scale companies, such as National Indemnity (a Berkshire Hathaway company) and the American International Group. Thus, at each level of the hierarchy, premiums are collected, claims are paid, and parties attempt to configure their optimal levels of risk.

You, the small business owner, pay premiums to an insurance company that indemnifies your business against insured risks. You may not have appreciated that your insurance company also pays premiums to a reinsurance company for indemnification against a certain portion of its risks. The reinsurance company, in turn, pays premiums to a retrocession company for indemnification against a certain portion of its risks. In other words, there is a great deal of risk-taking capacity supporting your business' insured risks.

Following a major disaster, commercial insurance rates rise dramatically. Workers compensation premiums, for example, can increase by 40% or more, even for companies with no loss experience. Rates on other commercial lines, such as commercial property and liability, can increase 100% or more. Many small business owners, faced with expensive insurance premiums in a less than robust economy, are confronting unpleasant choices. Some must choose between paying more expensive insurance premiums, cutting back on coverage, foregoing some coverage, or making cuts elsewhere, such as laying off employees. What is particularly baffling to many business owners is how a single catastrophic event could have such powerful consequences for rates. In this section, we will try to answer that question by explaining the economics of the insurance cycle. In addition, some practical tips about negotiating coverage in the postdisaster insurance market will be provided.

Consider the effects of disasters, or catastrophes that we are treating as super disasters, on the cash flow of an insurance company. An insurance company collects premiums from its policyholders, such as your small business. It invests these premiums in assets, such as high-quality bonds and blue chip stocks, to earn investment income. It pays out expenses, such as premiums, for its own reinsurance coverage, salaries to its employees, and so forth. It also pays claims to its policyholders for insured losses, or damages. The cash flow of an insurance company (premiums plus investment income less expenses less losses) is often expressed in terms of a combined ratio. The combined ratio is the sum of the loss ratio plus the investment ratio. A loss ratio of 100%, for example, means that for every dollar the insurance company collected in premiums, it paid out one dollar in claims and related expenses. An insurance company with such a loss experience stays in business by engaging in so-called cash-flow underwriting; that is, its insurance losses are more than offset by the investment income the insurance company earns on its premiums. In 1999, for example, insurance companies were paying out $1.07 in claims and expenses for every dollar it collected in premiums. You can appreciate how sensitive the insurance industry is to the financial markets.

In 1999, insurance companies could survive with a 107% claims ratio because they were enjoying a bull market. Returns to stock market investors and bondholders were robust. With such market conditions, insurance companies competed with one another to reduce premiums, preferring to build market share and believed that they could earn their profits in the financial markets. Some insurance companies did not purchase sufficient reinsurance coverage in order to reduce costs. For example, even before the September 11 catastrophes, trouble loomed. Companies such as Reliance Insurance Company, were offering property-casualty insurance policies at 25% less than what insurance companies with stronger credit ratings were prepared to offer. In 2000, Reliance Insurance Company came under the control of insurance regulators, as its financial strength continued to decline. It could not operate as an ongoing concern, in part, because its premiums were inadequate to cover the risks it was underwriting.

At the same time, the financial markets on which insurance companies had depended to earn their profits weakened. The implosion of Internet stocks, followed by major corporate bankruptcies, (e.g., Enron and Global Crossing) reduced the attractiveness of equity investments. Bonds, which comprise the largest class of assets in insurance company's investment port folios, were also a less profitable investment, as interest rates were at historic lows. Thus, even prior to September 11, 2001 and Hurricane Katrina, the scene was set for dramatic changes in the insurance industry.

Now, let's begin with the top of the hierarchy. The providers of retrocession coverage will pay claims to the reinsurance companies, which will pay their share of claims to the insurance companies and the insurance companies, in turn, will pay claims to their policyholders. Since the insurance industry had never conceived of major disasters causing damage on the scales we are now seeing, there will almost certainly be changes in underwriting policy.

In the past, fire insurance covered damage arising from fires and explosions irrespective of the cause, with a single exclusion for war and civil commotion. In most countries, terrorism was not identified in war exclusion clauses and so was assumed to be a covered risk. Prior to September 11, the most costly insured terrorist attack occurred on April 24, 1993 when a bomb exploded at Bishopsgate, London, causing $907 million of insured damage. While the human cost of such an attack is incalculable, the financial costs were below the costs of major natural catastrophes, such as hurricanes and earthquakes. Several countries particularly exposed to risks of terrorism—the United Kingdom, Spain, South Africa, and Israel—have special government support to cover these risks, but they are the exception. The United States joined this group when on November 26, 2002, Congress passed legislation known as the Terrorist Risk Insurance Act (TRIA). France and Germany have each passed similar legislation.

Most countries implicitly allowed commercial underwriting of terrorist risks. Unlike terrorist risks, natural disasters occur randomly and without design, but the probabilities and consequences of natural disasters are actuarially predictable. Prior to September 11, the risk of terrorism was covered, except in the four aforementioned countries, by the private market. Now, the new dimensions of terrorism call for some type of public sector-private sector solution. Until such a time as a solution is put forward, insurance companies will pay significant premiums for reinsurance cover, because they now realize that they cannot afford to be without it. A single terrorist attack with the concentrated deadly intent like that of September 11 could render bankrupt any single insurance company. As a consequence, insurance premiums are likely to remain high for the immediate future.

I predict that large corporations will become increasingly unwilling to pay such steep insurance premiums and will develop innovative means of insuring their risks. We have seen this phenomenon before, beginning in the 1980s with the development of the so-called alternative risk transfer market (ART). ART offered a portfolio of tools by which corporations could transfer their risks by means other than standard commercial insurance programs. One such tool in the ART portfolio was a captive program. Captives were insurance companies wholly owned by their corporate parents. They were typically domiciled offshore, in places such as Bermuda or the Cayman Islands, to benefit from favorable tax climates and fewer regulations. Captives allowed corporations the benefit of tax-deductible premiums to cover their risks while ensuring that profits remained in-house. Other means of transferring insurance risk included catastrophe bonds, in which insurance risk was transferred to the financial markets (imagine a bond whose return was measured by an insurance loss ratio), financial insurance (a hybrid product that transferred some elements of insurance risk, while financing others), and other innovative arrangements. Large corporations with significant loss exposures (such as pharmaceutical companies, oil companies, and other companies operating in industries with high severity/low frequency risks) will lead the way. Unfortunately, many of these solutions are not practical or cost-effective for small businesses. Nevertheless, the laws of supply and demand hold in the insurance market: When large corporations find alternatives to traditional commercial insurance, small businesses should benefit from declining premiums.

Meanwhile, there are some practical steps you should take to ensure that your business has adequate insurance coverage following a major disaster. Beware of the "paying more/getting less" phenomenon that occasionally follows a major disaster. Excluding risks that were previously covered by the small business owner's policy can sometimes dampen increases in insurance premiums. If you make an explicit assessment to forego coverage for certain risks to lower premiums, fine, so long as you understand the tradeoffs you are making. But don't fall prey to creeping exclusions. When time comes to renew your insurance—which is usually done annually—review your policy carefully, as you may not be comparing apples to apples with respect to current and last year's policies. Exercise caution with respect to policy wording and ask questions of your broker and insurance company if there is anything you don't understand. One question we might ask now, for example, that we hadn't asked in the past is, "Is an anthrax-laden letter delivered to my place of work a terrorist or criminal act? Is the coverage the same whether the letter is mailed by a local prankster or by a person from the Middle East?"

Do you remember the advice from Part One: Prepare of this book with respect to lowering your worker's compensation insurance premiums? I recommended that you verify the job classifications of your employees, as often small businesses over-pay their risks because they failed to properly classify jobs. I ask you to go back and repeat that exercise. In fact, you should verify, on an annual basis, that your information is current. As a consequence of the disaster, you may have had some attrition, or you may have hired new employees to assist in your recovery efforts and assume long-term responsibilities. Make certain that your information is accurate. There are more than 700 employee classifications and misclassification errors can be costly. A machine shop general classification, for example, costs $8.50 in workers' compensation premium per $100.00 in payroll. A "precision machinist," in contrast, costs $1.25 in premium per $100.00 in payroll. You can appreciate how easy it would be to make a mistake and pay more premiums than is required. It is worth the time and effort to review your employee data again.

I also advise you to comparison-shop with respect to insurance coverage. It is convenient to build a relationship with a single insurer, but in the face of postdisaster premium increases, you have to consider other options. One commercial insurance broker told me, "Yes, the market was becoming more expensive before Hurricane Katrina, but the rate increases were not as steep as what we are now seeing in the market . . . it's as if insurance companies think they have *carte blanche* to add 25% or 50% to the premium increases that they were going to demand anyway. Whether it is actuarially justifiable or not, that is what they are doing." Insurance premiums rose by 42% following Hurricane Andrew. Whether all small businesses should pay increases on this order of magnitude is debatable, particularly if they are not exposed to the risks that caused the original disaster. It pays to comparison-shop. Following a major disaster, I have seen a range of premiums quoted by different insurance companies to small business owners for similar risks. Compare and negotiate the best deal you can. You may be in a better position to control the premium increases your insurer is demanding if you can document the safety and security measures that your small business has in place that makes your company a better risk than its peers.

Speaking of peers, talk to your peers in the small business community following a disaster, after a suitable period of time to implement recovery efforts. Were they satisfied with their insurance carriers? Which insurance companies provided superior service and which ones failed to deliver? This is important information to have as you consider your business' insurance needs going forward. We can tell you from our experience that there is substantial anecdotal evidence in Lower Manhattan that one insurance company was the source of a disproportionate amount of disappointment following the September 11 disaster. In the first edition to this book, we wrote, "We would be reluctant to advise friends to seek coverage from this particular insurer, which has garnered some bad press." I was not surprised to see that insurance company attract bad press following Hurricane Katrina. Learn from your peers and help them to learn from you. In the next section, we will present some additional learning opportunities. Finally, be hopeful. Remember that after the last pre-Katrina benchmark natural catastrophe, Hurricane Andrew, insurance rates rose steeply, and then declined for five consecutive years. Expensive insurance premiums postdisaster are a common, but usually short-lived, phenomenon.

## LEARNING FROM THE EXPERIENCE

Experience is the best teacher and, having experienced a disaster that disrupted your business, you have learned some valuable lessons. Undoubtedly, there are some things you will do differently in the future. The changes you make to your contingency plan will not only improve the resiliency of your business should you be threatened with a subsequent disaster, but they will also improve your overall business processes, irrespective of whether disaster strikes again. Almost certainly, you learned some positive and encouraging lessons. You learned to appreciate the wonderful people you have in your life. The brush with disaster—assuming it was a more serious form of disaster—may have reframed your perspective. Sometimes, in our zeal to build our businesses, we occasionally neglect the people who mean so much to us and a disaster provides a not-so-gentle reminder of what really matters. You were likely impressed by the response of your employees and suppliers. Their commitment, their enthusiasm, and their hard work are responsible for the success of your rebuilding efforts.

A shared experience, such as a serious disaster and the subsequent recovery, builds a certain *esprit de corps*. I can tell you that the feeling of anonymity in the Big Apple disappeared following the events of September 11. I remember taking a subway to midtown and being a bit confused about where to go as my local subway station had been closed due to severe physical damage. Helpful strangers spontaneously volunteered the names of the working stations. During the subway ride, a neighbor who had recognized me from the elevator of my apartment building introduced herself and initiated a conversation. New York City, contrary to its reputation, is actually a friendly place, but it was never that friendly.

People will feel a need to talk about their experiences. Sharing and validating one another's experience seems to be an important part of the recovery process. During the period that Lower Manhattan was closed, a friend and I shared a bottle of wine with a Malaysian couple who were in New York City on an expatriate assignment. They had feelings of horror about the atrocity, a desire to stay and experience the more positive aspects of living in New York and, at the same time, a desire to return home to assure their families that they were safe. We certainly learn about our connections to one another during a disaster, but we also learn some very practical lessons about disaster recovery.

I have invested some time in talking to small business owners who were affected by the disaster, so that we could learn from their experiences and  share them with you, our readers. Of course, we have, throughout this book, shared our own experiences, but to the extent that we are more

IT- and insurance-savvy than most, we are likely not representative of the population of small business owners. Also, small businesses represent a range of different industries, and the experience of the restaurant owner or the commercial print shop may be different from our own and may hold valuable lessons for us. Few business owners anticipated a disaster on the scale and scope of September 11, 2001 or Hurricane Katrina. The combined effects of an economic recession and a disaster striking our financial capital were devastating to many small businesses. At the same time, we have to focus our attention on practical solutions we can implement as a result of this experience. Few small business owners have the resources to set aside capital in reserve to cover one or two years of expenses in anticipation of such a catastrophe. Let us focus our learning efforts on what we can practically do to mitigate the consequences of the next disaster—and hope it never comes.

I have, throughout this book, drawn on my experiences in Lower Manhattan, but a visit to the FEMA Web site will show you how frequently disasters strike. FEMA catalogs all major disasters in the United States and you will be surprised to see how many have occurred in the past few years. The floods in the Southern part of the United States or the storms in the Midwestern part of the country were disasters to those who were affected. I hope what we have learned can help you to prepare for disaster. You need to determine what the common factors with your business could be, because if you should ever experience a disaster, it will likely be very different from the one we experienced.

After spending considerable time with many small business owners worldwide since September 11, I have concluded that small business owners have learned a great deal about business interruption insurance and that their lessons often came at a high cost, occasionally, the loss of their businesses. The information presented thus far should serve to spare you these terrible losses. I presented basic facts about business interruption insurance as an endorsement to a property insurance program in Part One: Prepare of this book. Part Two:Respond advised you on how to calculate your insured loss and secure business interruption coverage. In Part Three: Recover, I have provided specific advice on resolving disputes over such coverage.

Now, I would like to share with you what I have found to be the errors most commonly made by small business owners in respect to their business interruption insurance. This is admittedly not an exhaustive study of the small business community, but often, anecdotal evidence can be the most persuasive. I hope that by sharing the lessons learned by small business owners in major disaster areas, you can better prepare your business to mitigate potential losses.

The most common error, by far, was a lack of business interruption insurance coverage for small businesses. Business property insurance covers damage to property (which is a direct loss) but not damage to business income (which is an indirect or consequential loss) unless the policy is specifically endorsed to provide this coverage. Relatively few small business owners requested this coverage, and if our sample has any significance, relatively few commercial insurance brokers thought to advise small businesses of the need for such protection. On September 10, 2001, a husband and wife team opened a pizzeria around the corner from my office. Unfortunately, without business interruption coverage in force, they had no means of covering their fixed expenses until they could repair and reopen the restaurant as they did not have the funds to do so. September 10, 2001 was the first and last day that their pizzeria served customers.

I have found that restaurant owners and medical/dental practices were the types of small businesses most likely to forego business interruption coverage. The irony is that these are the types of businesses that cannot operate from remote locations and so are in greatest need of income protection. Many of these business owners mistakenly believe that their property insurance will cover their losses in the event of a disaster. It will. It will cover the cost of repairing the damaged or destroyed assets, but, absent a business interruption endorsement, it won't cover the revenues lost during the period that the business was not operational. If you own and operate a small business in an industry with low switching costs for customers, you cannot afford to be without business interruption insurance.

Imagine that you run a paging or message service for physicians. Disaster strikes and you are temporarily without telephone service. The physicians won't have a choice but immediately switch to an alternate service provider that has not been affected by the disaster, as they require uninterrupted service. Once your telephone service is restored, you will not likely recapture all of the customers who defected. Switching service providers is inconvenient, and it is unlikely that all of your customers will switch back. To the extent that business interruption insurance can replace your revenues lost during the disaster, your business will have resources to fund the recovery.

The second lesson many small business owners learned with respect to business interruption insurance is the need to carefully evaluate the constraints on loss payments. Some business interruption insurance policies specify a staged payout; for example, 40% of the losses are paid to you within 30 days of the loss, 40% of the losses are paid within 60 days of the loss, and 20% are paid within 90 days of the loss. I recommend that you negotiate to remove any such payment limitation from your policy wording. There is no need for your business to provide interest-free financing to your insurance company. Following a major disaster, your small business will be in urgent need of funds. You will, for example, need to satisfy deductibles for your property insurance. A staged payout of business interruption claims is not in the interest of your business.

An extension (or corollary) to this lesson concerns waiting periods applied to business income losses. Insurance policies commonly impose waiting periods of one to ten business days or longer to business interruption endorsements. Many business owners often apply their own experience as retail insurance policyholders to the needs of their businesses and mistakenly believe that they are comparable. They are not. It may be, for example, entirely appropriate for you to have a 60- or 90-day waiting period for your personal disability income insurance policy (which dramatically lowers your premium), but it is not appropriate or advisable to apply a waiting period to your business interruption endorsement. When you budget for your personal expenses, you know that you must have sufficient savings to cover 60 or 90 days of your living expenses should you become disabled, if you have such waiting periods in your disability income policy. But it is more difficult to apply such budgeting methods to your small business following a disaster, at which time you will have to finance extraordinary expenses. With the exception of property insurance deductibles, few of these expenses can be forecast with any degree of certainty.

Small businesses typically suffer their greatest income losses immediately after a disaster strikes and slowly recover. A waiting period excludes those losses from coverage. In effect, a waiting period functions as an unknown deductible. I have business interruption insurance that covers my small business from the first day of losses, less a quantified deductible. Don't enter into a business interruption insurance program that specifies a waiting period. Substitute instead a deductible based on a fixed amount of capital. With a quantifiable deductible to satisfy, you know you must set aside a certain amount in reserve funds, but thereafter the business interruption insurance will make whole your small business for any losses.

The other complication that can arise with waiting periods concerns coverage. Consider a disaster that closes streets leading to your business. Take for instance, a hairdressing salon. Assume that you have a waiting period of seven business days. Within three days, the streets are reopened for pedestrian traffic and, in theory, customers can visit your salon. However, as a practical matter, they wait to resume visits to your business until such a time as all of the construction work on the street is complete. The insurance company can credibly argue that you do not have a valid business interruption claim because access to the salon was restored before the waiting period expired. It may take some time before pedestrians resume walking down the street where they can see that you are open for business. Business trickles back, but you suffered an uninsured loss. If you don't have a waiting period, you won't have such disputes with your insurer. Deductibles based on absolute dollar amounts of losses are subject to fewer interpretations.

Now consider what happens at the other end of the disaster timeline. Insurance policies often cover losses only until such a time as your business can reopen. But often, as in the preceding example, losses continue even after your facility has been restored. Consider obtaining an extended period of indemnity for your business interruption insurance. Revenues are often reduced for an extended period of time following a catastrophe. Observe how many months passed before passengers rebooked flights after September 11, for example. It may make sense for your business to have an extended period of indemnity clause for 30, 60, or 90 days for losses that continue to accrue following the date of the original claim. I have a friend who owns a corporate travel business based in Virginia. The attack on the Pentagon did not cause any damage to her premises, but she has learned from the lessons of others and will elect an extended period of indemnity when her existing policy comes up for renewal.

Before concluding our discussion of waiting periods for business interruption coverage, I would like to add a word about insurance deductibles. Many small business owners were unpleasantly surprised to learn that they had multiple deductibles to satisfy for their coverage. We suspect that this confusion may be the result of poor communication with their insurance brokers. All the personal finance books you will ever read advise you to reduce your premium by electing a higher deductible. Remember that, as in the comparison we drew between personal disability income insurance and business interruption insurance, personal insurance lines are not entirely comparable with commercial insurance lines. I investigated the source of confusion with at least two of my friends and determined that they had relied upon the cover letter from the commercial insurance broker that accompanied their policy documents and were misled as a result. The cover letter made reference to one of the deductibles. The cover letter is a social nicety of business correspondence; it is not a synopsis of the provisions of your policy. It is very important that you read your policy.

Turn to the page of your policy captioned "Common policy declarations." This is the document that lists the declarations, forms, and endorsements, which form your complete policy. It is typically presented by category, such as interline forms, property form coverages, liability form coverages, and umbrella liability coverages. Within each of these categories, you will find a reference to the coverage that is part of your policy. Let's examine the property form coverages as our example. Turn to the page of your policy captioned "Property Form Coverages Declaration." This is the part of the document that presents in explicit detail the coverages that were listed under the same heading of your common policy declarations. You may have a separate deductible applied to each coverage. For example, my policy provides for a $1,000 deductible to the personal property of others that applies only in the event of theft. If the personal property of my employees were destroyed in a fire, for example, the deductible would not apply.

This declaration also states the deductibles that apply to the other coverages that I have elected to include in my policy, such as business income, which states "actual loss sustained" and "no wait period applies." I have deductibles that apply to each of the other property form coverages in the policy, such as signs, valuable papers and records, and so forth. Now turn to the page of your policy captioned "Umbrella liability coverages." The document will identify your self-insured retention in the box marked "underlying insurance coverage." It would not be uncommon, for example, that you would have a $1,000 deductible for your property insurance standard form policy, but a $10,000 self-insured retention for your umbrella policy. The self-insured retention is the amount of losses your small business must pay (in other words, losses that your small business retains for itself) before the umbrella coverage becomes effective. Now review the entire policy with special attention paid to documents marked "declarations."

I ask you to do this so that you understand that you may have multiple deductibles to satisfy and that you may plan your reserve fund accordingly. I suspect that most small business owners would prefer to have a deductible of $500 to $5,000 to make premiums more affordable. In the case of the more "common" disasters, you may need to satisfy only a single deductible. In a catastrophe, such as the attacks on the World Trade Center or the Pentagon, multiple lines of insurance coverage will be required to cover your losses. This, in turn, requires your business to assume multiple deductibles. For small business owners who were devastated on September 11, the realization that multiple deductibles of $1,000 each aggregated up to $15,000 was painful. Electing a higher deductible may reduce your premiums, but beware that you may have to satisfy multiple deductibles should a catastrophe, not a disaster, strike. Build your cash reserves with that in mind.

The third lesson many small business owners learned with respect to business interruption coverage concerns losses incurred as a result of reduced access to your business following a loss or damage to your property. Consider, for example, the neighborhood restaurants that delivered lunches to workers in the World Trade Center. The destruction of the Trade Center resulted in a loss of 50,000 customers to those businesses. Contingent business interruption coverage would provide some assistance to those businesses for a period of time, which might be the cushion they need to recover.

Not all insurance lessons related to business interruption cover, but they were by far, the most common. Many small business owners learned lessons about providing contingency by means of their property insurance and will prepare for the future accordingly. The three most commonly learned lessons—again, this is not a rigorous study—concerned exclusions and limitations in policies, leasehold insurance, and property valuation methods. Exclusions and limitations are difficult, because they are common in insurance contracts and you often don't discover them until you sustain a loss and your insurance adjuster points out the fine print in your policy that excludes the loss from coverage. The only thing you can do is read your policy with great care. Ask questions and don't enter into a contract for insurance until each of your questions has been answered to your satisfaction. Determine if you need to supplement your insurance coverage, perhaps with an additional endorsement, and whether you are able to pay the additional premium required for such coverage. Do this before a disaster strikes.

In the context of this lesson, I ask you to carefully review your "all-risk" property insurance for those small business owners who elected such coverage. Remember that "all-risk" is a misnomer, and such policies frequently exclude from coverage losses from computer equipment, for example. We can name names of small business owners in our community who thought that their computer equipment was covered under their so-called all-risk insurance policies and were disheartened to learn that it was not. It was particularly disappointing because the most valuable fixed assets of a small business are often its computers and related hardware. Few small business owners would knowingly exclude such assets from coverage. You don't want to be surprised after a disaster to learn that your most valuable assets are excluded from coverage. Go back and review your all-risk policy now and purchase additional insurance coverage if you think you need it. We cannot reverse the losses that small business owners in Lower Manhattan or the Gulf Coast assumed as a consequence of these exclusions, but we can at least learn from them.

Leasehold insurance may protect your business if a disaster forces you to vacate your premises. Leasehold insurance will cover the unexpired portion of a long-term lease. Imagine that your office building is destroyed by fire. Leasehold insurance may pay the remaining rent due on your lease, so that you will satisfy that obligation. It also covers the difference between your existing rent payments and your future rent payments, should you lose access to your building or office in a disaster. This can be a significant benefit as scarce resources are expensive. If a fire, for example, destroys 100,000 rentable square feet of office space, the adjacent properties may become more expensive. I elected to forego this coverage for my businesses because we are very flexible with respect to our space requirements.

Finally, property valuation methods are a common source of contention following all major disasters. I strongly recommend that you insist on property insurance coverage that provides for replacement cost, based on current market prices for your insured assets. I also go one step further in my contingency planning. I annually update my inventory of business property, plant, and equipment to reflect the market values of our business assets. This gives us a clearer picture of our businesses' value of tangible assets and facilitates our capital budgeting exercise. It also gives us the information we need to make better business investment decisions. For example, I have been paying close attention to local and online auctions of business equipment with a view to making some good investments given the relatively weak prices of technology and capital equipment. Knowing the value of my existing assets enables me to make better purchasing decisions.

For every "lesson" that we have shared with you, there are many other small business owners who are saying to themselves, "if only I had known" with respect to some other aspect of their contingency planning. To address these needs through an ongoing dialogue, I have established a Web site where we may exchange information and lessons learned about best practices for disaster recovery. Further information is given at the end of this book regarding this Web site, www.preparedsmallbusiness.com. Meanwhile, I hope you will take to heart the lessons small business owners in disaster-affected areas learned the hard way.

## DEALING WITH EMOTIONS

You are likely to experience a range of emotions following a disaster. If the disaster was a minor computer malfunction, you may experience emotions of anger and frustration. Such trivial mishaps can have serious consequences for your business. They drain your energy and distract you from more critical tasks. The more serious forms of disaster, such as earthquakes, hurricanes, or acts of terrorism, can have more long-lasting effects. A natural disaster reminds us that our ability to chart our own destinies has its limits and we are all, to some extent, at the mercy of fate. Being displaced from your place of business, even if no one has been harmed, is stressful. We all develop our comfortable routines so that our minds go on "autopilot" for routine, repetitive tasks and we can focus our concentration where it is needed. But when our routines are disrupted, we need renewed concentration on our new environments and our new working conditions.

At the same time, there will be many people making demands of you during the recovery period. Some of these demands will be of a personal nature, such as a spouse who needs your support during a particularly stressful time or a child who has nightmares after the disaster. Many of these demands will relate to your business: You may have a customer whose needs are inflexible or suppliers who didn't devote the effort to contingency planning that you did. Recognize that the emotions you are experiencing in the recovery period are normal and expected. Indeed, this may be the first moment you have had since the disaster struck to catch your breath and take in all that has happened!

I am not a medical professional and so cannot offer medical advice. I am not a mental health expert and am not qualified to provide therapeutic services. I offer something else: practical real-world experience and understanding and support of what you will go through in the recovery period. I would like to accomplish two goals in this section of the book. First, I would like to share with you some of my personal reactions to the disaster that I experienced, so you will be sensitized to some of the reactions you might anticipate should you experience a major disaster. Second, I would like to share with you some of the things that we have learned about recovering from trauma. Even if you are the resilient type, and I am, this information will help you appreciate the different emotional reactions of those around you. Your extended small business family will need your attention in a different way following a major disaster.

Following the disaster that I experienced, my dominant feeling was one of disorientation. The subway stop nearest to my home was badly damaged on September 11 and so was closed by the police. The World Trade Center stops were obviously no longer available and some restoration work had to be done on the subways. Subway lines that offered express service offered both express and local service and there was always some confusion.

Since I walk to work, I often found that when I used the subway, I exited on the wrong stop or took the wrong line. The increased crowding on the subways compounded the confusion. Those who had taken the subway lines that were closed had to find alternate service, and so with fewer lines serving the same number of passengers, crowding increased. Walking about could be confusing, too. The twin towers served as a landmark; alerting me as to which direction was south or north and I could no longer rely on them.

Adding to the confusion was an unusual volume of noise and light at night. The work at the World Trade Center took place 24 hours a day, 7 days a week, as was necessary. Our ordinarily sleepy neighborhood became very noisy at night with trucks removing debris and jackhammers going at all hours. Outdoor lighting powered by mobile generators was brought to street corners to allow crews to work all night. Unfortunately, even with the shades drawn, many apartments in my neighborhood were lit up all night. The noise could be jarring; particularly since it often stopped and restarted in what appeared to be a random pattern. The residents who heard the planes crash into the towers were especially sensitive to loud noises. I remember being woken up at 3:30 A.M. one morning by a pair of F-16 planes overhead. As it turns out, the planes were not supposed to fly that route at that hour. The pilots presumably did not appreciate that the residents of Lower Manhattan were probably sleep-deprived and hyper-alert to such sounds. Having spent some time with small businesses in the Gulf Coast, I can tell you that they are going through exactly the same process.

Of course, the work had to be done and we are all glad that it was done so efficiently, but the noise contributed to a sense of disorientation. Instead of waking feeling well rested, I would wake up feeling fatigued. It wasn't just that the trucks removing debris would interrupt your sleep; it was that they would remind you of the event that required their presence: the terrible tragedy and the deaths of so many innocent people. The same association was made with the odors that emanated from the site, at least in the first few months after the disaster. I remember exiting the Wall Street subway station to a strong odor of smoke and the woman next to me asked, "Do you think we will ever get used to this?"

The feelings of disorientation worsened whenever I went to Midtown Manhattan, which was completely unaffected by the disaster. It is the most bizarre experience to leave a disaster area, enter a subway and exit to see people carrying on as if nothing had happened. At the same time, I found I was less tolerant of behaviors I would have ordinarily overlooked. I remember being in the office during a telephone conversation with a marketing person in Florida. She said something to the effect of, "I have never been to New York, but I guess you guys are just waiting for the other shoe to drop." At the time she made that comment there were ongoing warnings and rumors about further terrorist action. After the attacks, there were pranksters phoning in bomb threats to high-rise buildings. Apart from the inconvenience of unnecessary evacuations, and an abuse of the police and fire personnel who had better things to do than respond to pranks, it raised the overall level of anxiety in the City. Innocent and routine occurrences, like the subway stopping between stations with no explanation given, became anxiety-provoking events that led to speculation (e.g., maybe there is a fire at the next subway stop?). In the best of circumstances, this woman's remark would have been tasteless, but in this context, I found it offensive. Under normal circumstances, I would overlook such rude remarks, but this time I called an abrupt end to the conversation. Occasionally, these feelings were punctuated with guilt, as indeed, I realized that I was lucky to be alive and aggravated.

I share this with you because you may have the same emotional response to a disaster. If the road that you ordinarily take to work has been flooded, you will have to choose another route, and you may get disoriented from time to time during your new commute. If your community has suffered an earthquake or a hurricane, a great deal of work will be done to restore it. That will take time and delay the return to normalcy. Your children may be rerouted to a different school until their school has been restored after the disaster. The disruption of their lives will have consequences for yours.

Recognize that these reactions are not unusual following a traumatic event, such as a major disaster. You will likely have "normal" reactions to such an abnormal event. These reactions may include:

- Physical reactions

  - Fatigue

  - Nervous energy

  - Changes in appetite

  - Sleep disturbances, including insomnia and nightmares

  - Lack of physical coordination

  - Nausea

  - Chest pains/heart palpitations, changes in blood pressure

  - Chills, sweating

- Emotional reactions

  - Shock, numbness

  - Feelings of helplessness

  - Fear

  - Depression

  - Anger

- ○ Anxiety
- ○ Feeling unappreciated
- ○ Feeling isolated
- ○ Guilt
- ○ Irritability
- Mental reactions
  - ○ Intrusive thoughts about the event
  - ○ Flashbacks (to reexperience the event)
  - ○ Confusion
  - ○ Memory difficulties
  - ○ Difficulty making decisions
  - ○ Diminished attention
  - ○ Difficulty concentrating
  - ○ Avoidance of people, places, and activities
  - ○ Tendency to engage in workaholism
  - ○ Absenteeism
- Behavioral reactions
  - ○ Withdrawal
  - ○ Hyper-alertness
  - ○ Suspicion, aggression
  - ○ Pacing, fidgeting
  - ○ Increased consumption of alcohol or cigarettes

The reactions will run the gamut from numbness and indifference to hyper-alertness. The following suggestions may alleviate the symptoms:

- Follow your "normal" routine
  - ○ Maintain a normal schedule, with respect to sleep and work hours.
  - ○ Engage in regular exercise.
  - ○ Don't increase your consumption of alcohol or cigarettes.
  - ○ Don't change your dietary habits.

○  Stay in touch with friends and loved ones.

○  Get adequate, or additional, rest.

○  Practice being in the present moment. Remind yourself that the disaster is in the past and you are in the present.

○  Discuss your feelings with others and, if necessary, seek counseling if you need additional support coping.

Be alert to any difficulties your employees are experiencing. It is a good idea to be proactive about getting help, even if just to confirm to your employees that the reactions they are having (or may have in the future) are normal. Does your company's health insurance plan provide for counseling benefits? If so, discuss this option with your employees. If the disaster that struck your community was a major one, the Red Cross may have resources available to you to assist in counseling and dealing with the after-effects of the disaster. Check with your local department of public health or community hospital to see what other resources are available.

I strongly recommend inviting a counselor to spend an hour or so with you and your employees as a group to discuss the reactions to a traumatic event. An informative briefing can sensitize your employees to the reactions that they may experience and offer them assurance that such reactions are not uncommon following a disaster. At the same time, such instruction can alert your employees to the likely emotional reactions that their colleagues may experience following the disaster. With understanding comes tolerance and compassion. The session should end with instructions on how to get follow-up, one-on-one counseling. Don't pass on the opportunity to invite a counselor to visit your workplace, even if everyone seems to be coping. You don't know what nightmares people may be having when they go home at the end of the day. Be proactive in addressing these issues.

I would like to give you a few recommendations on dealing with these emotional reactions. Again, I cannot offer your professional advice in these matters, but I can speak from my own experience. The first recommendation is to attend a formal event commemorating what happened and grieving your loss, if possible. Participation in such an event may "validate" in your mind that yes, the disaster really did happen (extraordinary events can have surreal aspects to them). It may also afford a cathartic release of emotion in an appropriate setting. All cultures have rituals: We have rituals for celebrating birthdays, anniversaries, deaths, national holidays, religious observances, and so forth. Rituals can structure a shared experience and may be helpful to you in acknowledging what has happened, grieving the loss and moving on.

I attended the memorial mass for Firefighter James Coyle on October 24, 2001. Mayor Giuliani had asked New Yorkers to attend services for the police officers and firefighters who lost their lives on September 11, 2001.

When a firefighter or police officer dies in the line of duty, the City ensures that the loss is properly acknowledged. However, given the number of those who died on that date and the need for ongoing work at the World Trade Center, the City wanted to supplement the ranks of firefighters who could attend memorial services. I didn't know Firefighter Coyle. I read the schedule of memorial masses on the New York Fire Department's Web site. And yet I found myself crying in church for the loss of a total stranger. One of the most powerful memories I have of the memorial service was seeing the firefighters from Chicago, Las Vegas, Baton Rouge, and elsewhere. Their uniforms identified their origin. Many of them came in buses to New York City to support the family of Firefighter Coyle and the New York City Fire Department.

I keep the program for the memorial mass on my desk, and whenever I feel discouraged, I pick it up. The commitment and sense of purpose people displayed at that Mass is something I will never forget. When I saw the firefighters who had come from as far away as Louisiana and Nevada, I felt comforted.

I hope that the disaster from which your business is recovering did not result in any loss of human life. You may still find participation in a structured ceremony to be helpful. Perhaps your religious group may have a service to pray for the community. There may be events such as symbolic lightings of candles, or ceremonies to celebrate the reopening of key public places. Participation in such an event may help you acknowledge what has happened, away from the grueling schedule of readying your backup computer systems. It provides a forum for you to come together with others and to share your commitment.

My second recommendation is that you provide your employees (and your suppliers and customers, if possible) with some written commemoration of the disaster as a way of acknowledging their experience. Following the September 11 attacks, the Baptist Church distributed in our community a book titled *A Passage through Grief,* by Barbara Baumgardner. The author writes of how her life was shaped by loss: the loss of her husband, her father, and her 17-year-old granddaughter. She speaks frequently at hospice workshops and leads grief recovery groups. The book does not speak to any particular religious denomination; it is an interactive journal that guides the reader through a series of exercises to help them cope with their experience. The Baptist Church was kind enough to give me extra copies and I distributed them to people with whom I work. It is a way of letting people in your business life know that you care about them and that they are in your thoughts during this difficult time. You won't likely engage in mutual disclosures of highly personal information with your business contacts and you may never know the pain that others experience. This is one way of being sensitive to the experiences of others without being intrusive. There are other books that treat the same topic in different ways; select the one that is suitable for you.

My third piece of advice is that you listen to others who want to share. One of the common reactions that surprised us was the need people had to tell their stories. The experience was like the reverse of the poem by Samuel Taylor Coleridge, "The Rime of the Ancient Mariner." Instead of being obliged by the gods to *tell* our stories to everyone whom we meet (the fate suffered by the ancient mariner), we were obliged to *listen* to the stories of everyone we met! People really need to talk about it—where they were when it happened, what could have happened and thank God it didn't, what were the consequences of the disaster to them, and what happened to other people. You can be dashing out the door for a meeting and the mailman will stop you and tell you his story and you have to listen. People really need to talk and feel better after having done so—even those with whom you are only casually acquainted. I have learned to allow people to get the relief they need; if listening helps them, I am glad.

Now I am going to make a politically incorrect statement. Be attentive to the emotional needs of the men in your life. I was impressed by the men in my life and how many of them suffered silently and perhaps put themselves at greater risk of illness and injury. I remember being stopped in the hallway by the commercial insurance broker who had negotiated the lease for my office space. He poured his heart out about how his girlfriend, a Morgan Stanley employee who was in the World Trade Center on 9/11, had abruptly ended their relationship and appeared to be withdrawing from life. He appeared sincerely concerned about her, but I could see that he needed support, too. I was stunned by the candor of his disclosures, as this was not the nature of our relationship. This was completely unexpected as I was just leaving the office to pick up a package. I had not counted on this long session in the hallway. I thought of this incident when I read the newspaper report of the young man who was an emergency worker assigned to the recovery effort on the "pile": searching for the remains of those who had died. The newspaper report of his suicide noted that his coworkers had no idea he was so distressed. One would think the circumstances of his work would have suggested that he needed special care. Sometimes we forget the difficult burden of masculine conduct, so listen carefully and be particularly attentive to the men in your life who may have needs that they are too embarrassed to admit.

Finally, be aware that the most severe emotional reactions may occur months after the disaster, when you are supposed to have "moved on." This is exactly what happened to me when I faced the group in Huntington Beach, California. After several years of relative stoicism, I was embarrassed by an emotional reaction I could not control, a reaction provoked by the vivid televised images of devastation in the Gulf Coast caused by the hurricanes.

Fortunately for me, an angel appeared at the right time: Mike Semel, an IT expert who focuses on clients in the healthcare sector, particularly with respect to technology and compliance issues. Mike happens to be a Red Cross volunteer and grief counselor. He stepped up to offer me comfort and then told me and the rest of the group that my reaction was not unusual. Sometimes weeks, months, or years, after experiencing a major disaster, people experience strong and unexpected emotional reactions when provoked in some way. I am glad to report that the group was sympathetic, I overcame my embarrassment and I went with the workshop.

Informal inquiry among my friends who have survived major traumas, such as earthquakes, suggests that a delayed emotional response to a traumatic event is not unusual. Expect that emotional responses to the disaster can be delayed. Be sensitive to both your own well-being and that of your employees. And seek help if you need it. If you experience symptoms such as chest pains or sleeplessness or other unusual reactions following the disaster, help is available. You won't be able to look after your employees and your family if you are run down. Get the support you need.

# Epilogue

I hope this book has given you a great deal to think about and some specific tools with which to develop your small business contingency plan. I hope that disaster never strikes your family or your business, but should you experience a disaster, the preparation work you have done should mitigate your losses and accelerate your recovery. I would like to provide a forum for an ongoing dialogue with readers, as contingency planning is always a work in progress. Like you, I, too, revise my contingency plans and insurance programs annually to bring our level of preparation up to date with changes in our businesses as we continue to grow. I find that our contingency planning efforts yield tangible results in terms of improving our business processes, irrespective of whether a disaster strikes. I also find that we learn from the experiences of other small business owners and, I hope, some of them have learned from our experiences.

I have established a Web site, **www.preparedsmallbusiness.com,** to build a community with our readers. I hope that through this Web site we can share best practices with respect to contingency planning and provide updates to some of the information provided in this book. The Web site also offers bonus multimedia material and other special offers. I look forward to meeting you, at least in cyberspace!

# Resources

No single book can address all the needs of contingency planning and disaster recovery. In revising this book, I set out with the modest goal to give small businesses the information they need to develop a framework for a contingency plan and to share what I have learned about the planning and recovery processes. I hope you realize the benefits for your daily business operations from contingency planning. I also hope that the information in this book will make you a more knowledgeable consumer of information technology (IT) and insurance services as you develop your own plans. Certainly, many readers will require additional information beyond what is presented here. This book is a starting point.

The information in the book is a completely original work, unless indicated by footnotes to the text. Therefore, I have not included a bibliography or list of other references. However, I am providing a list of Web sites where specific details to any service can be found. I stress that I do not endorse any of these service providers and cannot guarantee their professional quality. Exercise care in determining if a specific service is appropriate for your business.

Contingency planning should always be viewed as a work in progress; as such, a list of other resources to consult would be subject to constant change. Therefore, do not treat it as complete. I have chosen to include Web sites that I think represent work with "staying power." I have also specified only home page references since subfolders on Web sites are subject to change anytime. For specific disaster recovery information you will most likely need to navigate through the particular site.

To begin, I would recommend www.ready.gov, a Web site of the U.S. Department of Homeland Security. The site opens a link to "Ready for Business," that provides information for businesses, small and large, to prepare for disaster. "Ready for Business" also presents the profiles of companies, including my own, that have worked through major disasters. Another benefit of the site is that it provides a convenient link to information for personal and family disaster planning, which can be helpful to your employees. If your business is based in Canada, visit the Canadian Centre for Emergency Preparedness, www.ccep.ca. In the United Kingdom, check out the site of the government's home office, Home Office UK, www.homeoffice.gov.uk

Otherwise, if you are not certain of your exact needs, start with the portal Web sites or associations. Here you will find a listing of Web sites that explain services and contain hundreds, sometimes thousands, of links to other Web sites. Be aware that some portal Web sites appear to be general in nature, but could be associated with specific consulting services, and therefore will reference only information with regards to other related Web sites of subsidiaries or related businesses.

I have deliberately omitted wholesale or retail stores that sell contingency planning IT, or other, equipment because my focus is on building general awareness of the contingency planning and disaster recovery processes. Were you to search for contingency planning or disaster recovery resources through an Internet search engine, you would retrieve thousands of linked sites. I include only those I thought would be helpful to small businesses.

Portals are a gateway to information and, as such, aggregate many sources of material through links to different Web sites. A portal is a rich way to begin the process of researching specific contingency planning needs, but it can be overwhelming! I recommend the following:

Business Continuity Institute, www.thebci.org

Disaster Center, www.disastercenter.com

Disaster Information Network, www.disaster.net

Disaster Recovery Information Exchange, www.drie.org

Disaster Recovery Journal, www.drj.com

Disaster Resource, www.disaster-resource.com

Information System Security Professionals, www.infosyssec.org

IT Audit, www.itaudit.org

Project Management Online, www.allpm.com

Risk Management Resource Center, www.eriskcenter.org

Risk World, www.riskworld.com

Many associations make available to their members and nonmembers information through their Web sites. Some of these sources might be overly technically oriented for the generalist approach I have adapted, and many have a focus towards contingency for large-scale organizations. In some cases, it may be possible for you to adapt the best practices in contingency planning for more complex and sophisticated organizations. Otherwise, as your business grows, these associations may assume greater relevance.

Association of Contingency Planners, www.acp-international.com

American Risk and Insurance Association, www.aria.org

Business Continuity Planners Association, www.bcpa.org

Business Recovery Management Association, www.brma.com

Disaster Preparedness and Emergency Response Association, www.disasters.org

Institute for Business & Home Safety, www.ibhs.org

International Disaster Recovery Association, www.idra.com

National Emergency Management Association, www.nemaweb.org

National Voluntary Organizations Active in Disaster, www.nvoad.org

Public Agency Risk Managers Association, www.parma.com

Public Entity Risk Institute, www.riskinstitute.org

Public Risk Management Association, www.primacentral.org

Public Utilities Risk Management Association, www.purma.org

Royal Society for the Prevention of Accidents, www.rospa.co.uk

Society for Risk Analysis, www.sra.org

UK Emergency Planning Society, www.emergplansoc.org.uk

You may also wish to consult the Web sites of specific categories of vendors:

- Consulting firms, for example, provide specific advisory, and in some cases, implementation services for contingency planning and disaster recovery. Many consulting firms make available "thought leadership" documents setting forth their views on best practices in the field. As such, the Web sites of consulting firms often offer provocative materials you can share and discuss with your colleagues.

- Web sites for financial services companies are relevant to all businesses to the extent we are all concerned with the financial health of our businesses. For small businesses operating in the financial services industry, they are particularly relevant as their focus is often on the management of financial assets and liabilities and diversification of such risks. Your bank and commercial insurance carrier likely have disaster preparedness information on their Web sites. You should familiarize yourself with any particular resources that your insurer offers. Many produce free guides with information on best practices for risk management.

- Telecommunication companies have devoted considerable resources to contingency planning and it is worth investigating what they have to offer.

- Government Web sites offer a wealth of information that may be of use to you. In particular, you may want to visit the Web site of your local government or municipality for contingency planning that is specific to your particular area. These sources are especially useful if your business is in a disaster-prone area, such as a flood zone.

In the text, I suggested that you consult with grief counselors and other staff and volunteers of your local Red Cross for free guidance on dealing with psychological and emotional responses to disaster. Certain cases may require medical intervention. I deliberately kept my remarks brief and limited to my own personal experience, as this is not my area of expertise. You may wish to consult the following source for more information:

Psychology, University of Illinois Extension, www.ag.uiuc.edu/~disaster

Relief agencies are not-for-profit organizations that offer charitable assistance to those affected by disaster. This is by no means a comprehensive list, but it is a good place to start.

Relief, Christian Disaster Response International, www.cdresponse.org

Relief, Red Cross, www.redcross.org

No doubt you will discover your own favorites through Internet search engines. However, this list of resources should help you identify additional information as your needs demand.

Let me close by encouraging you to visit www.disastersafety.org/business_protection/ to download a free *Open for Business*® Toolkit from the Institute for Business & Home Safety.

# Glossary

**Agent**  A licensed salesperson representing an insurance company to a buyer. An agent may also be a licensed broker.

**A.M. Best**  A rating agency that assesses the financial strength and claims-paying ability of insurance companies.

**Audit**  The creation of log files documenting how users interacted with your computer system. It is essential to detect suspicious activities and to determine which records to recover first from a backup, based on the frequency of record usage.

**Authentication**  The verification of the authenticity of either a person or of data, to determine that a message has indeed originated from its claimed source. Authentication methods are necessary for all forms of access control to systems or data files and should be periodically reviewed for maintaining security.

**Authorized**  An authorized insurance company is licensed to underwrite business in a particular state or jurisdiction. Authorized companies are also referred to as "licensed" or "admitted" companies.

**Backbone**  The backbone of the Internet, high bandwidth data transmission lines that connect ISPs that, in turn, provide access to you. Typically, an ISP hands over your data to another ISP, then to another ISP, and so on, until the data finally reach a backbone access point. Because the data may have to pass multiple routers on the way to the backbone, network latency rises, and running applications with a lot of small user feedback remotely (as in a disaster scenario), can become nearly impossible. It is better to use ISPs that are the original source of connectivity to the network, such as AT&T, Sprint, UUNET, AGIS, and BBN. But beware: Some companies also use resellers and intermediaries to provide connections to businesses and consumers alike.

**Backup**   Copies of computer files that can be restored if the need arises. Although users are generally aware of the need to produce reliable backups, they tend to lapse until they experience a system crash or accidentally delete some or all of their files. Backup media should be stored at a site physically removed from your office by at least ten miles.

**Bandwidth**   The transmission capacity of data lines, typically measured in kbps or mbps. Bandwidth is not guaranteed for any transmission over the Internet.

**Basic Form Coverage**   An insurance coverage that protects your business against fire, plus extended coverage, consisting of lightning, explosion, windstorm or hail, smoke, aircraft or vehicles, riot or civil commotion, vandalism, sprinkler leakage, sinkhole collapse, and volcanic action.

**BCP**   Business Continuity Plan. Large organizations typically produce an elaborate plan to ensure that the essential business functions of the organization are able to continue in the event of a disaster. The BCP is usually combined with a "Disaster Recovery Plan" (DRP) that deals with the immediate crisis to secure the health and safety of people and limits further damage to equipment. The DRP hands over the responsibility to the people who execute the BCP. The BCP will identify the critical people needed, their functions, and other systems and infrastructure needed to run a small emergency business operation and how to reestablish all the business functions.

For small businesses, although disaster planning is important, it does not need to be formalized in large BCPs and DRPs as immediate business continuity is typically of lesser concern. It is better to focus on simple, but effective checklists of "to-do" items for each person assigned in the event of a disaster.

**Broad Form Coverage**   An insurance policy that covers basic fire; extended coverage; and breakage of glass; falling objects; weight of snow, ice or sleet; and water damage.

**Broker**   A licensed salesperson representing the buyer to the insurance company. A broker may also be a licensed agent.

**Business Interruption**   An insurance that replaces lost income to cover fixed business expenses when a business has not yet resumed operations following an insured property loss.

**Business Owner's Policy**   Also known as a package policy. It combines property and liability coverage in one insurance policy for a small business with affordable premiums.

**Cable Modem**   Cables that transfer television signals are very well suited for carrying other high-frequency signals because of their shielded construction. Therefore, cable television companies can add a data signal on their existing cable infrastructure and offer Internet services. A cable modem is able to convert these high-frequency signals into an actual digital data stream.

Internet access via cable TV is especially interesting for households that typically have a cable TV box already installed. But Internet via cable is not usually available in commercial districts. DSL or dedicated data lines, like T1, are the preferred options.

**Casualty Insurance**   More commonly known as liability insurance. It protects the assets of your business against claims of negligence or wrongdoing.

**Centrex**   Basically the same as a PBX, but in this case the phone system is located at the phone company that offers similar functionality under the name Centrex.

**Commercial Auto**   A line of insurance that covers company-owned vehicles for both liability and physical damage.

**Contingency**   The additional effort to be prepared for unexpected or quickly changing circumstances. Typically a business continuity plan is developed with the hope it won't be put into use. It is important that such plans are not just theoretical papers, but actions that can be executed and tested even in nondisaster situations.

**Data Recovery**   Unlike data restored from a backup, data recovery refers to the process by which specialists using utility programs and disk software tools can "undelete" files that have been deleted accidentally or have been lost due to a hardware malfunction or a software issue. It is a time-consuming process with an uncertain outcome and you should not rely on it. Rely on the restoration from your backups instead.

**Data Restoration**   The process of restoring data from backup media. I have seen many people who made daily backups, but never attempted to retrieve their stored data. It can indeed become a little tricky if you are using backup software with proprietary formats and different generations of tape drives.

Small businesses should use backup mechanisms that are as simple as possible, such as the use of an additional hard disk as backup media that contain an exact copy of the primary disk from the prior day. Occasionally, a backup can be made from these hard disks in the form of a disk image and stored remotely, such as a server on the Internet. Please note that a disk image is only proprietary to the file system in use, but not to any application.

Please note that restoring files should always be done in a temporary space until you can verify that all data have been restored correctly. Otherwise, you might overwrite important changes that you or someone else recently made to your current file system.

**Data Safe**   A special safe made of heavy, fire-resistant, tamper-resistant, magnetically inert materials. Data safes are designed for the safekeeping of computer media, and important to have if you have vital business information that should be protected and cannot be copied to different places.

**Deductible**   The amount of losses a company must pay before its insurance policy pays a benefit.

**Dial-Up**   Refers to connecting a device to the Internet via a modem. Modem dial-ups can include security features like call-back.

**D & O**   Director's and Officer's Liability Insurance provides coverage in the event that directors and officers become personally liable for their actions on behalf of a company they serve.

**Disability Insurance**   Disability insurance replaces earned income to workers who are unable to continue their employment due to injury or illness.

**DMZ**   Demilitarized Zone. A separate subnetwork, typically directly attached to a firewall that shields off the main corporate network and its systems, but allows external parties from the Internet to gain access to systems in the DMZ.

**DRP**   See Business Continuity Plan (BCP) above.

**DSL**   Digital Subscriber Line. DSL uses a high-frequency signal that is superimposed on the analog, lower-frequency, voice signal. While regular analog modems use only the voice signal, DSL modems use the higher frequency, and can therefore transfer data at a much higher rate.

For a phone wire to be able to carry a high frequency signal, it must be in top working condition, and not more than one mile in length. There are various modifications of DSL. SDSL supports a symmetric data flow, which means that the in- and outgoing bandwidth is the same. ADSL has a much higher downloading bandwidth and is therefore especially suited for Web browsing. DSL does not usually come with guaranteed uptime, and thus is generally less reliable than a real data connection, such as a T1 circuit. Also, DSL data traffic is typically handed over through many parties until it finally reaches an Internet backbone connection, thus, network latency can be an issue on DSL lines.

**Employment Practices Liability**   Insurance for companies that provides protection in the event of employment-related lawsuits, such as claims of wrongful termination, sexual harassment, and so forth.

**Encryption**   Data encryption is a means of scrambling the data so that is can only be read by a person who has a "key" such as a password. Without it, the cipher cannot be broken and the data remain secure.

Often, the public key method is used. It uses a public key known to everyone and a private or secret key known only to the recipient of the message. When I want to send a secure message to my brother Dan, for example, I use Dan's public key from his Web site to encrypt the message. He then has to use a private key that belongs to the public key. Only with the private key is it possible to decrypt the message. The beauty of the solution is that anyone can send confidential messages to the receiving end, without having to communicate first with that person. This method is also often called asymmetric encryption because it uses two keys instead of one. Symmetric encryption thus uses only one key that both parties need to know in advance, which implies a higher security risk.

**Endorsement**  An endorsement is a written provision that modifies an insurance policy. An endorsement may add coverage for a specific peril, exclude coverage for a specific peril, or specify under which conditions losses arising from a specific peril will be covered under the terms of the policy.

**Ethernet**  A network technology that enables data to travel at 10, 100, or 1000 megabits per second. It requires Ethernet cards on each connecting device. So-called CAT5(e) cables are used when wiring an office using 10 Base-T Ethernet running on twisted pair cables. Patch cables are used to connect the cables from the office connection plugs to the network components. Patch cables look like phone cables but they are typically thicker and the modular RJ-45 plugs at the end are slightly larger.

**Excess and Surplus Lines**  Insurance underwritten by insurance companies that are not licensed to do business in the policyholder's state.

**Fallback Procedures**  Particular business procedures and measures, undertaken when events have triggered the execution of either a Business Continuity Plan or a Contingency Plan.

**FEMA**  An agency of the U.S. federal government that provides assistance to counties that have been declared disaster areas by the President.

**Firewall**  A system designed to prevent unauthorized access to or from a private network. Firewalls can be implemented in both hardware and software, or a combination of both. I recommend stand-alone units as firewalls, or solutions that are incorporated into network components, like routers, to create the least dependency from a more complex system, like a PC. Firewalls are frequently used to prevent unauthorized Internet users from accessing private networks connected to the Internet, especially intranets. All messages entering or leaving the intranet pass through the firewall, which examines each message and blocks those that do not meet the specified security criteria. You can also have a key word block on it, preventing children from accessing adult material.

**HA**  High Availability. Availability refers to the guarantee that is given that a particular system and the data on it are available for use when needed. Today, many systems require "high availability" (HA) setups. Think about e-mail and Web servers. Those systems should be located at data centers that can provide the required support. Please note that sometimes HA could also refer to a system that is available at just one particular time during each day. In general, however, HA refers to full 24/7 uptime guarantee.

**Hacker**  An individual whose primary aim is to penetrate the security defenses of sophisticated computer systems. "Benign hackers" are relatively rare. Most unauthorized access can be traced with intrusion detection systems.

**IDS**  An intrusion detection system (IDS) inspects all inbound and outbound network activity and identifies suspicious patterns that may indicate a network or system attack from someone attempting to break into or compromise a system.

**Insured**  A person or corporation entitled to receive benefits under the terms of an insurance policy. The named insured refers to the policyholder.

**Internet**  A global network connecting millions of computers, created as ARPANET in 1969 by the U.S. Army, to be a "self-healing" communications network in the event of a serious attack on the United States. That makes it valuable for disaster recovery purposes. Even during the September 11, 2001 World Trade Center Attack, although countless communication lines were severed, the Internet in Manhattan was completely functional.

The Internet evolved from this original network and is now controlled by regular businesses that provide the fast backbone communication lines. Over 100 countries are directly connected to this network which is decentralized by design. Each Internet computer, called a host, is independent. Its operators can choose which Internet services to use and which services to make available to the global Internet community. You use an ISP to connect to the Internet.

**ISDN**  Integrated Services Digital Network, an international communications standard for sending voice, video, and data over digital telephone lines or normal telephone wires. The 64 kbps data line is the base connection for all telephone and data communication lines. When you order ISDN service, you typically get two of these lines, both running over the same telephone wire, allowing you to access the Internet at 128 kbps. Or you can use one line for voice and the other for data. You need to have an ISP that accepts connections via ISDN. ISDN is still a good solution in areas where DSL or cable TV modems are not yet available and high bandwidth data lines are too costly.

**ISP**  Internet Service Provider, a company that provides access to the Internet. For a monthly fee, the ISP provides you with dial-up or a fast modem configuration, software that configures your system, and a username and password for authentication purposes.

The ISP will also typically provide you with an e-mail address and often access to your personal Web service. I strongly recommend not using either of them. If your ISP service fails in a disaster, or you simply want to change your ISP, you are out of luck, as these services are typically only accessible when connected through that particular ISP.

**Key Person Insurance**  Pays a benefit on the event of death or incapacitation of an owner or "key" employee of a business.

**Latency**  The time it takes for a theoretical zero-length data packet to move from source to destination across a network connection. While a packet is being sent, there is "latent" time, where the sending computer waits for a confirmation that the packet has been received. Latency and, for large data packages, network bandwidth, are the two factors that determine your connection speed.

**LCD**  Liquid-Crystal Display. LCDs are thin and flat displays that are used in a variety of products, from small portable devices, laptop computer screens, to desktop displays. An LCD display uses much less power then tube monitors, and can therefore extend the time a system can run on batteries. It has a lifetime about twice that of a regular monitor and thus fails less frequently.

**Leased Line**    An "always-on" network connection between two points set up by a phone company. It can transfer both voice and data signals. They are used by large companies to connect their worldwide offices, and allow them to make phone calls and exchange data within the company at a fixed price per year depending on the required bandwidth and the work required at both end locations. Today, it is often replaced with a VPN connection over the Internet. However, the Internet does not have guaranteed bandwidth on which you can depend, but leased lines do. If you live in a major metropolitan area, you can often get leased lines between two offices within the city at attractive prices.

**Liquidity**    Ready availability of cash and cash-equivalents. A company that has ready access to cash, for example, is liquid. A company that has little cash and must sell assets, such as real estate, to generate cash is said to be illiquid. In recovering from a disaster, a liquid business is at an advantage because it does not have to sell illiquid assets to generate cash to cover disaster-related expenses.

**Linux**    Linux (>leenuks<) is an operating system developed by Linus Torvalds; the source code was freely distributed and many people contributed to it. While initially an operating system for computer enthusiasts, it is now widely accepted as a cost-effective substitute for other operating systems, especially for server platforms. Today, you can buy IBM servers with Linux pre-installed, unthinkable ten years ago. Linux runs on a wide variety of processors from different manufacturers, such as Intel and Motorola.

**Media**    The items that store computer data, either fixed, built-in, or removable. Examples are Hard Disk, Diskette, CD, ZIP, Magnetic Tapes, etc. Each of these has its own community of fans, so you will find varied opinions on when to use which media. For data backups, you should note that CDs have the longest storage time of up to 100 years for archival CDs. Consumer CDs last about 30 years.

**Mirroring**    When you mirror data, you write the same data to two or more devices at the same time. You need this additional resilience many times for disaster preparedness. You can do this manually, or you can use RAID systems that automate the mirroring process.

**Modem**    Stands for modulator-demodulator. It allows the transfer of digital data over regular analog telephone lines. Modems are rather slow, but offer the advantage that the phone companies maintain phone lines with high priority in case of disasters, and modems work virtually anywhere in this country and around the world. Transferring data at high modem speeds, (e.g. 56 kbps), requires a high-quality connection.

**Mono-Line Policy**   Provides a single line of insurance, such as liability or automobile insurance.

**Murphy's Law**   The original Murphy's Law reads: "If there are two or more ways to do something and one of those ways can result in a catastrophe, then someone will do it." The term originated with E. A. Murphy Jr., who was working for the U.S. Air Force in 1949 and made this statement with regard to an experiment that he was working on when many unlikely failures occurred until he finally succeeded. The term "Murphy's Law" spread quickly within the aerospace community and is today often used to highlight the possibility that an unlikely event can occur.

**Network**   A network is two or more connected computers that are able to exchange data. Typically, you will connect today's computers via 100 Mbps Ethernet cables.

**NFIP**   National Flood Insurance Program, insurance coverage for floods provided by the Federal Emergency Management Agency.

**Non-Owned Automobile Coverage**   An insurance policy that covers the liability of a business for any damage caused when employees of the company use their personal automobiles for business purposes.

**OEM**   Original Equipment Manufacturer. Many PC sellers buy the same OEM products, but build them into different housings labeled with their own brand name. Therefore, it does not really matter which brand of computer you purchase. Inside the box, they are very much the same. Your choice of the PC supplier should depend on your individual needs, such as for technical support or specific usage requirements.

**PABX/PBX**   Commonly called a phone system, but the abbreviation stands for "Private Automated Branch Exchange." It is a unit that allows you to make internal phone calls and share your actual phone lines among various employees. If you have one, you need to think about a UPS unit to ensure that some basic functionality will be available if you have an electrical power outage.

**Package Policy**   Combines two or more mono-line insurance policies to cover two or more lines of insurance for a single policyholder.

**Partition**   Before you format your hard drive, you need to decide how many logical sections you want to divide it into. This is important for performance reasons, and you might have different file systems on different partitions. Each partition shows up as a separate logical disk drive.

**Peril**   A cause of loss, such as fire or earthquake.

**Physical Security**   You need to have these protection measures in place that will safeguard your assets in case you have to evacuate your building, and you are not certain when you are able to return, and who will have access to your files. There are various forms of equipment that protect your assets against fires, tampering, theft, or vandalism.

**Policyholder**    The person or business whose name appears on the insurance policy.

**Premium**    The payment a company makes to obtain insurance coverage for certain risks.

**Property Insurance**    Property insurance protects the physical assets of a business against the risk of fire, theft, and other perils.

**Professional Liability Insurance**    Professional liability insurance provides coverage against claims of malpractice or negligence brought against professionals, such as physicians, engineers, lawyers, or architects, as they render their professional services.

**RAID**    Redundant Array of Independent Disks or Redundant Array of Inexpensive Disks. RAID allows you to store your data automatically over various physical hard disks. Logically, however, these disks will appear as only one drive to the user. RAID systems can be used for performance enhancements, but they are typically used to protect data from hard disk failures. If a hard disk fails, you can simply exchange it, and your RAID system will rebuild the data on that hard drive with the information from the other disks.

They have been in use for a long time by data centers, but in the last couple of years, low-cost PC cards have been introduced that allow you to have your own inexpensive RAID system in your PC.

**RAM**    Random Access Memory. The memory of the computer that holds temporary data accessible at high speeds. You want to have sufficient RAM for your particular use of your PC for optimal performance. Too little RAM and your computer is really slow because it has to write and read data from the hard disk. When buying a computer, it is generally a good idea to double or triple the RAM that is offered in its original configuration.

**Recovery**    The process by which utility programs and disk software tools can "undelete" files that have been deleted accidentally or have been lost due to a hardware or software issue. It is a time-consuming process with an uncertain outcome, and you should not rely on it. Rely on your backups instead.

**Resilience**    The ability of a system to withstand adverse conditions and remain stable.

**Restore**    I have seen many people who made daily backups, but never attempted to retrieve their stored data. It can indeed be a little tricky if you are using complex backup software or certain tape drives. Therefore, I recommend that small businesses use hard disks as backup media that hold an exact copy of the original disk. Occasionally, a backup can be made from those hard disks in form of a disk image that does not use a proprietary format.

Please note that restoring files should always occur in a temporary space first, until you can check that all data have been correctly restored.

Otherwise, you might overwrite important changes that you recently made to your original file system.

**Rider**   A document referenced in the insurance policy that amends the original policy.

**Router**   A device that determines if data on the network are intended for an outside network, such as the Internet, and therefore passed on to it. You can use routers for access control, auditing, and keeping statistics on your network traffic. Consumer and small business units most often include firewall functionality.

**Server**   A computer that shares the information stored on it with other computers in the network. There are many types of servers, such as mail servers, Web servers, etc. Most of them belong in a professionally managed computer center. In most instances, a small business needs only a file server on which to back up data.

When buying a server, please note that the price of a server configuration is usually justified compared to a desktop PC. Servers often use dual processors, high bandwidth bus systems, and fast hard disks.

**Shareware**   Shareware are programs that are free to download from the Internet and that usually come with an evaluation period of about 30 days. After that time, if you like the program and would like to continue to use it, you can purchase the full version often directly over the Internet.

Choose and try as many programs as you like, and then decide which one works best for you. Shareware programs are usually best when you look for small system utilities, such as file synchronization tools. Please take a look at www.tucows.com or www.shareware.com.

**Special Form Coverage**   An insurance program that provides basic and broad form coverages and other losses that are not specifically excluded from the policy.

**Software Inventory**   A detailed list of all software licensed to the organization, cataloging the license numbers, program name, version/release number, cost, locations of installation, and the employees authorized to use this software. The software inventory should be part of a large asset control mechanism. You will need the software inventory for auditing purposes and to claim insurance benefits in the event of disaster.

**Stability**   A computer that is unreliable because it does not operate in a stable manner is a nightmare for users and system administrators alike. Computers become unstable for a variety of reasons caused by either software or hardware. You might see the system simply crashing, or freezing, or hanging in an infinite loop. Typically, you have to restart the system and you lose all the changes that you made on a document since the time you last saved it. It is a good idea to use only operating systems that are used in large deployments, and install only compatible applications.

**Surge Suppressor**   An electrical device that protects electronic equipment from surges in electricity. It contains a fast-reacting circuit breaker, and usually you must replace the whole unit after a surge event.

**System Administrator**   The individual who manages a computer system to provide services to users on a day-to-day basis. It is not a good idea to use generic or built-in administrative accounts. You should always use administrative rights that you assign to user i.d.s to allow auditing of who made which changes.

**T1**   A dedicated data line that transfers digital signals at 1.544 megabits per second. A T1 line can support about 50 people browsing the Internet depending on usage, fewer if you are running a busy Web server internally. A T1 connection is about five times the price of a similar DSL connection. However, the greater stability and reliability justifies the extra expense. Please note that in rural areas, T1 lines are assessed surcharges according to the distance to the next data communication center. Often, you have the opportunity to share a T1 line with several businesses around you, called fractional T1 access, something that might be a cost-effective solution for your small business.

**T3**   A T3 is about 30 times faster than a T1 line and supports a data transfer rate of about 44 megabits per second and bundles 672 individual data channels at 64 kbps each. Large companies and Internet backbone providers use these lines.

**Tape Drive**   Primarily used for backing up data. The drive acts like a tape recorder, reading data from the computer and writing it onto the tape. Since tape drives have to scan through lots of tape just to read small amounts of randomly scattered data, they are slow for retrieving specific data. This is why they are used almost exclusively for data backup. However, reasonably fast tape drive devices are fairly expensive, so that a tape drive makes sense only if you are storing hundreds of gigabytes of data.

**Umbrella Policy**   An umbrella policy provides excess liability protection to a business and pays a benefit to the insured only when the limits of the basic, underlying insurance policy are exhausted.

**Unauthorized**   An insurance company not licensed in a state or jurisdiction is an "unauthorized" or "unlicensed" or "nonadmitted" insurer.

**UNIX**   The UNIX operating system was created in the 1960s at Bell Laboratories. It became popular in the 1980s for scientific computing. Since Internet hosting is often done on UNIX machines, the platform gained popularity in the 1990s. There are a variety of UNIX derivative operating systems available. They are all known for their excellent performance and stability.

**UPS**   Uninterruptible Power Supply. You should have at least one UPS unit that ensures that a critical piece of hardware has continuous power during a power outage. The UPS unit will initiate an orderly shutdown of the hardware shortly before its battery is depleted.

**Version Control**   Version control has been used for software developers for decades. Now it is also often used in companies to include version control of documents written by a group of people. The advantage is that you can always roll back to an earlier document state because version control systems store the changes that you made to a base document. From time to time, you want to rebuild the base document to incorporate all changes to date and to reconcile conflicting changes that might have been independently been made by two or more work groups.

**Voice Mailbox**   It works like an answering machine, but the message is digitally recorded by a third party and sent to your e-mail address via the Internet. It is essential that you have at least two such services in place so that you can listen to your messages from any Internet terminal, even if your office has been destroyed in a fire, for example.

**VPN**   Virtual Private Network. It is an emulation of a private network over the Internet using sophisticated authentication and encryption methods combined with a "tunneling" network protocol.

**Workers' Compensation**   Workers' compensation provides a benefit to workers who have experienced a job-related accident or illness. The insurance pays for medical costs and disability income to the injured workers as well as death benefits to the dependents of a worker whose death was job-related.

**ZIP**   In the context of this book the term "ZIP" refers to a product from Iomega. The company makes a removable storage device called a Zip Drive. It holds 100 and 250 MB Zip disks, and has a wide distribution. Zip drives are less frequently used for backup, but are often for transferring large files or to keep data stored at a secure location when not in use.

# Index